PREGNANT ON ARRIVAL

Difference Incorporated

Roderick A. Ferguson *and* Grace Kyungwon Hong

SERIES EDITORS

Pregnant on Arrival

. . . .

Making the Illegal Immigrant

Eithne Luibhéid

Difference Incorporated

University of Minnesota Press
Minneapolis
London

Portions of chapter 1 are reprinted from "Childbearing against the State? Asylum Seeker Women in the Irish Republic," *Women's Studies International Forum* (special issue on "Representing Migrant Women in Ireland and the E.U.") 27, no. 4 (October–November 2004): 335–50. Reprinted with permission from Elsevier.

An earlier version of chapter 4 was previously published as "Sexual Regimes and Migration Controls: Reproducing the Irish Nation-State in Transnational Contexts," *Feminist Review* (special issue on "Sexual Moralities"), no. 83 (Summer 2006): 60–78. Reprinted with permission of Palgrave Macmillan.

Portions of the Introduction, chapter 5, and the Conclusion were previously published as "Nationalist Heterosexuality, Migrant (Il)legality, and Irish Citizenship Law: Queering the Connections," in *South Atlantic Quarterly* 110, no. 1: 179–204. Copyright 2011 Duke University Press. All rights reserved. Reprinted by permission of Duke University Press.

Published by the University of Minnesota Press
111 Third Avenue South, Suite 290
Minneapolis, MN 55401-2520
http://www.upress.umn.edu

A Cataloging-in-Publication record for this book is available from the Library of Congress.

ISBN 978-0-8166-8099-3 (hc)
ISBN 978-0-8166-8100-6 (pb)

Printed in the United States of America on acid-free paper

The University of Minnesota is an equal-opportunity educator and employer.

20 19 18 17 16 15 14 13   10 9 8 7 6 5 4 3 2 1

Contents

A Note on Terminology

When discussing migrants who are variously characterized as illegal, irregular, unauthorized, undocumented, nonstatus, clandestine, *sans papières, sin papeles,* and so on, word choices are never neutral. Rather, they reflect specific histories and political perspectives in a deeply polarized debate. Moreover, debates about terminology are inseparable from questions about how we conceptualize the subjects, objects, and processes of analysis.

In this book I generally use the term "illegal migrant." Many who are critical of migration policy strongly object to the term, arguing that while individuals may be in irregular situations, no human being is ever illegal. Moreover, the term attributes criminality to migrants who, in the vast majority of instances, have committed no crime, and it fails to shed meaningful light on their actual circumstances. Ruhs and Anderson argue for moving away from a binary of legal/illegal (or regular/irregular, or authorized/unauthorized) to instead explore how migrants' compliance with different aspects of law falls along a varied spectrum.[1] Goldring, Berinstein, and Bernhard propose the concept of "precarious status" as a means to capture "varied forms of irregularity [and the ways that] there may be movement among various forms of irregularity, and between these and legality."[2] I agree with these arguments, and the materials that follow contribute to advancing them. Yet, as Anderson and Ruhs explain, "states . . . typically use the term 'illegal.' They tend to present 'illegality' as a problem to be solved through stronger borders (internal and external), strict enforcement of immigration and residence controls, and, increasingly, cooperation between the state and civil society."[3] Moreover, "'illegality' is also the term that is often used by those elements of the mass media that promote and reinforce negative public attitudes to immigration, and illegal immigration in particular."[4] In this book I retain the term "illegal migrant" because I seek to critically historicize, problematize, and denaturalize how states, media, and publics have participated in constructing the figure of the "illegal" migrant as a problem to be solved within the logics that Anderson and Ruhs describe—and the role of sexualities in these processes.

I generally use the term "migrant" to refer to anyone in Ireland who does not hold Irish citizenship status and is therefore subject to the state's immigration control apparatus. The Irish state differentiates among migrants by assigning them statuses including employment permit holder, student, immigrant investor, spouse or civil partner of an Irish national, asylum seeker, and so on, to which differential rights and constraints attach. Whether the migrant is from the European Union/European Economic Area (EU/EEA), a visa-required non-EU/EEA country, or a non-visa-required non-EU/EEA country further significantly shapes the migrant's possibilities and constraints. For children who are born in Ireland but without Irish citizenship, their parents' country of citizenship and legal status is generally determinative of their status.[5] Rather than uncritically reproducing these state-based distinctions, I make such distinctions primarily when speaking factually about how a migrant has been officially categorized; critiquing such distinctions; or addressing how migrants try to transition among the statuses. I use the word "immigrant" to refer to official state laws, policies, and control measures that are directed toward migrants.

Introduction

Justice officials [in Ireland] reported late last year that some 80 percent of women of child-bearing age who sought asylum in the previous 12 months were visibly pregnant when they lodged their applications. It is a safe bet that many of these people would drop their asylum claims once they had become mothers, and instead claim residency.

And so it came to pass that being visibly an immigrant and visibly pregnant—or even in charge of a baby in a buggy—was enough to provoke hostile reactions from passers-by who perceived this as evidence of "circumventing" normal immigration controls.

Alert to the fact that what has become known as the "Irish born child" route to residency was increasingly being used by people who did not otherwise have a claim to live here as refugees, the authorities had long since resolved to do something about it.

—Nuala Haughey, "Residents of Limbo," *Irish Times*

IN THE 1990s, Ireland became transformed from a nation drained by centuries of emigration into what U.S. investment firm Morgan Stanley dubbed the "Celtic Tiger," a destination that was sought out by migrants from around the world.[1] They included not only workers from the European Union (EU), United States, Asia, and elsewhere but also asylum seekers who were often from West Africa and Eastern Europe. Asylum seekers are migrants who gain admission on the grounds that they fear persecution. This book focuses on the Irish government's and public's responses to pregnant asylum seekers who acquired legal residency by giving birth to children rather than by state verification of their claims of fearing persecution. These women and their male partners rapidly became viewed as "illegal" migrants who falsely claimed asylum as a means to enter the country and then, through birthing children, transformed themselves into legal residents who had been neither selected

nor screened by the state. The fact that migrants were successfully gaining residency through childbearing was considered to provide an "incentive" for growing illegal migration. Headlines in the mainstream
media, such as "State Alert as Pregnant Asylum Seekers Aim for Ireland," capture the mindset that prevailed.[2]

Focusing on the period between 1997 and 2004, when the controversies over pregnant migrants were at their peak, the chapters in this book
analyze the claim that pregnant migrants were "really" illegal migrants
and the responses and changes that this claim provoked. Chapters explore several interlinked questions: how did pregnancy become constructed as "proof" of illegal migration? What changes in law and policy
were implemented as a result of the controversies over pregnant migrants? How did these changes, rather than preventing illegal migration,
instead expand the grounds on which migrants became designated as
illegal? How did efforts to control so-called illegal immigration both
draw on and reconfigure nationalist sexual norms?

In posing these questions, this book does not seek to resolve whether
migrants were "really" illegal, nor does it propose policy changes that
might assist in better policing against unauthorized migration. On the
contrary, drawing from the rich scholarship about the social construction of the illegal migrant, the book argues that events in Ireland offer an
important opportunity to denaturalize and ask critical questions about
the processes through which states construct migrants as legal or illegal.
By analyzing the emergence of the pregnant migrant as a paradigmatic
figure of illegal migration, the book explores the role of sexual norms
specifically in shaping how states draw the line between legal and illegal
status, which is an issue that has been undertheorized in the rich scholarship on the social construction of migrant illegality. Queer theory offers
valuable tools to analyze the issue; through such analysis, queer theory
in turn becomes stretched to more fully account for the importance of
geopolitics and immigration processes in sexuality struggles. Much is at
stake in understanding these processes, for designating migrants as illegal does not keep them out of national territories but instead renders
them vulnerable, marginal, and exploitable, even to the point of death.
Yet, as a result of being designated illegal, migrants become constructed
as having caused their own vulnerability and exploitability even while
the role of states, employers, and general publics in their circumstances
becomes elided, naturalized, or beyond scrutiny.

Materials focus on the Irish Republic (hereafter Ireland), but the experiences analyzed in this book shed light on many regions of the world where pregnant migrants in particular and questions of migrant sexualities in general have generated significant controversy in recent years, including in Costa Rica, France, Germany, Hong Kong, Israel, New Zealand, and the United States.[3] Moreover, nation-states routinely draw from one another when developing migration controls; for example, Irish officials drew on U.S. immigration laws and practices in order to address concerns about pregnant migrants. Subsequently, as U.S. politicians, the media, and the general public became engaged in heated debate about whether children born to undocumented migrants should receive citizenship at birth, some critics began to view Ireland's approach as offering a useful model. The links between struggles over pregnant migrants in Ireland and elsewhere suggest that nationalist sexual norms are being contested and reconstructed at local, national, and global levels through immigration and citizenship laws and practices. Struggles over gay and lesbian migration, marriage migration, sex trafficking, and related issues are also part of the process.

The following sections describe the book's theoretical framework, explain major developments in Ireland between 1997 and 2004 concerning pregnant asylum seekers, discuss the materials and methods on which the chapters are based, and preview the upcoming chapters.

Queer Theory and Migration Scholarship: Building Critical Dialogue

People rarely framed the controversies over pregnant migrants as entailing struggles over sexuality and its associated intimacies. Indeed, the controversies usually proceeded without explicit reference to sexuality at all. The fact that pregnancy—which is clearly linked with sexual experiences—is often not associated with sexuality, whereas a kiss between two people of the same gender is often seen as "flaunting" sexuality, reflects the powerful operation of heteronormativity in everyday life. As queer theorists explain, heteronormativity refers to "the institutions, structures of understanding, and practical orientations that make [the dominant sexual order] seem not only coherent" but also natural, timeless, and unquestionable.[4] Heteronormativity normalizes sexuality channeled into childbearing within patriarchal marriage, especially among members of the dominant racial/ethnic and class group, as the standard to which everyone is expected to aspire.[5] Yet the ongoing production of that norm is naturalized and rendered invisible.[6] Analysis of the controversies over pregnant migrants offers a means to denaturalize and critically explore how sexual norms are established, what work they perform, and how they become transformed.

Queer theory's analysis of heteronormativity reflects a political and theoretical move away from treating sexual identities as "stable, transhistorical, or authentic."[7] Instead queer theorists explore the production of sexual subjectivities and the distinction between normative and non-normative sexualities. Thus, they critically examine how the idealized heterosexual norm not only produces a homosexual/heterosexual binary but also what Michel Foucault might characterize as a "distribution" of sexualities around the norm.[8] Gayle Rubin provides one model of distribution through her image of a pyramid: "Marital reproductive heterosexuals are alone at the top of the erotic pyramid. Clamoring below are unmarried heterosexuals in couples, followed by most other heterosexuals. . . . Stable, long term lesbian and gay male couples are verging on respectability, but bar dykes and promiscuous gay men are hovering just above the groups at the bottom of the pyramid."[9] The distribution of populations on the pyramid varies by time and location and carries consequences. Rubin explains, "Individuals whose behavior stands high in this hierarchy are rewarded with certified mental health, respectability, legality, social and physical mobility, institutional support, and material benefits. As sexual behaviors or occupations fall lower on the scale, the individuals who practice them are subjected to a presumption of mental illness, disreputability, criminality, restricted social and physical mobility, and economic sanctions."[10] This book will show that efforts to police against pregnant migrants remade not only Ireland's sexual pyramid but also different groups' positions on the pyramid, and the penalties or privileges associated with each position.

Queer of color scholarship makes clear that the sexual pyramid is organized not just by sexual and gender hierarchies but equally by race, class, and geopolitical inequalities that cross-cut one another.[11] The controversies over pregnant migrants certainly affirm that analysis. As Cathy Cohen explains, "The roots of heteronormativity are in white-supremacist ideologies that sought (and continue) to use the state and its regulation of sexuality . . . to designate which individuals were truly 'fit' for the full rights and privileges of citizenship."[12] Thus, sexual subalterns in a heteronormative order usually include not just diverse lesbians and gay men but also poor and racialized women who birth children, interracial couples, sex workers, and others who are variously citizens and migrants. Accordingly, Cohen envisions the creation of queer coalitions that challenge and transform hierarchies of every kind. She suggests that these coalitions must be rooted not in claims to shared identities or histories but "in our shared marginal relationship to dominant power that normalizes, legitimizes, and privileges."[13] Cohen's analysis, when applied to the controversies over pregnant migrants, invites us to consider possibilities for queer coalitions that substantively address the impact not only of sexuality, gender, race, and class but also legal status in creating complex regimes of privilege and subalternity. This issue is further addressed in the book's concluding chapters.[14]

Rich scholarship on sexualities and nationalisms has particularly theorized the role of the state in mandating and enforcing the sexual pyramid. As the scholarship shows, nation-states need normative heterosexuality not only for biological and social reproduction of the citizenry but also for the cultivation of particular kinds of social, economic, and affective relationships.[15] Processes for distributing populations on the sexual pyramid are also deeply implicated in nation-state efforts to renegotiate their positions within transnational fields and neocolonial hierarchies. For instance, Cindy Patton suggests that Taiwan began allowing openly gay men to serve in the military as a means of demonstrating the state's modernity, its distance from its own past, and its difference from neighboring countries.[16] Alice Miller argues that asylum cases involving sexual persecution offer opportunities for transnational looking and judging among nation-states.[17] Queer migration scholarship, to which this book contributes, asserts that immigration controls provide a particularly important means for nation-states to reaffirm or remake dominant nationalist sexual norms in ways that reposition the nation-state in relation to global fields while also subjecting migrants and citizens to normalizing regimes of power.[18]

Analysis of the experiences of gay and lesbian migrants has been particularly important in developing queer migration arguments.[19] Yet the larger goal of the scholarship has never been to simply "add" gay, lesbian, and transgender experiences to the historical record, although this is very important, but to also transform migration scholarship as a whole so that it systematically addresses heteronormativity as an overarching system that unevenly distributes and governs all migrants.[20] In accordance with that goal, this study engages, expands, and queers the rich scholarship on the social construction of the "illegal" migrant by addressing two issues: how heteronormativity shapes the allocation of migrants' legal statuses and, at the same time, how migration struggles remake the nationalist, heteronormative, sexual pyramid. Employing a queer theory framework and centering the pregnant migrant as a figure of illegal immigration allows for such an analysis.

First we must situate the figure of the pregnant migrant in relation to the general scholarship on the social construction of migrant illegality.

Constructing Illegal Immigration through Changing Immigration and Citizenship Laws

In recent decades, illegal immigration has been described as threatening national sovereignty; undermining social, welfare, health, and labor market benefits; spawning crime; challenging social control; and, in worst-case scenarios, enabling terrorism.[21] As a result, efforts to control and prevent illegal immigration have risen to the top of the agenda in global northern states, leading to extensive changes in both immigration and citizenship laws.

Yet claims about illegal immigration and efforts to prevent it generally overlook the important scholarship about the social construction of migrant illegality that shows that designations of illegality and legality are products of law, politics, and society.[22] Indeed, migrants' status stems not from their "personal" characters, as is often suggested by mainstream discourses and policies, but from the contradictions between the larger structural dynamics that drive migration and individual nation-state regimes for immigrant selection.[23] Restrictive citizenship regimes further reinforce that contradiction. Thus, as more and more nation-states have opened their doors to the globalization of capital, goods, information, and services, increasing numbers of people have been mobilized for migration.[24] Recent migration flows have followed in the tracks of older migration routes, including those forged between specific nation-states and regions based on histories of colonialism, capitalist intervention, warfare, and cultural exchange. Migration has also expanded into new routes, including into countries such as Ireland that were historically emigrant-sending rather than immigrant-receiving nations. Once migration movements are initiated, they become self-sustaining in a process that Massey and his colleagues describe as cumulative causation.[25]

Nation-state citizenship and immigration laws and practices are the critical interface where these processes converge to construct some migrants as legal and others as illegal. Citizenship law plays a fundamental role, since only noncitizens are subject to immigration requirements, rules, and enforcement. The very fact of not holding citizenship in a nation-state means that one cannot freely cross the border into that territory but instead becomes subjected to that country's immigration laws. Immigration law, in turn, determines whether one crosses the border as a legal or illegal migrant.[26] Although explicit racism is no longer written into most immigration law, selection criteria nonetheless continue to discriminate along multiple axes, including in regard to racial, economic, cultural, and sexual hierarchies that are central to nation and citizenship. As Catherine Dauvergne describes, "Migration law is typically a site of permissible discrimination designed to meet state objectives. This is called 'immigrant selection' rather than discrimination," and this logic of "discriminat[ing] between applicants on the basis of choosing those who best meet the needs and values of the nation-state has not been impugned overall."[27]

Immigrant selection criteria regularly change in accordance with broader shifts in "political economy and cultural politics."[28] Thus, in recent decades, selection criteria, including in Ireland, seek out migrants who can serve neoliberal regimes of capital accumulation and forms of social life that valorize entrepreneurship, individual responsibility, privatization, and reduced or nonexistent social spending.[29] In the process, opportunities to legally migrate have become increasingly restricted even while the number of people who have been mobilized for migration has grown.[30] Immigrant selection criteria generally admit migrants based on labor needs, migrants' ability to provide investor capital, or family ties to citizens or legal residents. A small number of migrants are also admitted under refugee and asylum programs although, as we will see, the asylum track in global northern countries, including Ireland, has been drastically restricted in recent decades.

Although labor, investment, family, and asylum constitute different tracks for legal admission, in reality they are not entirely distinct. For example, "attempts by policy-makers to make clear distinctions" between asylum seekers and labor migrants are often undone by migrants' "mixed motivations," which frequently combine flight from violence with economic considerations.[31] Equally, migrants who seek admission based on family ties to a labor migrant very often become workers themselves. These migrant experiences illustrate the somewhat arbitrary nature of state migrant admission categories—which contributes to routing some migrants into illegal status.

Indeed, migrants who cannot fit themselves into these state admission criteria are unable to enter legally. Those who do manage to fit themselves into the admission categories may receive some form of legal status but remain subordinated and vulnerable in an ongoing way. This is because, as Matthew Coleman describes, "the border—and border enforcement—is increasingly *everywhere*," operating at "myriad, conflicting scales" that involve various authorities.[32] The immigration enforcement apparatus extends well beyond the territorial border and border officials to encompass police, education, welfare, health care, and other workers who are frequently required to verify legal status and perform other immigration control–related functions.[33] Migrants who are initially admitted based on labor and family criteria may nonetheless lose their legal status if their visas expire, if they fail to follow bureaucratic rules, if they are accused of a crime or misdemeanor, or on other grounds. Asylum seekers are even more vulnerable to the loss of legal status precisely because their status is inherently transitional. Being an "asylum seeker" gives the migrant the right to remain in the territory—although under very restrictive conditions—only while the state reviews the migrant's claim for protection from persecution. Once the review is complete and all appeals have been exhausted, some asylum seekers become redesignated as refugees or holders of other comparable statuses. But the vast majority whose claims for protection are not recognized become redesignated as deportable and illegal.

This book analyzes how childbearing emerged as a pivotal site of struggle between migrants and the state over whether they would acquire more durable legal status than they currently held, or alternatively, become redesignated as illegal and deportable. It builds on scholarship that shows how, since the late 1990s, the Irish asylum system's processes, like those of its EU neighbors, shifted in ways that were intended to deter migrants from seeking asylum, or, when that failed, to ensure that most asylum claims were not recognized, thereby routing migrants into illegal status. Yet those who acquired residency through a child were not just asylum seekers but also other migrants. The book therefore also builds on recent works that highlight the role of the Irish state and Irish employers in transforming various labor (and, in some cases, family) migrants from legal to illegal status after their entry. For instance, a majority of those interviewed for a 2007 report by the Migrant Rights Centre Ireland had entered Ireland legally but subsequently became illegal for reasons that included "employers not renewing work permits, businesses or companies closing, illness, exploitation by employers which caused workers to leave, lack of knowledge of their responsibilities, rights and entitlements and a lack of flexibility on the part of the Department of Justice, Equality and Law Reform (DJELR) in the face of a wide variety of unforeseen circumstances experienced by migrant workers."[34] A report 2009 by Crosscare exhaustively documents multiple ways that the Irish immigration system contributes to making various migrants illegal over time, including through lack of procedural clarity and transparency; consistent unresponsiveness of staff to requests for information; migrant status options that are effectively inaccessible; and "inadequate planning, consultation, and dissemination of immigration policy and procedural changes."[35] By centering on childbearing, however, I provide an original analysis of how sexual norms contributed to those processes.

In theory, migrants may eventually reduce the vulnerability associated with their status by acquiring citizenship (i.e., by naturalizing).[36] Indeed, migrants often do naturalize not just for reasons of identification with their new "homeland," as the mainstream immigration narrative suggests, but also for strategic reasons including a desire to reduce their vulnerability and enhance their security and opportunities. Yet, Mae Ngai describes, the promise of naturalization applies only for migrants who are legally present, who manage to maintain legal presence for the requisite number of years (which varies depending on the rules), and who meet additional requirements.[37] This reveals another important way that immigration and citizenship laws converge to construct illegality: presence in violation of immigration law generally precludes the possibility of eventually acquiring citizenship (though there are some exceptions, for instance, amnesties for certain groups of "worthy" illegals). Because of this convergence, many migrants become frozen into permanently subjected status.

The construct of the illegal migrant has emerged from and is continually redefined through these ongoing dynamics. In recent years the dynamics have intertwined with Europeanization processes.

Europeanization and the Expansion of Migrant "Illegality"

Beginning in the 1970s European states began to redefine the rules of entry, residence, and work; in the process constructs of immigrant illegality were both expanded and redefined. For example, Franck Düvell cites a study showing that in Britain, "by constantly refining the definition of 'undesired aliens' . . . and [by] successively developing the concept of 'illegal entry,' the number of people considered as 'illegal entrants' increased ten-fold in the decade between 1970 and 1980."[38]

The expansion of grounds on which migrants could be designated as illegal accelerated after the signing of the Single European Act in 1986.[39] The act's purpose was to create new economic space through which EU citizens could move freely "for accumulation of assets and wealth."[40] But in the process much migration from outside of the EU zone became redefined as illegal even while migrants from within the European Union became newly legal.[41] Measures to securitize, disable, and criminalize non-EU migration were steadily implemented. Non-EU asylum seekers in particular became equated with illegal immigration for reasons that are further explained later.

Düvell captures the intersecting forces that converged not simply to construct the illegal in new ways in the European Union but also to expand the range and kinds of migrations that would become deemed as "illegal": "the emergence of large scale undocumented migration during the 1980s, and its rise during the 1990s, is based on a complex relationship of new migrations, new socioeconomic framing conditions, new migration politics and discourses. It is closely related to a period of transition from an old to a new world order."[42]

Düvell also details migration policies within the European Union that constructed the illegal immigrant in new ways. As he describes, "Throughout the 1980s and 1990s, visa regulations were imposed by all OECD countries and successively extended into an increasing number of countries, 'reducing freedom of movement' but preparing the ground for what became undocumented immigration."[43] Controls on entry, stay, and employment were adopted; carrier sanctions (i.e., penalties on airline companies, trucking companies, and other transportation businesses that brought migrants without proper authorization) were imposed. Buffer zones developed, which pushed migration controls outward onto countries that ringed the European Union; these countries' cooperation in controlling migration was secured through financial incentives or the prospect of joining the European Union in the future.[44] EU agreements on development and trade routinely included immigration provisions.[45] Laws and policies began to codify that migration that occurred outside of these authorized controls was "illegal" and subject to criminal or administrative procedures. Repatriation and readmission agreements were signed so that "illegals" could be deported.[46] At the same time, possibilities for legal migration by non-EU migrants became "increasingly limited to the privileged few."[47]

These developments and individual nation-states' implementation of them, including in Ireland, support scholars' argument that, contrary to dominant discourses, "illegal immigrant" is not an inherently undesirable "type" of person but rather a position of social and political vulnerability that is constructed through multiple relations of power. Scholars have shown that histories of colonialism, racism, and global capitalism are particularly central to the ways that certain groups of migrants are more likely than others to become designated as illegal.[48] This book extends their arguments by suggesting that normative sexual regimes also importantly shape where and how the line gets drawn between legal and illegal immigrant status.[49] At the same time, I argue, normative sexual regimes become redefined through efforts to control illegal immigration.

Ireland, Immigrant "Illegality," and Normative Sexuality

In the 1990s globalization, combined with Irish government efforts to reposition the country as a "knowledge economy," produced the Celtic Tiger, with growth rates that outpaced the rest of Europe. These changes went hand in hand with neoliberalization processes that "prioritised individualism, entrepreneurship, mobility, flexibility, innovation and competitiveness both as personal values to be cultivated by the individual . . . and as dominant social values."[50] Ireland began to experience significant in-migration, which was initially dominated by returned Irish migrants, whose numbers increased continually between 1987 and 2002, peaking at twenty-seven thousand that year.[51] Non-Irish migrants initially came primarily from the United Kingdom, "with the rest originating in roughly equal amounts from the rest of the European Union, the United States, and the rest of the world, respectively."[52]

Migrants' origins shifted between 2001 and 2004, however, when migrants from outside of the EU/EEA began to dominate the flow. They arrived in response to changing Irish labor recruitment initiatives; opportunities for third-level education; and the search for asylum, as these avenues for admission interacted with shifting geopolitics and the changes wrought by neoliberal capitalism. For example, when the Irish government began recruiting nurses in Asia, Filipinas dominated nursing flows in the early years of the new millennium. By 2008, however, India had become the largest source of migrant nurses in Ireland.[53] In contrast, students from the United States and China particularly predominated among those arriving in Ireland for study.[54] Applicants from Nigeria and Romania predominated among asylum seekers until 2007, when Romania became a member of the European Union. After that Romanians were no longer eligible for asylum, but Nigerians continued to seek asylum in significant numbers.[55]

In 2003 the Irish government adopted a policy of "sourc[ing] all but the highly skilled and/or scarce labor from EEA countries."[56] The policy significantly skewed admission possibilities to favor EU/EEA citizens—even while who counted as an EU citizen shifted. Ten new countries joined the European Union in 2004, and two more joined in 2007. Ireland was one of just three countries that immediately opened its labor market to migrants from the ten countries that joined in 2004. Accordingly, in-migration became dominated by EU/EEA migrants, particularly those from the ten new EU accession countries.[57]

The 2006 census revealed the extent of change, which occurred within a relatively short period: "There was a total of 420,000 non-Irish nationals living in Ireland in April 2006, representing 188 different countries" and accounting for 10.1 percent of the population.[58] The top ten countries of origin of these nonnationals were the United Kingdom, Poland, Lithuania, Nigeria, Latvia, the United States, China, Germany, the Philippines, and France. These ten groups represented 82 percent of all nonnationals in Ireland. The ten next biggest nationality groups came from India, Slovakia, Romania, Italy, Spain, South Africa, the Czech

Republic, Pakistan, Russia, and Brazil. The census also highlighted the heterogeneity of the groups: "While there are some remarkable similarities among the different groups there are also areas of strong dissimilarity. For example, while the Polish are largely here to work, the Chinese are here to study; the U.K. nationals live mainly in rural areas while the Nigerians are highly urbanised; the U.S. nationals are concentrated in the higher social classes while those from accession states tend to be working in the manual skilled areas."[59]

These high levels of in-migration presented challenges. Initially, Ireland had few legislative or administrative procedures in place for managing migration and no provisions to allow for permanent migration. Workers could enter but were expected to leave at the end of their term of employment or residence. The government clung to the idea that Ireland was not a nation of immigration. A process of settlement was somewhat envisioned only for refugees and asylum seekers who were considered to be unable to return to their countries of origin.[60]

But as the numbers of asylum seekers grew, from 39 in 1992 to 11,634 a decade later, there came claims that most were "really" illegal immigrants, not "genuine" asylum seekers, and that childbearing was enabling them to circumvent migration controls and settle down permanently.[61] Asylum seeking—as opposed to labor migration—was therefore the area where immigration was initially diagnosed as most out of control, and as demonstrating the need for the government to redefine and expand its controls, even though labor migrants were far more numerous than asylum seekers. Indeed, responses to numerically small but politically "troublesome" migrant groups often give definition and legitimation to larger systems.[62] Through the concerns about pregnant asylum seekers specifically, heteronormativity would become central to the ways that migration into Ireland was problematized: new strategies for managing migration were developed, the construct of "illegal immigrant" was discursively produced, and norms of good citizenship were rearticulated.[63]

The growing mistrust of asylum seekers in Ireland reflected wider EU trends. In the 1990s, as EU countries experienced rapid growth in asylum applications, policymakers began to suggest that most asylum seekers were illegal migrants who were faking or inventing stories of persecution. Therefore they suggested that harsher measures were needed so ministers and bureaucrats could effectively distinguish between migrants who had strong claims for refugee protection and illegal migrants who were merely posing as persecuted. By defining the problem as a matter of determining underlying "truth," officials obscured the fact that neither "refugee" nor "illegal migrant" refers to empirically verifiable or clearly distinguishable social groups. Instead, as I have described, the "illegal immigrant" is produced by states in changing ways through administrative and legislative means. The same is true for the category of "refugee."[64] As Liisa Malkki cogently explains, refugees "do not constitute a naturally self-delimiting domain of . . . knowledge."[65] Rather, the management of displacement in Europe after World War II constitutes one of the crucial histories through which the contemporary figure of the "refugee" emerged. Technologies of power, including the refugee camp, regimes of knowledge production and documentation, the rise of administrators and bureaucrats trained in "refugee management," and the crafting of global legal instruments, are among the key mechanisms through which the modern refugee and, later, the asylum seeker were produced. Crucially, the 1951 Geneva Convention and the 1967 Protocol defined as refugees those who had crossed an international border and who had experienced or feared persecution on account of race, religion, nationality, political opinion, or membership in a particular social group. While these agreements uphold the individual's right to leave one's country to seek asylum, they do not require nation-states to actually grant asylum.

By the late 1970s the humanitarian framework that dominated in the management of refugees and asylum seekers in Europe began to be replaced by what Ashkaan Rahimi describes as a "realist" frame that viewed asylum seekers primarily as "foreigner(s) entering the country who must be controlled."[66] The goal became not to respond to asylum seeker needs but rather to reduce their numbers. After the fall of the Berlin Wall and the collapse of the Soviet Union, policies and practices were further developed that sought to either prevent asylum seekers' arrival in the first place or, when this failed, to variously disqualify their claims for protection.[67] After September 11, 2001, strategies of state securitization further negatively affected the treatment of asylum seekers.[68] Indeed, according to Düvell, "the 'fight against illegal immigration' including the prevention of allegedly 'illegitimate asylum applications' has been analysed as the main driving force behind the creation of a common EU migration policy."[69]

As EU countries made it harder to reach and cross their borders, those fleeing persecution frequently resorted to modes of entry that were associated with illegal migration—including entering without official documents, entering without inspection, and paying smugglers. Effectively, many had to *become* illegal migrants if they were to have a chance to gain asylum (which shows how categories are themselves interlinked and the boundaries between them shift). Yet this further contributed to the conflation of asylum seeking with illegal migration and justified increasingly draconian controls in a steadily spiraling process.[70] Effectively, these new laws and policies allowed EU states to redefine the boundary between the categories of "asylum seeker" and "illegal migrant" in ways that expanded the latter group.

Ireland's refugee regime initially promised a less draconian approach than was evident in the rest of the European Union. The 1996 Refugee Act, in an exciting departure, recognized sexual orientation, gender, and trade union membership as additional grounds on which persecution might occur. Yet only a few sections of the act were initially implemented. Over the next few years, as asylum seekers arrived in increasing numbers, attitudes changed. Siobhán Mullally describes the development of "a culture of disbelief and a desire to dispense with asylum claims with ever increasing speed. Securing effective protection to those fleeing persecution has become a secondary concern."[71] The pervasiveness and persistence of "disbelief" concerning asylum claimants is captured by Ronit Lentin and Robbie McVeigh, who report that "in May 2005, in response to a parliamentary question about the high cost of deportations, [the Minister for Justice, Equality and Law Reform, Michael McDowell] claimed that asylum seekers tend to tell 'cock and bull stories,' stating he 'would prefer to interview these people at the airport, but the UN insists that I go through due process.' "[72]

In line with EU trends, Ireland sought to preempt the arrival of asylum seekers in the first place and, when this failed, implemented procedures that resulted in an overwhelming majority of their claims becoming invalidated on bureaucratic and technical grounds.[73] What made the Irish situation different, though, was that pregnancy and childbearing became an important means through which asylum seekers—and, indeed, all migrants—could redefine their legal status. This was possible because of two interlinked factors: first, until January 1, 2005, Ireland granted birthright citizenship to anyone born on Irish soil or seas. Second, in 1990 the Supreme Court had ruled in the *Fajujonu* case that nonnational parents of Irish citizen children were entitled to reside in Ireland unless the state could provide a compelling and exceptional reason to prevent them from doing so.

Nationalist Heterosexuality: Necessary yet Destabilizing

The *Fajujonu* decision reflected a larger historical reality about how dominant Irish nationalism, like most nationalisms, operates through gendered, heterosexualized, and racialized metaphors of family that came to shape social and legal structures in profound ways. Historically, Irish people were racialized and colonized including through discourses about their supposedly aberrant sexuality.[74] In the nineteenth century sexual norms were significantly transformed and cohered in a manner that differed from those of their British counterparts. As Clair Wills describes, the growing alliance between the Catholic Church and Catholic nationalists in the late nineteenth and early twentieth centuries resulted in forms of domesticity and heterosexuality that "eschewed the bourgeois ideals of 'privacy' or 'intimacy.' "[75]

After the partitioning of the island and the creation of the Irish Free State (which later became the Irish Republic) in the south in 1922, a "particular construction of sexual and familial roles became the very substance of what it meant to be Irish."[76] The Catholic Church and state worked in tandem to enforce these constructions, which were codified by the 1937 Constitution. The constitution described the family as "the natural primary and fundamental unit group of Society, and as a moral institution possessing inalienable and imprescriptible rights, antecedent and superior to all positive law."[77] Article 41.3.1 added, "The State pledges itself to guard with special care the institution of Marriage, on which the Family is founded, and to protect it against attack." Women were positioned as reproducing the state and the nation through their childbearing, mothering, and work in the home. Alternative sexualities of any kind were not spoken of and were to be exported through emigration or hidden away through locking people in institutions such as Magdalene Laundries. Consistent with the constitution's reproductive logic, all children born in the southern state were automatically citizens at birth.[78]

The heterosexual norm generated Othered populations: gays and lesbians, sex workers, unmarried mothers, fornicating bachelors, and others. Moreover, it implicitly racialized Irishness: as recent scholarship argues, the model of Irishness that was envisioned by the constitution was of white, Catholic, and settled people. Other Irish people, however, including Blacks, Travellers, Jews, and Muslims, were not the ones whose childbearing was imagined as reproducing the nation.[79] Irish state managers continued to articulate claims about Irish "sexual difference" as a marker of nationalized distinctiveness forged in opposition to the former colonial master, including while negotiating Europeanization processes.[80]

The *Fajujonu* decision, which offered migrants a route to legal presence through birthing a child in Ireland, carried the weight of these longer histories of Irish state-endorsed heteronormativity. But by the late 1990s the decision was seen as presenting the Irish government with a significant difficulty—one that would effectively necessitate refashioning the heterosexual norm. The difficulty, according to mainstream media and politicians, was that migrants with no legitimate basis for their presence in the state nonetheless entered by claiming asylum and then transformed themselves into legal residents and possible future citizens by birthing citizen children. The fact that childbearing could lead to residency for migrant parents was characterized as an incentive for continued, and growing, illegal migration. Migrants who gained residency through childbearing were portrayed as parasites, spongers, and an undesirable "type" of being who threatened Irish economic growth. African women were particularly singled out, even though Eastern Europeans comprised a significant number of asylum applicants, and their childbearing became portrayed as a form of supposed racial and cultural deviance.[81] Pregnancy rates and childbearing patterns became the primary form of knowledge about migrant women that was produced and disseminated in ways that reduced them to their sex organs.[82]

Selectively ignored was the fact that gaining residency in this way was perfectly legal; there was a process in place to facilitate it; government officials often actually recommended to migrants that they seek residency if they had a child (although they have since denied this); and migrants other than asylum seekers gained legal status in this way. Moreover, the ways that childbearing intersected with individuals' migration circumstances was incredibly varied rather than simply cynical, instrumental, or exploitative, as explained in chapter 2.[83] Thus the attribution of illegality to migrants who gained residency through birth of a child represented a discursive construction that was frequently unattached to technicalities of law.[84]

Nonetheless, in response to the concerns about pregnant migrants, successive ministers for justice, whose remit includes immigration control, vowed to take action. Michael McDowell, the minister for justice from 2002 to 2007, first sought to address the 1990 *Fajujonu* decision that had made it possible for migrants to gain residency through their Irish citizen children. Ironically, McDowell himself had represented the Fajujonus in their successful suit. Yet in a case known as *L&O*, he brought two migrant families, the Lobes from the Czech Republic and the Osayandes from Nigeria, to court. Members of each family had filed claims for asylum but were refused on technical grounds.[85] While their cases were being processed, each wife gave birth to a child in Ireland and, on that basis, the families claimed the right to remain. The minister sought to deport them and, in the process, to secure a ruling that ended the granting of residence to migrant parents based on their citizen children's rights. The Supreme Court ruled on the *L&O* case in 2003, allowing the state to end the practice of granting residency to migrants based on their parentage of a citizen child.[86]

In 2004, in response to continuing concerns about pregnant migrants, the government proposed a referendum to amend the Irish constitution's citizenship rules. Rather than automatically awarding citizenship to any child born on Irish soil or seas, the government proposed that only children who were born to migrants who had been legally present in Ireland for three of the last four years should acquire citizenship at birth. Notably, time spent as an asylum seeker or an international student did not count toward meeting that three-year requirement. Furthermore, children and grandchildren of the largely white Irish diaspora remained eligible for citizenship through descent, even when they had never set foot in Ireland. The referendum passed by a margin of 79.17 percent to 20.83 percent, and the revised citizenship laws came into effect in 2005.

As chapters in this book explore, these changes actually expanded the grounds for migrants to become designated as illegal—without necessarily reducing or preventing migration. At the same time, they refashioned rather than abolished the dominant sexual norm. They starkly reveal, as Jacqui Alexander describes, how "heterosexuality is at once necessary to the state's ability to constitute and imagine itself, while simultaneously marking the site of its own instability," including in the context of immigration controls.[87]

The Line between Legal and Illegal Status

Chapters in this book are linked through a shared concern: Mae Ngai's claim that "the line between legal and illegal" status can be crossed in both directions.[88] Ngai's claim encapsulates several key points. The most important is that migrants should never be conflated with their legal status—even while we should also never overlook how deeply legal status shapes migrants' life possibilities. Yet legal statuses do not describe "types" of people; rather, they are imposed on or taken up by migrants in the context of multiple forms of power.[89]

"Legal" statuses are not singular; rather, states offer diverse legal statuses for migrants, each with associated rights and restrictions that may change. Acquiring legal status is not a one-time event; rather, as explained earlier, one's status may expire or be terminated for various reasons. Consequently, migrants must engage in ongoing efforts to not lose their legal status. Migrants may transition from one kind of legal status to another (e.g., from student to laborer, legal to illegal, or illegal to legal). Migrants may be in compliance with one aspect of the law governing their status but not with another (e.g., they may be legally present but illegally working).

Conflating migrants with their status misses the opportunity to understand how statuses are struggled over, changed, and remade (though not abolished). This includes through struggles at the macro level (e.g., as authorities pass new immigration laws), the micro level (e.g., every time someone engages with the immigration apparatus), and everything in between. Conflating migrants with their status effectively reifies the state's legal status categories, mystifies the categories' production, and ultimately sanctions various forms of state violence toward or differential inclusion of migrants.[90]

The claim that the line between legal and illegal can be crossed in both directions indexes these issues. Building on this framework, chapters in this book explore struggles between the Irish state and migrants over where to draw the line between legal and illegal status. When I conducted my research, the struggles significantly centered on asylum seekers. In Ireland, as elsewhere, "asylum seeker" is a transitional status that allows migrants to be legally present, although subject to considerable restriction, while the state evaluates their claims of persecution or feared persecution. Asylum seekers usually hope that the state's evaluation process will eventually lead to a more secure status, such as that of recognized refugee, which in Ireland carries the right to long-term residence and employment.[91] While I was conducting research, however, the Irish state's evaluation processes almost inevitably led to denial (including as a result of expedited processing, narrow interpretations of the Geneva Convention, rules that invalidated asylum claims on technical or bureaucratic grounds regardless of merit, and so on).[92] Once an asylum claim is denied and all appeals are exhausted, the asylum seeker no longer has a basis for continuing legal presence. Effectively, he or she transitions from being an asylum seeker to becoming an illegal and deportable migrant.

In this context, childbearing became an important site of struggle between asylum seekers who wanted a more secure legal status and the state that sought dismiss their claims and redesignate them as illegal. Other migrants also sought to secure or enhance legal status through childbearing. Therefore, chapters 1 through 5 use controversies over childbearing to explore different aspects of the struggle between migrants and officials over legal status. In so doing, the chapters break down monolithic constructs about "being illegal" and instead convey what is at stake for ordinary (and extraordinary) migrants in struggling for various legal status possibilities. Given that childbearing is centrally tied to sexual norms, the conclusion addresses the importance of sexual norms generally and the relations of power that they uphold in shaping migration struggles.

There are many theoretical benefits to this approach. Most importantly, it frees us from the grip of the dominant framing ("are these asylum seekers really illegal migrants?"), which treats state migration statuses as natural, self-evident, and without history. Instead we are invited to explore the processes through which the statuses emerged, the relations of power in which they are embedded, the centrality of sexuality in shaping these status designations, the migration regimes that the statuses serve, and the people who benefit from these regimes.

Reframing the dominant debate also enables us to establish different kinds of relationships to the various actors involved. For example, it allowed me to reframe my relationship to the migrants with whom I interacted. Instead of seeing them solely through the lens of state categories as either helpless victims needing "rescue" or cynical criminal spongers, I could appreciate them as diverse people who variously participated in the larger struggle over where and how the line between legal and illegal should be drawn, without their lives being reducible to these questions or to the inscriptions of the state. At the same time I better understood the motivations of those engaged in antimigrant activism even though I disagreed with them.

Reframing the debate also invites us to imagine other approaches through which migration control might be organized: approaches less dedicated to serving the interests of states, big corporations, and privileged classes against the interests of everyone else and less sanguine about the violence that is intrinsic to contemporary migration control.[93] Indeed, throughout the book I characterize migration controls as violent even though I recognize the extraordinary difficulties of having that characterization taken seriously. As Geraldine Pratt explains, because migration controls are sanctioned by law, citizens don't generally think of them as violent or else they legitimize the violence as necessary and acceptable. Pratt challenges this perspective by describing that migrants, whatever their status, remain caught between the contradiction that liberal, democratic states claim to not discriminate yet the treatment of migrants as a separate, less entitled, and more vulnerable population is thoroughly institutionalized in law and policy. Migrants' structural subordination is required for and symbolically and materially underpins the supposed freedom and equality of the citizen.[94]

Consequently, although the material, symbolic, and subjective violence attendant on migration controls, including in so-called liberal and democratic states, has been extensively documented, this has not markedly contributed to changing hearts, minds, or policies. Even when the violence manifests as a systemic pattern of deaths at borders, there is little political will to rethink migration policies because the deaths have become normalized through "distanciation, neutralization, or authorization of the harmful effects of government policies," including by "recasting border-related deaths as the product of risky personal choices, the unfortunate price to be paid to secure the nation, or as fitting sanction for illegal action."[95] This book challenges strategies of normalizing the violence that migrants routinely experience.

Methods, Materials, and Upcoming Chapters

This interdisciplinary text uses a range of materials, including those based on participant observation that I conducted in Dublin, Ireland, in the summers of 2001, 2002, and 2003. During these times, I volunteered in workplaces and activist sites that allowed me to learn firsthand about how conflicts over migration were playing out.[96] Thus, for one summer I volunteered in a law office in Dublin where I assisted with compiling documentary support for asylum claims, particularly those based on sexual orientation.

Another summer I volunteered for twenty hours a week at the Vincentian Refugee Centre in Phibsboro, Dublin, which served significant numbers of Ireland's newcomers. In addition to teaching English to asylum seekers, I spent one hour a day teaching Irish history to a young asylum seeker from Uganda who was trying to complete her Leaving Certificate (i.e., high school diploma) and many other hours doing whatever else was needed—sitting in on interviews, routing people, making and serving cups of tea, minding babies while mothers got assistance, playing with the teenage asylum seekers who dropped in, hanging out and chatting. These everyday experiences offered invaluable insight into the everyday challenges facing asylum seekers and their resourcefulness in responding.

Residents Against Racism (RAR) also provided important learning opportunities. Every Saturday, from noon until around 2:00 p.m., members of RAR stood in front of the Bank of Ireland in College Green, one of Dublin's busiest intersections. The RAR banner was tied to the railings behind us; laminated news clippings about the struggles facing migrants were taped below the banner; the folding table was set out, with its donation can and stacks of information. Then we handed fliers to passersby. One side of the flier described RAR and the other side gave an account of a migrant individual's or family's struggle, urging the passerby to contact the minister for justice to protest. The stories varied. I learned the fine art of fliering—encouraging people to take the material while minimizing direct confrontations. Standing with RAR was like becoming a human Rorschach inkblot: passersby came up to express their views on migration (some sympathetic and troubled, others angry and troubled) or even, on occasion, to overturn our table and try to remove our materials. Through these encounters I learned much about how migration, especially asylum issues, was being understood and lived. Sharing the space in front of bank with other activist groups and occasional street traders, some of whom were migrants, also contributed to my learning. For instance, one Saturday RAR fliered side by side with an antiabortion group, several of whom vehemently insisted that RAR's politics supported the killing of "unborn children."

In seeking information I consistently followed the one rule that Sr. Breege, the Vincentian Refugee Centre director, insisted upon: I never asked anyone why or how they came to Ireland, although people were free to tell me if they wished to, and many eventually did. Some readers may believe that I missed a valuable opportunity to collect important research data that would have furthered my study. I understand those concerns; I shared them. But after living and working among migrants who in many instances had experienced great danger and suffering in the process of their journeys, who were constantly called on to justify their presence to multiple hostile and suspicious publics, and who were negotiating very stressful conditions, I came to believe that Sr. Breege's rule represented the best practice. Indeed, as my research framework shifted toward thinking about the struggle over how the state was drawing the line around legal status, it became less important to know why or how people came than to accept that they were here now, and to learn how they were participating in the struggle for legal status. Anything else, I felt, would have replicated the violence of the Irish state, which constantly asks migrants to justify their presence while establishing itself as the final arbiter of whether they were telling the truth and whether their reasons for being present were "legitimate."

My interactions with people, both migrant and citizen, were continually shaped by the play of "différance," a term coined by Jacques Derrida that combines the concepts of "differ" and "defer." Stuart Hall explains, "This second sense of difference challenges the fixed binaries which stabilise meaning and representation and shows how meaning is never finished or completed, but keeps on moving."[97] Hall uses Derrida's framework to challenge constructs of fixed or authentic cultural identities and to underline the importance of history, power, and processes of transculturation in shaping who we are and what we are becoming.[98] In my case, "différance" shaped my research partly because I am among a generation of Irish people who went abroad during the economic struggles of the 1980s. Over time I learned to see myself through the eyes of U.S. people's varied images of Irish migrants even though the images often had little direct connection to my experiences. I also learned the histories of capitalism, colonialism, and mass migration that created bridges between Ireland and the United States along which I had moved, and that shaped my social position in the United States, although not in any singular way. At the same time I never stopped seeing myself through the eyes of family members and friends who remained in Ireland and through the discourses of the Irish nation-state for whom emigration carries very different meanings and histories than for the United States.

In the summer of 2000 I was visiting my family when a taxi driver in Dublin regaled me with the narrative about non-Irish migrants who were entering by whatever means possible and then acquiring residency by birthing a child. According to the taxi driver, most of the migrants were living off social welfare while regular Irish people worked hard and paid taxes to support them. Some of the migrants had as many as ten children, the taxi driver insisted, to boost their social welfare allowance. Yet he was anxious that I not think that he was a racist; he had hardworking friends who were black and brown, he said, and they shared his views because they were badly affected by the negative public opinions about the scamming childbearing newcomers.

I offered little response; indeed, I couldn't quite imagine how to respond effectively. Very likely the taxi driver was "reading" me as one among the hundreds of thousands of Irish-born and -reared people who were returning from every continent to participate in the Celtic Tiger miracle, and whose existence received official acknowledgment through the state category of "returned emigrant," which was enumerated side by side with—yet as different from—the non-Irish migrants who were also streaming in.[99] However, although I was arguably part of the Irish diaspora (to use yet another state category), I was not exactly a returned emigrant because my employer was a United States university. The economic stability that accompanies full-time employment, combined with summers off, meant that I could finally return to Ireland where family members still live, and which I had never decisively left.

At the time of my encounter with the taxi driver, I was finishing the writing of *Entry Denied,* a book that explores how sexual regimes shape migrants' possibilities for being legally admitted to the United States and analyzes how sexual regimes intertwine with gender, race, and class to produce complex registers of inclusion and exclusion. That conflicts over immigration may manifest themselves through exaggerated claims about migrants' childbearing, resulting in troubling legal and policy changes, was familiar. Indeed, my knowledge of how sexual and immigration struggles converge was based on both research and experience. My experiences included participating episodically in the Irish Lesbian and Gay Association's efforts to be included in rather than banned from the St. Patrick's Day parades in the United States; marching against California's Proposition 187, which demonized migrant women and their childbearing in order to supposedly stem illegal immigration; and hearing more than once from white Americans that I must be delighted to have "escaped" from living in such a sexually "backward" country as Ireland (a remark that does not allow for shades of nuance or complexity but simply maps geopolitical and cultural binaries).

I was also familiar with the ways that sexuality and migrant legal status may connect. In the 1980s some two-thirds of all Irish migrants in the United States were undocumented. I was fortunate to be exempt from the struggle over legal status, but I learned in visceral ways from Irish and other migrant peers about why people may feel compelled to migrate, even without legal status. I understood that migrants without legal status are not members of an alien species or a dangerous criminal class. Later, as a doctoral student, I learned how laws, policies, histories, and global economics converge to shape who has, or does not have, legal status. I also learned that governments can do something to transform undocumented migrants' situation, as when the U.S. Congress introduced a visa lottery that allowed thousands of illegal Irish migrants to gain legal status. That process, however, also underscored how deeply race, class, gender, and sexuality are tied up with legalization opportunities, for the visa lotteries disproportionately benefitted Irish and European migrants people as part of a racial calculus that was driven by fear of the "browning" of America.[100] At the same time, the lotteries incorporated class and educational requirements while failing to address the struggles facing many gay and lesbian migrants who are unable to gain legal status because the system is geared for married middle-class heterosexual couples and their children. All of these experiences meant that when I encountered the discourse of "illegal immigration" in Ireland, I was ready to be skeptical, ask hard questions, and turn a critical eye on state policies that prioritize state security over human security. Irish scholarly and news articles that underline the gap between the Irish government's advocacy on behalf of undocumented Irish migrants in the United States and its criminalization of non-Irish migrants in Ireland also raise these important questions.[101]

Although I brought my experience and knowledge to bear on the taxi driver's narrative, Breda Gray offers a valuable warning about the limitations of trying to understand others' histories through analogies or

forms of identifications that are insufficiently attentive to différance.
Gray analyzed public discourses that suggest that in light of Ireland's
sustained and painful history as an emigrant nation, it is imperative to act
humanely and ethically toward new migrants in Ireland. Yet Gray suggests that equating Irish people's experiences of emigration with those
of current migrants into Ireland erases différance: "The specificities of
contemporary immigration, which includes asylum-seekers, economic
immigrants, and returning Irish migrants of different gender, ethnic,
class, and other backgrounds are elided. The predicaments of contemporary immigrants" are recognized only to the extent that they mirror and
confirm Irish emigrant experiences.[102] The resulting identifications
and politics involve "assimilating the other to the self; that is, the experience of the other is interpreted only with reference to one's own prior
experience. . . . The effect is the annihilation of 'the other' because she
is deprived of her specificity, her unique existence and character. . . .
Furthermore, the motivation is not to engage with, or 'encounter' the
other for herself" but to affirm one's own narrative of self.[103] A more ethical approach, Gray suggests, is provided by Kaja Silverman's model of
"heteropathic identification," which "maintains openness to radical difference that may not be easily recognizable, and to 'experience beyond
what is known by the self.' "[104] Building on Gray, this project does not
seek to stabilize the identities of either researcher or researched but instead to reflect the continued flow of différance across migration circuits
and to trace some of the relations of power involved.

There can be no doubt that being Irish born, looking white, speaking
English, and being highly educated shaped my ability to establish the
ties needed for participant observation. The passports that I hold materially enabled me to move across borders to conduct the research—even
while other travelers were always being visibly immobilized and questioned by officials as I passed through checklines and borders. No doubt
many migrants in Ireland viewed me primarily as another white Irish
person, although some knew that I had substantial ties to the United
States to which they hoped to eventually migrate. Irish people often had
complex relationships to me since those who have lived abroad are figures of différance and ambivalence. I was often conscious of how my
speech sounded, how my clothes were cut , how I occupied space, and a
thousand other details that revealed my mixed status. Yet, while differ-

ent, I was hardly distinctive; I met Irish people who had "returned" from every continent, and each encounter was like interacting with incommensurate funhouse mirror images of Irishness. In the end, as Stuart Hall describes, "return" is never possible. I eventually experienced the research not as an effort to return but as a process of building new ties and learning new knowledge about a society that had undergone sweeping transformations.

Different chapters in the book use different kinds of materials. The process of participant observation provided invaluable insights and understandings that could never have been gained through documentary sources alone. Yet rather than claiming to "represent" the experiences of migrants or the diverse Irish people with whom they engaged, this work focuses on raising questions and reframing critical debates. Thus, it draws not only on participant observation but also on legal and policy documents, as well as on representational materials such as interviews, newspaper and television coverage, records of parliamentary debates, and reports about asylum seekers issued by community, religious, labor, and asylum seeker groups. It also engages with secondary scholarship that has emerged.

Chapter 1 analyzes critical speeches delivered by then minister for justice John O'Donoghue in 2001, in which he characterizes migrant women's pregnancies as "evidence" of growing illegal immigration and describes his strategy for tackling this. Chapter 2 draws on interview narratives and participant observation in order to reframe the minister's concerns about migrant pregnancies. Interviewees suggested that Ireland's immigration control system was reactive, poorly planned, and exclusionary; in this context, childbearing offered some migrants a means to negotiate multiple barriers. Interviewees' reframing contributes to scholarly understanding of how state immigration laws actively construct forms of migrant illegality.

Chapter 3 uses fieldwork materials, government documents, and archives to explore the material and subjective experience of being an asylum seeker in Ireland today. Focusing on the social welfare system, I analyze how it attempts to transform asylum seeking migrants into dependent, demoralized, and impoverished subjects. That transformation facilitates the state's denial of the vast majority of asylum claims and asylum seekers' reclassification as illegal and deportable migrants. Until

2003, however, giving birth to an Irish child enabled some asylum seekers to avoid these outcomes and to instead become legally resident, independent, and socially valued subjects.

Chapter 4 reviews a Supreme Court decision concerning a Nigerian asylum seeker who sought to avoid deportation by arguing that she was pregnant and that the Irish constitution promises to "defend and vindicate" the "right to life of the unborn." This extraordinary case, which deployed conservative sexual arguments for immigrants' rights purposes, allows me to explore how pro-life discourses affect state immigration controls; immigrants' opportunities to resist deportation and acquire legal status; and Irish women's sometimes contested right to travel overseas for abortions, which remain illegal within the state. Interconnections among these issues are also revealed.

Chapter 5 analyzes the 2004 Citizenship Referendum, which ended the practice of automatically granting citizenship to migrants' children who were born in Ireland. I suggest that the referendum reveals the temporal—rather than spatial—dimensions of immigration control, which seek to create an exclusionary national future by managing heterosexual reproduction. The citizenship referendum created a national future in which the citizen/noncitizen distinction, with associated inequitable access to resources and opportunities, was restabilized; migrants' children were subjected from birth to immigration law, which rendered them vulnerable to becoming designated as illegal and deportable; and Irishness was transformed from cultural into biological property that is transmitted through heterosexual sex and childrearing.

Chapter 6 provides an overview of what happened to migrant parents with citizen children after the passage of the citizenship referendum, and then describes further conflicts over sexualities and migrations—this time in regard to heterosexual marriage migration, same-sex couple migration, sex work, and domestic work—that subsequently emerged.

The conclusion brings the book's arguments together by reviewing how pregnancy became the basis for claiming that certain migrants were "illegal," and then implementing laws and policies that made them so. It then addresses how the production of the figure of the illegal migrant is integrally related to the conceptualization and institutionalization of the norm of the desirable migrant and the good citizen in ways that rearticulate sexualized, gendered, racialized, classed, and geopolitical hierarchies.

It suggests that, despite the state's framework of "national interest" that legitimized these outcomes, state migration controls have been and remain contested. Yet questions of sexuality have rarely factored into opposition arguments or alternative visions; what would happen if we were to factor sexuality in? The chapter concludes by reviewing areas for further research.

Shifting Boundaries through Discourses of Childbearing

NATIONAL, COLONIAL, AND RACIAL RELATIONSHIPS have historically depended on discourses about women's sexed bodies to establish hierarchies of differences. Actual women's bodies were often studied, exhibited, or otherwise used to affirm and naturalize these hierarchies.[1] One of the most infamous examples of a woman whose body was used in these ways was Saartjie, or Sarah, Baartman, a young Khoisan woman from Southern Africa who was exhibited in Europe between 1810 and 1815.[2] She was exhibited particularly so that Europeans could gaze upon her buttocks and genitalia, which were primary sites used by scientists at the time to establish racial and colonial differences and hierarchies. When Baartman died in France at the age of approximately twenty-eight, the famous Georges Cuvier conducted her postmortem. His sixteen-page report devoted nine full pages to her sexual anatomy and only one paragraph to her brain.[3] A wax mold of her genitalia was made and kept at the Musée de l'Homme in Paris.

It is not simply that writings and representations concerning Baartman's body were inaccurate but, more importantly, that they were distressingly productive. They constructed and legitimized a powerful set of ideas whose consequences we are still living with today. The circulation of images and ideas about Baartman's body in scientific writings and popular media, including newspapers, cartoons, and vaudeville, helped to reconsolidate racial, national, and colonial hierarchies in new ways. Baartman's unhappy experiences underscore that racial, national, and colonial boundaries and hierarchies are never static but are continually redrawn, and that subordinated women's bodies—especially their sexual and reproductive organs—are often used to facilitate these processes. Irish audiences were among those who saw Baartman when she was exhibited.[4]

Framed in the shadow of Baartman's legacies, this chapter begins by providing an overview of how discourses about women's childbearing bodies have been implicated in the construction of colonial, racial, and national boundaries that involve the Irish Republic. I particularly highlight the importance of migration—both emigration and in-migration—in shaping these processes. The second section describes narratives about migration and sexuality that emerged in Ireland at the turn of the millennium when some migrants began acquiring residency through birthing children. The third section focuses on remarks that were made by Minister for Justice, Equality, and Law Reform John O'Donoghue in December 2001, in which he characterized pregnancy as a means for unwanted illegal immigrants to transform themselves into legal residents and described his plans for tackling this.

Irish Women's Childbearing and the Boundaries of Empire, Race, and Nation

Historically, Irish women were forced to become familiar with the connections among constructs of women's sexed bodies and colonial, racial, and national hierarchies. In the nineteenth century, while Ireland remained under British rule, the Celt became located in an intermediate position within the racial hierarchies of the time. As often occurs in racialization processes, this location was justified by supposedly objective physical traits. For example, Dr. John Beddoe's "index of nigrescence" claimed to prove that Celts became increasingly Africanized as one moved from east to west in the British Isles, with inhabitants of western Ireland registering an index of 70 percent African.[5] Such allegedly objective physical differences were believed to reflect the existence of a biologically based racial hierarchy.[6]

The extent to which theories and studies of women's bodies were used to articulate a Celtic/Saxon distinction remains to be firmly established.[7] But there is some evidence that this occurred. For example, in 1855 Dr. Richard Tuthill Massy, a lecturer at the Royal College of Surgeons in Ireland, published *Analytical Ethnology,* in which he tried to challenge Anglo-Saxon racialism through inversion. Like the scientific racists of the day, he used physical criteria as grounds for discussing race, but he tried to argue that these criteria were proof of Celtic superiority. Moreover, he used women's bodies and arguments about the allegedly greater beauty of Celtic women to try to make his point, offering such claims as "with the large calf of the Celtic woman you have a small breast; with the large thigh of the Saxon woman you have a large breast."[8]

Supposedly biologically based racial differences between Celt and Saxon were believed to result in specific cultural traits. Thus, the bodies of manual laboring men most frequently represented ideas of Irishness in Britain, with the men constructed as stupid, uneducated, dirty, violent, and drunken. Irish women's representation within the symbolic economy of racism took a different form. Like men, Irish women comprised the backbone of many low-wage occupations in Great Britain, but they were often racialized through reference to their childbearing:

> Irish women's bodies were implicitly present in stereotyping
> through their role in the process of reproduction, especially their
> "excessive" fertility. . . . The rhetoric focuses on families and their
> threat to the English way of life both biologically and culturally.
> These include through "swamping" and racial degeneration, the
> weakening of Protestantism, unfair demand for resources and
> lack of control over bodies, both their own and those of unruly,
> dirty, and over-numerous children.[9]

This description not only highlights the racialization of Irish women through claims about their supposedly uncontrolled fertility and inappropriate childrearing practices but also identifies migration as the context for the discourse's production.

Indeed, migration processes massively transformed what constituted normative sexuality within Ireland.[10] This was dramatically evident in the period after the Great Famine of 1845–52 when, under British rule, a new economic and social order was in the making. An economy dependent on the potato, which had given rise to supposedly "improvident" marriage and childbearing among the poorer classes, was swept away and replaced by an economy based on livestock.[11] Sexuality remained organized through reference to marriage, but marriage was now restricted to one son who inherited the land, and one daughter who was dowried. Tom Inglis indicates some of the connections between transformations of the economy and of sexuality: "In the supposed cycle of events after the Famine, the segregation of the sexes led to the control of sex. The control of sex helped the control of marriage. The control of marriage helped the control of population and, finally, the control of population helped improve the overall standard of living."[12]

In practice, things were never that simple. Nonetheless, emigration emerged as a crucial mechanism for trying to establish and maintain a desired balance between sexuality, population, and economy. For example, Inglis describes that "in most families those sons and daughters not selected for marriage had a choice of remaining sexually inactive, or emigrating."[13] J. J. Lee is more pointed: "A callously efficient socialisation process postponed marriage and effectively denied the right to a family to a higher proportion of the population than in any other European state. . . . The dispossessed were reconciled to their fate by emigration."[14]

Jim MacLaughlin suggests that bourgeois Irish nationalists' ability to eventually capture the state from Britain was significantly enabled by post-famine processes of economic restructuring and mass emigration, which allowed this class "to add, literally, field to field."[15] We can extend MacLaughlin's analysis by suggesting that the emerging sexual order was also an important element of the formation of an independent state, including because it served the economic and social interests of the bourgeoisie. That sexual order at once borrowed and differed from its metropolitan counterparts. Clair Wills describes that it prescribed domesticity and sexuality channeled into heterosexual marriage, which were also the standards for the United Kingdom and the United States. Yet, because of Irish-specific conditions, including land war, mass emigration, and the struggle for independence, sexual norms became routed through and used to serve anticolonial Catholic nationalism. Domesticity became "deployed in the service of Catholic-nationalist hegemony" while other aspects of the modern middle-class home, particularly "conjugal love, romance, free choice, were rejected."[16] Rejection "came not only from the Church, but crucially from the economic requirements of small farmers," who relied on matchmaking based not on love, romance, or sexual desire but on strategic calculation to ensure continuity in land settlement and transmission.[17] The Catholic Church's growing monopoly on discourses about sexuality contributed to this configuration.[18]

After independence, social ideals became institutionalized, including in the 1937 constitution, which imagined a nation organized through patriarchal heterosexual marriage—one where women were relegated to the roles of wives and child bearers within the privatized home, and there were no same-sex interests or alternative sexualities of any kind.

Moreover, the vision and version of Irishness that was enshrined in the constitution and reflected in social policy was not simply patriarchal and sexually normalizing; it also conceived "Irish" people as settled, Catholic, "white," and bourgeois.[19] Immigrant, Black, Jewish, and Traveller women were not generally the women whose childbearing was envisioned as perpetuating the nation.[20]

To understand how childbearing in independent Ireland could become a site for constructing cultural, ethnic, and racial distinctions, it is helpful to follow McVeigh and Lentin's suggestion that Irish racism has been formed at the juncture of two distinct processes: the racialization of Irishness by outsiders, particularly the British colonial state; and majority Irish people's racialization of both "internal" others within the nation-state and of indigenous and minority groups encountered during experiences of diaspora.[21] Thus, on one hand, relegating women to the role of child bearer for the nation entailed an effort to "answer back" to colonialist logics (or in McVeigh and Lentin's terms, to respond to the racialization of Irishness by powerful outsiders). But at that same time, a particular vision and version of nation, and of Irishness as race, was enshrined.[22] For although heterogeneous groups were gathered together under the umbrella of the postcolonial state, dominant constructions of Irishness were not equally available to all.[23] The elevation of childbearing by certain sectors of the population represented a moment for the second aspect of Irish racialization dynamics to take place: that of differentiating internal others from "properly" Irish people.[24] For example, Helleiner describes that Irish Travellers, a historically subordinated group within Ireland, were racialized through reference to their childbearing (e.g., they were described as "infesting" remote areas and "breeding like rabbits").[25] According to Helleiner, these "discourses of inferiorization reflected and reproduced the construction of Travellers as an internal threat to moral community/nation."[26] Claims that Travellers were birthing many children but rearing them improperly became central to how the state conceived and justified its policies toward the Travelling community.[27]

Yet the intertwined forces of poverty and emigration continually threatened the postindependence imaginary of a nation organized around normative marriage and childbearing. Women's high rates of emigration, and the loss of their childbearing capacities and unpaid labor, generated particular anxieties and public commentary. Pauric Travers describes that the Fíanna Fail party leader, Éamon de Valera, "came to accept that the success of his party's policy of establishing as many families as possible on the land was dependent ... on persuading young women to marry into small farms" rather than resorting to emigration.[28] Others shared his views; a priest in County Cork suggested the introduction of a "marriage bounty to encourage young women to marry into small holdings rather than emigrate."[29] De Valera favored the idea of subsidizing the building of dower houses on existing land holdings into which newly married couples could move. Although it was regularly considered, the dower cottage scheme as well as proposals for what was effectively a state dowry never got off the ground, and high levels of emigration continued.[30]

In the 1950s continually high emigration—particularly by young women of childbearing age whose departure left "parishes ... [without] a single young girl"—and a faltering economy generated great anxieties that the Irish might become "a vanishing race."[31] The government accordingly sought once more to redress the perceived imbalance between sexual norms, economic development, emigration, and state and nation building. The 1954 Commission on Emigration and Other Population Problems "considered, but rejected, the possibility of introducing marriage loans and grants in order to encourage marriage. They argued instead that measures to improve the general level of economic and social development would lead to an improved marriage rate" while reducing emigration.[32]

Also in the 1950s the government had to address how in-migration fit into the mix. In 1956 Ireland ratified the 1951 Geneva Convention Relating to the Status of Refugees and participated in the UN High Commissioner for Refugees (UNHCR) program for resettling Hungarians who had been displaced during the Soviet invasion. Despite initial enthusiasm for the program, the government expected that it could carefully select who was admitted and "exclude those deemed incompatible with Irish society."[33] Catholic families were selected for resettlement since Catholicism and normative familialism were deemed compatible with Irish social norms *and* were expected to minimize the labor market impact (since only husbands were expected to work).[34] But less than two months after the arrival of the Hungarians, the state decided to encourage them to relocate overseas.[35] Their Catholicism and familialism were apparently not sufficient to allay fears about the cultural and economic impact of their presence.

While emigration threatened to remove young, childbearing women from the nation at rates that were seen as potentially catastrophic, it also had benefits. In particular, it became a central mechanism for sustaining the sexual and gender order with its associated cultural, ethnic, and racial logics, all of which tied to the economy and to nation and state building. While the state never promoted emigration, individuals resorted to it as a way to negotiate the pain and penalties that they faced as a result of nonconformity to the dominant gender and sexual order. Marella Buckley explains that Irish women internalized an image of emigration to Britain as offering an "escape hatch" in case of reproductive crisis, such as unwanted pregnancy.[36] The extraordinary history of continued migration by young women who were pregnant outside of marriage has been well documented (see chapter 4).[37] Numerous writings also describe that, until the 1990s, lesbians and gay men understood that they were expected to emigrate, if possible, since homosexuality was deemed incompatible with Irishness.[38] Íde O'Carroll has suggested that some women (and no doubt men) who suffered sexual abuse or incest resorted to migration in response.[39] Emigration was also important for those involved in interracial or cross-religious intimate relationships, including as a strategy to negotiate racial, religious, and cultural norms of Irishness when children were born.[40] Effectively, decisions about emigration and actual emigration strategies were shaped by sexuality—although sexuality often remained shrouded in silence or operated as a tacit, unspoken force.

All this suggests that emigration was central to the emergence, consolidation, and maintenance of the modern Irish sexual order in the context of famine, land struggles, and the independence struggle. The emigration/sexuality nexus also became central to Irish state- and nation-formation processes, and their associated gender, sexual, racial, class, cultural, and geopolitical hierarchies.[41] These hierarchies became renegotiated when migration by nonnationals into Ireland grew substantially in the 1990s.

Migration, Childbearing, and Residency: Struggling over Multiple Hierarchies

In the 1990s, as the Irish state sought to reposition Ireland within the world economy, migration continued to shape sexual norms. But now, along with continuing emigration overseas, migration *into* the state commenced on a significant scale and rapidly diversified to the point that that by 2006 migrants from 188 countries constituted more than 10 percent of the population. Growing in-migration meant that sexual encounters across lines of race, ethnicity, nationality, and legal status became everyday possibilities and often realities in villages, towns, and cities throughout Ireland. Systematic research about how in-migration altered Irish sexual cultures and norms has yet to be conducted. But there can be no doubt that sexuality was an important means through which individuals both experienced and made sense of rapid changes brought about by in-migration.[42]

A white Irish lesbian captured some of the complicated ways that sexuality shaped everyday encounters between Irish people and migrants at the start of the new century:

> There's a man from Uganda who I often run into, and we always talk about going for a drink but then it never happens. I was starting to be concerned that the man might think I was fobbing him off [i.e., not being sincere]. Then one day I ran into him again, and this time he was accompanied by a group of other asylum seekers, all of them eager and pleased to meet an Irish woman, and hinting they'd like to go out with me. One asked if I was married, and I said yes. Asylum seekers are used to Irish women saying they're married, even though it's usually a lie, so I felt bad answering him in that way, even though in my case it's true. "Are you married to an Irish man?" one of the men asked, implying that I, like other Irish people, "stick to my own." I said, "no, actually, to a Welsh woman." The men had *no* idea what to say![43]

The account highlights some of the dynamics that structured people's negotiation and interpretation of social interactions at that time. Almost anyone living in Ireland was aware that migrants could become legal residents through giving birth to a child in Ireland. Residency was possible because, as described in this book's introduction, Ireland granted birthright citizenship to anyone born on Irish soil or seas. In addition, in 1990 the Supreme Court had ruled in the *Fajujonu* case that Irish citizen children were constitutionally entitled to the company and care of their parents, and this right was exercisable within the state. Thus, migrant parents of Irish children could become residents (and possibly citizens in the future) through their children.[44] It should be noted that the parents' residency hinged not on heterosexual marriage but on biological parentage combined with ongoing, active parenting once the child was born. Extensive media coverage, everyday interchanges, and politicians' pronouncements about migrants who gained residency through childbearing meant that male/female interchanges, not to mention flirting, dating, and sex across lines of legal status, became burdened in complicated ways by the implications of these rules, as my informant suggested. Moreover, the entire process was deeply heteronormative and heteronormalizing. Lesbians and gay men, including my informant's female partner, remained largely invisible throughout the debates on migrants' childbearing and migration more generally. As she described, the mention of marriage between two women reduced everyone to awkward silence.[45]

Various narratives about the connections between childbearing and migrant residency were in steady circulation at the time.[46] One common narrative suggested that asylum-seeker men were taking advantage of naïve Irish girls, impregnating them so that the men would gain residency. For instance, after a group of Romanian asylum seekers were temporarily housed in Wexford, "an editorial in the *Wexford People* . . . argued that 'some young asylum seekers were intent on striking up relationships with impressionable young girls, fully aware that a baby would ensure permanent residence in this country.' "[47] Other Irish women were also characterized as susceptible to the wiles of asylum-seeker men who "exploited" them for residency. Drazen Nozinic describes, "There is a pamphlet titled 'Blacks' that has been disseminated to Black refugees' letter boxes throughout Dublin over the last two years. It says: '. . . Blacks from Africa come to Ireland trying to find unattractive, insecure women who cannot find a husband, and fall easily into the trap of an African hunting.' "[48] The pervasive image of asylum-seeker men "preying" on naïve or insecure Irish women and girls prompted a young white woman to suggest to me that Irish culture has absorbed what she described as "the American myth of the Black rapist." On further inquiry, she explained she felt that the media constantly ran stories suggesting that Black men were "threatening virginal Irish women." The stories, she said, always focused on Irish girls who were young, seventeen or eighteen, and who were getting engaged to African men. "It's not said, but definitely implied, that he's taking advantage of her and he probably has a wife and twenty kids back in Africa."[49] Irish narratives, however, added new complexities to "the American myth," since they also racialized Eastern European men as predators, albeit in a different way. Such images of asylum-seeker men as predators, according to Katrina Goldstone, recapitulated events in the 1920s when Jewish men were portrayed as threatening Christian Irish women. The narratives implicitly "whitened" the Irish women involved while constructing white womanhood as a condition of vulnerability for which protection was needed. Yet, as Goldstone observed, "the threat of foreigners attracting Irish girls seems more important than the fact that Irish girls are routinely abused by figures of authority and, indeed in some cases, members of their own family."[50]

Narratives, rumors, and speculation also abounded about asylum-seeker men taking advantage of asylum-seeker women. These often coalesced into discussions of sexual coercion or trafficking. For instance, "it is claimed criminals in Lagos organize transport to Ireland for pregnant women."[51] The narratives seemed primarily interested in exoticizing and racializing asylum seekers through implicit claims about their "cultures" (which were supposedly composed of unrelentingly patriarchal and cruel men who behaved as sexual predators and women who were completely helpless sexual victims). Chandra Talpade Mohanty has trenchantly critiqued the construct of migrant or third-world women as helpless victims of supposedly timeless and patriarchal culture.[52] These narratives not only colonize and racialize but also make it impossible to thoughtfully address the needs of migrant women who do find themselves vulnerable and coerced in the context of migration.

Narratives about Irish women who became intentionally involved with asylum-seeker men also developed and circulated. For example, some poor or working-class inner-city women who were pregnant but unmarried were described as colluding with asylum-seeker men by listing them as fathers when the babies were born. The men got residency while the women received cash payments from the men. The *Irish Times* described, "Ms. Olivia Mitchell (FG, Dublin South) referred to a 'serious and sinister abuse' which has been reported to her. This was the practice of paying single Irish mothers to register a non-national as the father of their children. 'In one case, I heard of a pregnant girl being approached at a bus-stop in Dublin and being offered £1,000 to accept and declare a non-national as the father of the child.' "[53] Other negative depictions of

Irish women who intentionally became involved with asylum-seeker men were produced. A former garda (police officer) described honestly, "An Irish man dating an asylum seeker woman is okay—she's exotic and a 'good ride.' But an Irish woman dating an asylum-seeker man is a tramp."[54] Antiracist activism by white women was easily cast within this heterosexualized and racialized logic. A young white Irish lesbian who regularly distributed leaflets in the center of Dublin to protest government racism toward immigrants and asylum seekers described that a group of young white men regularly taunted her by shouting that she was must love having sex with Black men. A white British woman who also protested described that a passerby came up and said, "I hear that you like black pudding" (i.e., black penis; black pudding is also a food).[55]

Narratives of older Irish white men with significantly younger, often "hot" looking (and sometimes far better educated) asylum-seeker girl-friends and wives also circulated but, as described by the former garda, rarely evoked censure.

All of the narratives deployed different combinations of social actors in a drama around heterosexual sex. They compulsively repeated the founding national narrative, that participation in heterosexual reproduction makes one a member of the national community. Yet they displayed great unease with migrants becoming members in that way. They also proposed new heterosexual figures. The Irish figures included the "innocent" Irish girl, imagined as white, young, and probably rural, who was being taken advantage of; pregnant, unmarried inner-city women or girls who accepted cash for lying about the father's identity; Irish women who were sluts and disloyal to the nation because of their supposed desire for sex with Black men; and Irish men who had new opportunities for sexual adventure, though this was rarely problematized (thus replicating the "double standard" that shapes Irish sexual, gender, and racial ordering). These Irish figures were rendered "Irish" in part through their contrast with various migrant figures—predatory men and women who are victimized through their sexuality. The narratives nonetheless implicitly acknowledged that Irish people were actively involved the processes through which some migrants transformed their status through birthing a child.

The most consistent public narrative, however, centered on pregnant migrant women who supposedly "abused" the system by claiming asylum, then birthing children and claiming residency on that basis. The women were blamed for creating a health care crisis, escalating the costs of social welfare, encouraging crime, and inciting continuing migration by undesirable people. That narrative is the focus of this book.

Constructing Pregnant Asylum-Seeker Women as "Illegal" Immigrants

Narratives about pregnant asylum seekers as "really" illegal immigrants took varied forms. Here I focus on an important narrative that was generated by the minister for justice, John O'Donoghue, and circulated by the *Irish Times* on December 1, 2001. I use the concept of "problematization" to analyze the narrative. As Jonathan Inda explains:

> Government is inherently a problematizing sphere of activity—
> one in which the responsibilities of administrative authorities
> tend to be framed in terms of problems that need to be addressed.
> These problems are generally formulated in relation to particular
> events . . . or around particular realms of experience. . . . The goal
> of governmental practice is to articulate the nature of these
> problems and propose solutions to them.[56]

Problematizations mobilize specific regimes of power and knowledge, which make issues thinkable and manageable in certain ways while foreclosing other possibilities. I am interested in how the minister problematized childbearing by asylum-seeker women; how he connected their childbearing to a supposed threat of illegal migration; and how his framing suggested that illegal migration could therefore be acted upon by targeting migrant women's bodies, especially their sexual and reproductive organs.[57] Since the minister is empowered to propose, implement, and change immigration law on behalf of the Irish state, his perspective and action plan are especially important.

I selected this instance of ministerial problematization because it was directly connected to the Supreme Court's 2003 *Lobe and Osayande* (L&O) decision that effectively ended migrant parents' ability to gain residency based on their Irish citizen children. Since the minister did not make available a text or speech that officially represented his problematization, my analysis draws from the two articles that were published in the *Irish Times,* Ireland's newspaper of record, on December 1, 2001.[58]

The minister did not challenge or refute any of the claims included in the articles. Instead, he offered very similar remarks in other media outlets throughout the month.

"Increasing Numbers of Heavily Pregnant People Were Entering Ireland"

For some time, Minister O'Donoghue had expressed concern about the fact that the *Fajujonu* decision enabled asylum seekers to gain residency by birthing a child rather than because the state officially recognized their asylum claims.[59] According to the *Irish Times,* asylum seekers who gained residency through childbearing remained "a political hot potato, particularly in the run-up to the elections next year. Already, it has been raised by individual representatives of the three main parties." The two articles reported a significant new development, however: the minister had settled on a course of action to address the issue. According to the *Irish Times,* he planned "for the first time" to try to deport asylum seekers whose applications had been denied and who were parents of Irish citizen children. To that end, he had issued deportation orders to several such families. The deportation orders would be contested in the courts, thereby providing an opportunity to articulate why *Fajujonu* should no longer serve as the standard to guide his decisions. Cases—in the form of individual asylum claims that became cases to be tried in the courts— were therefore to serve as the minister's instrument for change.[60]

Michel Foucault has described the case as "a means of control and a method of domination."[61] Lauren Berlant provides further information about how cases reflect and extend governmental relations of power. According to Berlant, cases are arguments about why things must change. They move from the singular and individual to the generalizable. In the process they "make up" knowledge about a group, ordering diversity and eliminating individuality (except to the extent that individuality can be referenced to a normative group aggregate). Such knowledge not only "makes up" the group in a certain way, but also, makes them actionable— available for interventions and management. The processes also redefine who is an expert, who has authority.[62]

The cases that the minister selected to overturn *Fajujonu* functioned in all of these ways while at the same time enabling the production of a striking discourse about the connections between women's reproductive sexuality and illegal immigration. The cases concerned two families whom the Irish public would come to know as the Lobes, a Czech Roma family, and the Osayandes from Nigeria.[63] The articles do not provide details about the substantive basis of the Lobes' claim, and the Osayandes are described simply as seeking asylum because of religious persecution. Both families had applied for and been refused asylum in Britain, after which they traveled on to Ireland to apply again. But the Dublin Convention, which governs asylum processing in the European Union, denies asylum seekers the right to reapply elsewhere after their asylum claims are turned down by an EU state. As chapter 2 explains, the convention has a number of serious shortcomings, including that it does not address variations in how EU/EEA countries process asylum claims, which means that the success of any claim may depend as much on the country where it was filed as on the substantive basis for the claim.[64] Because of the convention, however, the Lobes and Osayandes were technically ineligible to even apply for asylum in Ireland, and the fact that they did so meant they fit easily into the dominant narrative about "bogus" asylum seekers who were "really" illegal immigrants.

Since they were ineligible to seek asylum, the government issued a deportation order against each family shortly after their arrival. But Mrs. Lobe "was in advanced stage of pregnancy. In October . . . [she] was rushed to hospital as she was threatened with deportation. The Garda decided not to proceed with the deportation at that time and the woman gave birth to the couple's fourth child in November." In terms of the second family, the Osayandes, "the British and Irish authorities agreed to return the couple to the U.K. without hearing an asylum application in Ireland. The Garda decided not to enforce the deportation because the mother was pregnant. She gave birth to a son in Galway in October. However, the Department is still seeking to deport the father, for the same reasons cited in Case A." In both cases, then, the women's "advanced" pregnancy prevented the garda from speedily deporting families whose search for asylum had been denied on technical grounds. Once the Irish children were born, however, the families applied for leave to remain based on the birth of children—who were citizens only because the garda had delayed the families' deportations.[65] Accordingly, the families appeared to be calculating, ungrateful, and cynically deploying childbearing to thwart the state's efforts to control immigration.

Statistics were mobilized to bolster the claims that asylum seeking in general, and pregnancy in particular, provided a means to circumvent immigration controls.[66] Like cases, statistics depersonalize individuals, order diversity, and reduce complexity to a manageable, governable group called "asylum seeker" about which averages and aggregates can be known, and against which individuals can be assessed and normalized. Like cases, statistics entail relations of power, for it is the state that determines what information should be collected about asylum seekers (never vice versa). As Nikolas Rose describes, the production of statistics "can be neither ideologically nor theoretically innocent: hence the social enters the statistical through the 'interests' of those who undertake this task. . . . Expectations and belief are embodied . . . in the form of explicit or implicit theories shaping what is counted and how it is to be counted."[67] Yet statistics continue to have the aura of impartiality. If the government can mobilize statistics to back up its assertions about asylum seekers (and asylum-seeker women's pregnancies), then they cannot be acting from prejudice; there must be a real problem, according to popular thinking.[68]

In the *Irish Times* articles, several kinds of statistics are provided. First, the article gives statistics about the numbers of asylum claims filed in Ireland in recent years, which show a steady climb. Implicitly, the two test cases are referenced to these larger numbers—even though the cases are hardly "representative" of the aggregate numbers. Rather, attorneys that I interviewed speculated that Minister O'Donoghue selected these two cases precisely because they were particularly weak, juridically speaking. Yet from the minister's point of view, their weakness was precisely their strength since this offered the best opportunity to secure a court ruling that would unbind him from the *Fajujonu* decision. Moreover, such an outcome would not be confined to the two families but instead generalized to reshape the government's handling of *all* asylum cases involving migrant families with Irish citizen children.[69]

In addition to numbers of asylum claims, other statistics are provided. We are told that by the end of October 2001, "4,500 [applications to remain in Ireland based on parentage of an Irish citizen child] have been lodged this year, representing one-third of all asylum claims." The specific referent at the end of the sentence is unclear; for instance, since fewer than 13,500 asylum applications were filed in 2001, then 4,500 cannot be one-third of claims for the year. It cannot be one-third for all asylum claims ever filed, either. It may (or may not) represent one-third of all unprocessed claims.[70] Yet, although the referent is unclear, the implication is that the one-third of asylum seekers who have filed for residency on the basis of parentage of an Irish citizen child likely have asylum claims that are weak, unfounded, or bogus. Moreover, the sentence teaches readers to read statistics about asylum claims side by side with statistics about applications for residency based on parentage, creating a simple correlation while ruling out complexities. For instance, the fact that other categories of migrants, not just asylum seekers, received residency based on parentage of an Irish child is rendered invisible.[71]

Metaphor and statistics combine to suggest that rates of asylum seeking, and subsequent rates of residency for asylum seekers based on childbearing (rather than on state determinations that their asylum claims are valid), are growing at an alarming rate. The first article opens with a reference to a "surge in births"; the second speaks of applications to remain based on parentage as "soar[ing]." In his *Essay on Population,* Malthus famously introduced the distinction between arithmetic versus geometric growth. According to Malthus, food increases at an arithmetic rate (1, 2, 3, 4, and so on), whereas population grows at a geometric rate (1, 2, 4, 8, 16, and so on), which presents the possibility of a doomsday scenario.[72] Similarly, the numbers of asylum seekers entering Ireland, and the numbers of migrants claiming residency based on birth of an Irish child, seem to be increasing at a rate that is closer to geometric than arithmetic.[73] The language of "doomsday" had already been evoked to describe the impact of these developments on maternity hospitals. On August 4, 2001, an *Irish Times* article, "Holles Street [maternity hospital] Can't Keep Up with the Baby Boom," opened with an imaginary scenario in which the (presumably Irish citizen) reader is pregnant, her contractions are closer together, she's ready to deliver, and she rushes to the hospital—only to be turned away because the hospital is overwhelmed, including by nonnational women. The master of the Holles Street maternity hospital, Dr. Declan Keane, was quoted as saying, "The three big Dublin [maternity] hospitals are facing a 'doomsday scenario,'" since they cannot keep up with the numbers.[74] In general, as Pat Guerin describes, "the sense of a deluge of asylum-seeking immigrants 'flooding' into Ireland became a feature of Irish print media from 1997 onwards."[75]

In short, the statistical link that is created between asylum seeking and acquiring residency through childbearing singles out women's bodies in a manner that reduces them to their sexual and reproductive organs. In the *Irish Times* articles discussed here, Minister O'Donoghue describes pregnancy rates in vague terms: "A significant proportion" of women are pregnant on arrival. Over time, the claim became more specific, involving government statements that 50 percent, then 80 percent of asylum-seeker women are pregnant on arrival.[76] Maternity hospitals also became important producers of data that reduced asylum-seeker women to their pregnancy rates.[77] The Irish Medical Association weighed in, too, with its study of the rates of perinatal mortality for pregnant asylum seeking and refugee women in Ireland.[78] The statistics were often murky—for example, conflating childbearing rates for all nonnational women (including legal migrant workers, visitors, students, and others) with that of asylum seekers.[79] Nonetheless, statistics about pregnancy rates become one of the most significant forms of knowledge about migrant women that circulated in Ireland.

"Making Up" Illegality through Sexual Reproduction

Statistics about pregnancy rates also became the means to suggest that migrant women, especially asylum seekers, who had children were likely to "really" be illegal migrants.[80] Several key links between childbearing, asylum seeking, and illegal migration are evident in the following passage:

> The number of asylum-seekers applying to remain here on this parentage rule has soared in the past year. . . . With Ireland being the only EU member to grant citizenship automatically to children born in the State, the Department believes many failed asylum-seekers are using this loophole to stay in the country. It also believes some women are coming here specifically to have children. The Minister for Justice, Mr. O'Donoghue, last month said Ireland's unusual legal position was "well known abroad." "A significant proportion" of female asylum-seekers were pregnant upon arrival here and their decision to seek asylum was partly motivated by the benefits they could obtain through having a child in Ireland, he said.[81]

Here, the minister describes Ireland as unique among EU countries in granting birthright citizenship (not to mention in granting residency to migrant parents of an Irish child). This makes Ireland a special "target" for immigration "abuse," by his reckoning. Practices of targeting are shown, in his view, by the fact that "a significant proportion" of women are pregnant upon arrival. One may wonder how the department gathers information about the pregnancy rates of arriving asylum seekers, but such efforts certainly illuminate that women's heterosexualized bodies easily become sites for knowledge production that is used for immigration control. The minister's comments also implicitly reference several highly publicized instances when migrant women immediately went into labor upon arrival in Ireland.[82] Claims that women were arriving in advanced stages of pregnancy (which placed particular stress on the maternity hospitals) became an important element of the mainstream construction of illegal immigration and its consequences—as well as fostering the sense of Ireland being "flooded," as described earlier.

A second important element of this passage is the claim that pregnant migrant women are not merely "targeting" Ireland but doing so to gain benefits. Those who enter as asylum seekers, specifically, are supported at government expense because asylum seekers are not permitted to engage in paid employment (see chapter 3). Once their children are born asylum-seeker women have grounds to acquire residency, which allows them to access the regular social welfare system with its more generous entitlements. They may also attend government-sponsored training courses and enter into paid employment. Their children are entitled to the full range of benefits and opportunities that attach to Irish (and EU) citizenship. As Pat Guerin describes, "informing public attitudes to asylum seekers in Ireland is the belief that most applications were in fact 'bogus' and aimed at defrauding the Irish welfare system. . . . 1997 marked the beginning of a focus on refugees and asylum seekers as expensive welfare cheats."[83]

Moreover, mainstream discourses employed zero-sum logic to suggest that benefits received by asylum seekers reduced benefits that were available to Irish people. As Bryan Fanning describes, "asylum seekers were depicted as welfare scroungers, in competition with indigenous groups for welfare resources."[84] Indeed, some public discourses suggested that asylum seekers received more generous benefits than the Irish poor and working classes. For example, the *Irish Examiner* reported:

> The rumour mill has gone into overdrive with stories of largess being made available for the benefit of asylum seekers. From

2FM's Gerry Ryan to the morning chat shows on local radio stations, the myth mongers are having a field day. Apparently they are getting more than "our own." Asylum seekers, at taxpayers' expense, are allegedly getting subsidised cars, which don't need to be insured; free mobile phones; and lump sums in social welfare payments which are being spent on toys and sweets for their numerous children. That's on top of the electricity bill being paid by the State and free TV licences. Anyone with common sense knows it's complete bunkum.[85]

Thus, economic struggles facing poor and working people during the period of the Celtic Tiger were easily attributed to costs associated with asylum seekers rather than to economic policies pursued by the government that produced growing social and economic gaps. As described in chapter 3, claims about asylum seekers as welfare (ab)users eventually contributed to a social transformation whereby, for the first time, certain benefits became tied to citizenship status, and differentiations among migrants (as well as between migrants and citizens) would be increasingly institutionalized, articulated, and experienced through differential regimes of social welfare.

Claims of welfare sponging were never empirically substantiated but were nonetheless repeated, including from the highest levels of government. For instance, five days after the minister's claim that pregnant asylum-seeker women were primarily motivated by the prospect of benefits rather than by the desire to escape from persecution, Taoiseach (prime minister) Bertie Ahern stated, "Many of those working in the maternity hospitals have highlighted the enormous growth in the numbers of pregnant women who come to the hospitals within a few days of arriving here, and these people are quite clear on their entitlements and what it means if their babies are born in Ireland."[86] In sum, mainstream discourses suggested that pregnant migrants were users of (but not contributors to) social welfare benefits; their access to benefits served as an incentive for growing numbers of pregnant women to "target" Ireland; and ordinary Irish people were being hurt by these policies toward asylum seekers, with no end in sight.[87]

A third concern, implied by Minister O'Donoghue's remarks but made more explicit elsewhere, is that the supposed targeting of Ireland by pregnant migrant women threatened to erode national sovereignty and remake the racial and cultural order. For example, three days after

*Billboard from Amnesty International Ireland's 2001 campaign for Leadership
Against Racism, showing the faces of the minister for justice, the taoiseach,
and the tánaiste, as displayed outside a pub in Galway. Image by author.*

the minister's remarks, the *Irish Examiner* ran an article that was head-
lined "State Alert as Pregnant Asylum Seekers Aim for Ireland."[88] Noel
O'Flynn, a member of parliament, argued, "'the asylum crisis is out of
control and the country is being held hostage by spongers, wasters, and
con-men' [including by those who use (or abuse)] . . . the maternity-
residency clause in the constitution."[89] Expanding on this theme, Ireland's small anti-immigrant group, the Immigration Control Platform
(ICP) dropped leaflets into mailboxes in Dublin 7, which was an area of
the inner city with a high concentration of refugees and asylum seekers,
urging people to "stop the invasion and colonisation of Ireland." The
leaflet mentioned the maternity-residency clause as the mechanism for
invasion and colonization.[90] ICP founder Áine Ní Chonáill "described
the current government policy on asylum seekers as 'a charter for invasion,'" and Ireland as becoming a maternity ward for West Africa.[91] The
concerns about national sovereignty became explicit in the *L&O* case,
with the defendants arguing that their deportation would violate the

constitutional guarantees to protect the family—while the minister counterargued that their deportation was necessary to ensure the "integrity" of the immigration and asylum system, which is crucial for national sovereignty.

Finally, migrants having babies also became conflated with organized crime. Guerin describes that the media had contributed to the criminalization of asylum seekers through "numerous sensationalist reports on asylum-seeker involvement in criminal activity."[92] The association of asylum seeking with illegal immigration was certainly one crucial dimension of the process. In terms of childbearing women, in particular, the *Irish Examiner* reported, "criminals in Lagos organize transport to Ireland for pregnant women. The majority of births to asylum seekers in Dublin hospitals are to Nigerian women."[93]

Making the Case

Many groups voiced concerns about the possible connections between asylum seeking, illegal migration, and childbearing. But only the minister and the Department of Justice were in a position to take action. Thus, the minister's framing of the problem was crucial.

In a nutshell, Minister O'Donoghue believed that Ireland's migration regime offered a direct incentive for illegal immigration. He argued that illegal immigrants were entering Ireland by claiming asylum and then securing residency by birthing Irish children. With residency, these unwanted and undesirable migrants could make claims on the state including for welfare, health care, and education. As a result, illegal immigration threatened to grow at an exponential rate. A standard governmental response to illegal immigration is deportation—but in Ireland, migrants who gave birth to children could circumvent deportation, not to mention bypass standard state immigration controls. Thus, the minister was hampered in his ability to effectively respond to illegal immigration—unless the *Lobe and Osayande* (*L&O*) case enabled him to convince the court to change the rules.

In this account pregnancies were constructed as the literal means through which illegal immigration was taking place. Migrant women's pregnancies became understood within a framework of calculating consumer choice, welfare sponging, or criminal intent rather than through the lens of the complex, diverse histories that shaped migration into and through Ireland. Pregnancy became the predominant discourse through which everyone came to "know" or know something about migrant women. At the same time, there appeared to be nothing beyond their pregnancies that one needed to know.[94] Effectively, migrant women were reduced to their vaginas and pregnant bellies, which were paraded before the public. Like modern-day Sarah Baartmans, their figures rendered normative heterosexuality problematic. The minister's planned solution neither acknowledged nor problematized normative heterosexuality but instead involved reconfiguring normative heterosexuality along more obviously racialized lines and as an explicit technology for border control.

The minister's framing did not materialize from thin air. It drew on discourses and practices that had already developed to "make up" asylum seekers in certain ways. Scholars, activists, and members of the public have described the approach as exclusionary, alarmist, and unwelcoming. It included the development of a legal regime that focused on preventing asylum seekers from ever arriving, and, if they did, ensuring that their applications would be processed in ways that likely resulted in denial. It also included the development of the policies of dispersal and direct provision, which scattered asylum seekers around the nation into segregated housing facilities that were generally operated for profit by private corporations. The minister's framing also drew on widespread narratives about sexual activity across lines of legal status that transformed migrants' possibilities. Finally, the minister drew on—but clearly intended to rework—the historic connections between women's childbearing and national belonging that had been institutionalized through the 1937 constitution.

The minister's effort to "make the case" for changing the existing system worked not only through the information that he used but equally from the information that he did not use. For example, the role of the Irish state in generating migration—including through its membership in the EU, its trade policies, and its tacit participation in ongoing United States wars—was not acknowledged. EU and Irish migration regimes—which focus on increasing "free movement" for EU nationals in order to increase prosperity while at the same time steadily criminalizing migration by all others—exacerbated the problem since they did not address the root causes of migration but rather simply criminalized those who crossed nation-state borders without state permission. The voices and views of asylum seekers and migrants were not considered by—not permitted to disrupt?—the minister's framing of the problem. The role of Irish men and women in enabling migrants to acquire residency through childbearing was silenced. The fact that migrants other than those categorized as asylum seekers were also acquiring residency through a child was rendered invisible. For instance, in 2002, 4,027 people gained residency through an Irish child, including 3,027 people who were or had been in the asylum system and 950 migrant workers and international students.[95] The omission of all of these issues meant that alternative ways of conceiving the connections between childbearing and asylum seeking were shut down. Consequently, the contention that most asylum seekers were really illegal immigrants—who used childbearing to avoid deportation, and as a route to residency—was made to seem plausible, reasonable, and self-evident.

Minister O'Donoghue's framing was critical because the Department of Justice is in charge of establishing and managing immigration controls. Subsequent chapters track governmental actions that were undertaken in light of the minister's framing. Although he defined the problem by focusing on asylum seekers, the problem's resolution would affect all categories of migrants, not just asylum seekers—and would reshape the meaning of "being Irish."

CHAPTER 2

Counternarratives of Migration Law and Childbearing

MINISTER FOR JUSTICE JOHN O'DONOGHUE'S REMARKS, ana-lyzed in chapter 1, reflect the viewpoint of global northern state officials who consider unauthorized human migration across interna-tional borders to be a very serious problem. The remarks also reflect and further contribute to the framing of childbearing migrants, especially asylum seekers, as "really" illegal migrants who are cynically exploiting the system for their own gain. According to the minister, this necessi-tated further efforts to criminalize them.

Catherine Dauvergne captures the paradox that faces states when they try to reduce illegal migration primarily through expanded crimi-nalization: "Each extension of the law regulating migration increases il-legal migration through defining increasingly larger categories as being outside the law. In addition, states have stepped up migration enforce-ment. This too increases the number of illegal migrants through tech-nologies of surveillance. . . . The current 'crackdown' on extralegal mi-gration cannot help but increase it."[1]

This chapter uses nonstate narratives to complicate and critique state approaches to addressing unwanted migration that primarily involve ex-panding criminalization, or creating incentives and disincentives, with-out addressing the global dynamics and multiple inequalities in which migration processes are rooted. It shows how these state approaches set up various migrants to become designated as illegal, and how childbear-ing enabled a relatively small number of migrants to avoid that outcome. The narratives are drawn from many sources, including interviews that I conducted in the summer of 2001, when I volunteered at a Dublin law office that handled many immigration and asylum claims. Using the contacts that resulted, I asked twenty-six people to share their views on the claim that "illegal" immigrants were entering Ireland by requesting asylum and then using childbearing as a means to gain legal residence, thereby bypassing state scrutiny and immigration controls. Most interviewees were Irish born and raised, white, and drawn largely from community-based groups, nongovernment organizations, legal services, and activist organizations. Their comments were enhanced by participant observation at the Vincentian Refugee Centre, where I got to know some asylum seekers in depth and made connections with many others, ten of whom I formally interviewed.[2]

The interviewees overwhelmingly challenged the stereotype of "pregnant asylum seeker who is really an illegal immigrant" and instead speculated about the heterogeneous origins and varied migration experiences of the women who had become reduced to that stereotype. They pointed out that migrants were generally not illegal in the sense of lacking legal authorization for their presence but instead were vulnerable to being made illegal as a result of both Ireland's confusing, exclusionary patchwork of immigration and asylum laws as well as the effects of exclusionary laws in other EU states. In that context, interviewees suggested, childbearing may have offered some migrants a means to negotiate multiple difficulties and jeopardies.[3]

Interweaving interview materials with published sources, this chapter therefore provides information about asylum and migration laws in Ireland, discusses how the laws set up various migrants to become designated as illegal, and addresses how pregnancy and childbearing may have offered some migrants a means to negotiate these difficulties and barriers. It indicates the diversity of individuals, communities, and circumstances that were lumped together under the stereotypical discourses about "illegal" migrants. And it treats migrants' pregnancies and childbearing not through the lens of state discourses—as either timeless expressions of unchanging cultural essence or difference, or as evidence of Othered women's sexualities being harnessed for undesirable, criminal, or fraudulent ends—but as complex, historically situated, multiply structured processes and experiences through which some migrant women established legal presence despite the exclusionary efforts and discourses of the Irish state.[4] The chapter also makes clear that not just migrants but also many citizens found much to question about the state's migration control strategies. Since interviewees differentiated between women who were already pregnant when they arrived and women who became pregnant after arrival, the chapter is organized accordingly.

Pregnant Asylum Seekers Arriving from Other EU States

Some interviewees focused on women such as Mrs. Lobe and Mrs. Osayande (discussed in chapter 1), whose asylum claims had been denied in another EU state and who consequently faced the likelihood of deportation to their countries of origin. Rather than waiting to be deported, however, the women instead traveled to Ireland where they reapplied for asylum. The women were pregnant when they arrived, and since the processing of asylum claims generally took considerably longer than nine months, the women could expect to become eligible for residency on the basis of birthing Irish citizen children, regardless of the outcome of their asylum claims.[5]

The Irish government regarded such women with dismay. Dominant discourses, not only in Ireland but also in other EU countries, described them as engaged in "asylum shopping," a disparaging term that reduced their actions to a matter of calculating "consumer choice." The Irish Refugee Council explains, "This term relates . . . to the perception that asylum seekers may choose one EU Member State over another on the basis of a higher standard of reception conditions or social security assistance."[6] The Dublin Convention, which requires individuals to apply for asylum in the first EU country in which they arrive, was introduced to address this concern. Under the Dublin Convention, if individuals can be shown to have passed through the border of another EU member state, or to have lodged asylum claims in another EU state, they may be returned to that state for their asylum claims to be considered. As well as addressing "asylum shopping," the Dublin Convention was intended to remedy the problem of "refugees in orbit," which involved asylum seekers whose claims were passed from one state to another without any state assuming final responsibility for making a determination.

No study has ever shown that asylum seekers deliberately select a country based on the levels of its welfare benefits, which suggests that the discourses of "asylum shopping" misrepresent migrants' actions and intentions. Studies have shown, however, that the underlying premise of the Dublin Convention is debatable. As the Irish Refugee Council describes, the Dublin Convention "relies upon the assumption that the asylum seeker will receive equal protection and equal access to justice in each EU Member State. However, European national legal systems have divergent views on asylum procedures, particularly in relation to the

definition of a refugee, the definition of a safe third country and the definition of agents of persecution."[7] These differences are reflected by the
divergent rates among EU member states in their recognition of asylum
claims. For example, in 2005 the overall EU recognition rate was 15.5 percent, but individual member-state recognition rates varied from 0 percent to 63.1 percent (Ireland's rate was 8.7 percent).[8] In 2006 the overall
EU recognition rate was 22.3 percent, with recognition rates ranging
from 0 percent to 73 percent (with Ireland's rate at 9.3 percent).[9] This
suggests that contrary to claims about the harmonization of asylum procedures across the EU, the outcome of one's asylum case still seems to
significantly depend on the country where one applies.

Many interviewees with whom I spoke were aware that asylum processing is not standardized throughout the EU. Moreover, they knew
that there are reasons why migrants may seek asylum in a specific country, including the presence of family connections, language ties, or an
established community that can ease the transition.[10] Thus, interviewees did not necessarily regard migrants who sought and were refused
asylum elsewhere and who then came to Ireland, as "shoppers," cheaters,
manipulators, or effectively "illegal." This included when the migrants
were pregnant on arrival.

Migrants Who Needed Complementary Protection

Some interviewees understood that in addition to disparities among EU
states in terms of their rates for recognizing asylum claims, there are also
disparities in terms of "complementary protection." Complementary
protection is important for migrants who do not meet the Geneva Convention standards for refugee status but who need protection anyway.
For example, the Organization for African Unity recognizes the need for
protection among migrants who, "owing to external aggression, occupa-
tion, foreign domination or events seriously disturbing public order in
either part or the whole of [their] country of origin or nationality, [are]
compelled to leave [their] place of habitual residence in order to seek refuge in another place." Similarly, the Organization of American States'
Declaracíon de Cartegena recognizes that migrants who flee "generalized violence, foreign aggression, internal conflicts, and massive violation of human rights or other circumstances which have seriously disturbed the public order" may need protection. But these kinds of needs

are not recognized under the Geneva Convention, which governs asylum processing in the EU.[11]

At the time that I conducted my research, Ireland did not officially offer complementary protection to migrants who did not meet Geneva Convention standards but were nonetheless at risk. Rather, migrants could appeal to the minister for justice, equality, and law reform for humanitarian leave to remain, based on section 3(6) of the Immigration Act 1999. Significantly, this section of the act concerns not protection but deportation. Migrants, including those whose asylum claims are refused, receive a notice of deportation. The notice explains that they may leave voluntarily; report for deportation at a given date, time, and location; or, within fifteen days, submit a written representation to the minister that explains why the deportation should not occur. "Humanitarian considerations" is one of the grounds for making such a representation. Ursula Fraser clarifies that "Section 3 of the Immigration Act 1999 is not designed to act as a scheme of complementary protection," but in the absence of other alternatives, it came to assume that role.[12] Effectively, migrants had to wait until they received a notice of deportation before it was possible to even initiate an application to remain on humanitarian or other grounds.[13] Moreover, decisions about whether to grant humanitarian leave were (and are) made entirely at the minister's discretion in a nontransparent manner.[14]

In October 2006 a more systematic effort to provide complementary protection was introduced into Irish law.[15] After that date a migrant who was refused refugee status could apply for "subsidiary" (i.e., complementary) protection in addition to applying for leave to remain on other grounds.[16] Only certain migrants were eligible to be considered for subsidiary protection: those who "a) are not a national of a Member State of the European Union, b) have been refused a declaration as a refugee in Ireland, and c) substantial grounds have been shown for believing that, if returned to the country of origin, or country of former habitual residence, an individual would face a real risk of suffering serious harm."[17] The numbers granted subsidiary protection are low; according to Corona Joyce, "by the end of 2008 some 2,896 applications [for subsidiary protection] had been received . . . some 9 cases [were] granted Subsidiary Protection status, with 545 cases refused."[18] In 2009, the most recent year for which statistics are available, there were 2,089 applications for subsidiary protection made in Ireland; 24 were granted and 635 were refused.[19]

The Immigration, Residence and Protection Bill (IRPB), first introduced in 2008, proposed to create a single process under which migrants
could apply to be considered for refugee status and, failing that, for subsidiary protection. As Brian Barrington explains, the current process
"leaves a person who is clearly eligible for subsidiary protection, but not
for refugee status, having to apply twice for protection and to wait longer
than he or she should have to. It is also inefficient since essentially the
same file has to be examined twice over, giving rise to delay and increased cost."[20] While migrants' cases are being examined and reexam-
ined, they are forced to remain within the direct provision system (see
chapter 3 for critical analysis of the system) rather than being able to get
on with their lives. Thus, a single process for considering migrants' protection needs promised to provide significant advantages—if, as Barrington noted, it was implemented properly, with sufficient resources,
and in a manner that ensured fairness. With the fall of the government in
early 2011, however, progress on the IRPB, including the possible introduction of a single procedure, came to a halt.

People that I interviewed were not aware of exactly how complementary protection worked or did not work. But most understood that migrants might need protection even when they did not meet the Geneva
Convention guidelines, and that such protection was very difficult to
get. Thus, some interviewees suspected that women were arriving pregnant in Ireland because they had been denied asylum and complementary protection in other EU countries—yet, given the strictness of asylum and the limitations on complementary protection in Ireland, having
a child was the only way for some people in difficult circumstances to
establish legal residence.

Difficulties accessing complementary protection may shed light on
the experiences of the Lobe family, who sought to gain residency through
their citizen child when their asylum claim was refused. As explained in
chapter 1, the Lobes had traveled from Britain to Ireland after Britain
denied their asylum claim. They reapplied for asylum in Ireland even
though they were ineligible to do so under the Dublin Convention. The
Irish state sought to deport them but eventually delayed doing so because Mrs. Lobe was heavily pregnant and ill. When their child was
born, the family sought residency based on the child—but instead, the
minister for justice used them as a test case through which to effectively
void the *Fajujonu* decision that had given residency to migrant parents of

citizen children.[21] Throughout these events, official documents provided no information whatsoever about the substance of the Lobes' asylum
claim. *Irish Times* journalist Nuala Haughey's interview with David
Lobe, however, suggests that the family may have needed complementary protection:

> He left his home near a Roma village outside Most [in the Czech
> Republic] in 1999, having sold his house and car. He says his
> Roma wife, Jana, who had had a job cleaning buses, was beaten
> while travelling on a bus into town one day. She was pregnant at
> the time and lost the baby. "They didn't like Romas there," he
> says. "If you were walking in the street in our town they call [to]
> us 'Jews go to gas' and nasty words."
>
> The couple and their then three children travelled to the U.K.,
> which they had learned from the newspapers was multicultural
> and without too much racism. They didn't fare well there, as their
> claim to be refugees fleeing persecution was rejected within four
> months. Their appeal too was turned down, but it was almost a
> year before it was processed and a deportation order was made
> against them.
>
> Meanwhile, Lobe's mother, father and sister had also left the
> Czech Republic and were living in Bandon, Co. Cork, [Ireland]
> also as asylum applicants. Lobe says his diabetic father was ill and
> his mother implored him to move to Ireland. Facing deportation
> from the U.K., Lobe and his young family had little to lose, so
> they travelled to Ireland in March, 2001. At the time of her
> arrival, Jana was pregnant. Within five months, the family's
> refugee application and its appeal had been refused. They were
> faced with deportation from Ireland while Jana was in an ad-
> vanced stage of pregnancy and severely anaemic.[22]

Racist, anti-Roma violence that led to a miscarriage may not have qualified the Lobe family for refugee status under the Geneva Convention.
But it does raise questions about whether the family needed complementary protection. However, the family received neither complementary protection nor residency based on their Irish child; instead, they became
one of two families whose cases were used to end the practice of granting
residency to migrants with Irish children. Lobe described that throughout

the legal deliberations over his family's future, he kept asking himself, "Why me? Why me? Why my family?" He concluded, "If I'm being honest with you, I give up. I don't hope. I couldn't win because what I am? I am nothing. I am just an immigrant and the Government they have the power."[23]

Migrants Who May Have Been Trafficked or Smuggled

Some interviewees suggested that women were pregnant on arrival because they were being trafficked by organizations that were aware of Ireland's "maternity residency" policy. As grounds for their suspicions, Irish interviewees mentioned that on arrival, some migrants clearly did not know what country they were in, and some had never even heard of Ireland.

Separately, several asylum seekers vividly described to me how disorienting and frightening it was to find themselves in a country that they had never heard of. Partly this was because of the colonial geographies that they had learned in school, which described Northern Ireland as part of Britain but omitted to mention the existence of a Republic of Ireland. None of these asylum seekers described themselves as being trafficked; indeed, they provided no details about their means of arrival, and I did not inquire. But it is certainly likely that some migrants had been trafficked. Others may have been smuggled. The silence surrounding such experiences is compounded by the conceptual confusion around definitions of trafficking, smuggling, and unauthorized migration.

Trafficking has become a pervasive concern in global northern states in recent years. Definitions of trafficking and laws and policies to address it generally build on the United Nations Protocol to Prevent, Suppress, and Punish Trafficking in Persons, Especially Women and Children (2000). The protocol defines trafficking as involving three crucial elements: as "an *action* consisting of 'the recruitment, transportation, transfer, harbouring or receipt of persons'; as [an action] which occurs by *means of* 'the threat or use of force or other forms of coercion, of abduction, of fraud, of deception, of the abuse of power or of a position of vulnerability or of the giving or receiving of payments or benefits to achieve the consent of a person having control over another person'; and as being undertaken '*for the purpose of exploitation.*' "[24] This definition is far from clear, with the result that trafficking is frequently conflated with smuggling, unauthorized migration, or prostitution, which generates problematic laws and policies that further subordinate and victimize the migrants involved.

The Platform for International Cooperation on Undocumented Migrants (PICUM) offers a working definition of the distinction between trafficking and smuggling: "The smuggling of migrants, while often undertaken in dangerous or degrading conditions, involves migrants who have consented to the smuggling. Trafficking victims, on the other hand, have either never consented or, if they initially consented, that consent has been rendered meaningless by the coercive, deceptive or abusive actions of the traffickers."[25] PICUM identifies another key difference between trafficking and smuggling: "[Trafficking in human beings] involves the subjection of trafficked persons to forced labour, which is the means by which traffickers make profits on their activities. People smugglers will charge fees for facilitating the crossing of national frontiers, but need not remain involved with the smuggled person after the crossing of the border."[26] Moreover, "trafficking *need not involve a violation of immigration regulations*, and can also take place when people have a right of entry and residence in the country of destination, but have nevertheless been coerced into making the journey. In these circumstances the act of trafficking would not involve infringement of immigration regulations at all, though the element of coercion would make it a crime against the individual."[27]

As this suggests, reliable distinctions between trafficked, smuggled, and unauthorized migrants are often difficult to make.[28] Moreover, smuggled migrants may become trafficked migrants in the course of their journeys; and smuggled migrants, like those who are trafficked, routinely experience exploitation. Indeed, Bridget Anderson and Rutvica Andrijasevic argue that definitions of trafficking that rely on exploitation raise a critical difficulty: "how to distinguish trafficking from legally tolerated employment contracts (and also from legally tolerated forms of exploitation of women and children within families)? . . . How to draw a line in the sand between 'trafficked' and 'not trafficked but just-the-regular-kind-of-exploitation' migrants?"[29] For this reason, scholars including Anderson and Andrijasevic have proposed that we need to consider migrants as experiencing a spectrum of exploitation that does not divide neatly into trafficked/not trafficked.[30]

Importantly, the UN definition of trafficking, on which much policy- and law-making builds, is part of a protocol against *transnational crime,* rather than a protocol concerned with human rights.[31] As Kamala Kempadoo describes, "Anti-trafficking in this framework is synonymous with a war on international crime, and represents an attack on the movement of persons, weapons, or drugs that defy or circumvent legal boundaries and borders."[32] Thus, ramped up immigration controls have become the preferred method for addressing trafficking. Yet "prioritizing crime, punishment, and immigration control . . . supports the neoliberal economic interests of corporations, multilateral agencies, policy experts and national governments, rather than those of the world's working and poor people."[33] For instance, strengthened immigration controls do not address the conditions that give rise to trafficking (or smuggling or undocumented migration) in the first instance. Rather, strengthened immigration controls *reinforce* relations of power and forms of exploitation of migrants. Effectively, they strengthen the hand of traffickers and employers over migrants by criminalizing the migrants' presence and activities.

At the time that I conducted my research, Ireland had little legislation in place to address trafficking. The gardaí (police) operated under the Illegal Immigrants (Trafficking) Act 2000, which was primarily enacted to criminalize and control illegal immigration into Ireland. As the title suggests, the law conflated smuggling, trafficking, and unauthorized immigration.[34] Furthermore, Eilís Ward and Gillian Wylie note that despite the reference to trafficking in the title, the law makes no reference to exploitation, which remains central to most definitions of trafficking.[35]

In 2003 the Garda National Immigration Bureau (GNIB) launched Operation Quest to address criminality, prostitution, and human trafficking in the lap-dancing industry, which employed migrant women.[36] More than one hundred people were arrested and ten prosecutions resulted. Wylie comments, "It is notable that these prosecutions were all related to breaches to visa regulations or work permits and were not prosecuted as trafficking cases. . . . By identifying the women primarily as violators of visa regulations, they became categorised immediately as illegal migrants and liable to be deported. The question of whether they had been trafficked therefore receded from sight, although suspicion remains that this was the case."[37]

Also in 2003 Pauline Conroy published a study on children who were believed to have been trafficked to Ireland.[38] In 2006 the U.S. State Department's deeply problematic but highly influential annual Trafficking in Persons Report suggested that Ireland was both a transit and destination country for human trafficking, and this conclusion was repeated in subsequent versions of the report.[39] In 2007 Ward and Wylie published the first survey of the extent of trafficking of women over eighteen years of age into Ireland for purposes of sexual exploitation. Their study raised concerns about how to appropriately define trafficking, including because of ambiguities in the international definition; the fact that the Irish state offered no official definition; the ways that discussions of trafficking for sexual exploitation get bogged down in polarized debates about whether prostitution inevitably constitutes abuse or whether some women may exercise agency within the constraints of their circumstances by selling sex (which, in turn, raises complicated questions about whether the sale of sex should be addressed as a moral or a labor issue); and how various institutions, especially governments, have a vested interest in generating particular kinds of numerical data about the issue.[40] As the authors note, "definitional differences are not simply ideological but affect the nature of the data."[41] The authors addressed these difficulties by allowing "those interviewed in the research process to offer their own definitions of trafficking," while nonetheless noting that "most cases detailed to us contained elements of the main ingredients of trafficking—deceptive recruitment, transfer and exploitation without consent."[42] Based on this approach, Ward and Wylie concluded that at least seventy-six women had been trafficked into Ireland for the sex industry between 2000 and 2006.[43]

Although most attention was focused on the trafficking of migrant women and children for sexual exploitation, the Migrant Rights Centre Ireland (MCRI) drew attention to migrants who were being trafficked for other kinds of forced labor and urged the government to make administrative and legal changes that would address migrants' needs.[44] According to MCRI, migrants were being trafficked to Ireland for domestic, agricultural, restaurant, care, construction, seafaring, and circus work.[45]

The government passed and implemented the Criminal Law (Human Trafficking) Act of 2008, which forbids trafficking in adults or children for the purposes of sexual or labor exploitation or to sell their organs.[46] It also makes it an offense to sell or offer for sale or purchase or offer to purchase any person. Section 5 makes it an offense to solicit a trafficked person for prostitution.[47] To ensure a comprehensive and coordinated response to trafficking, an anti–human trafficking unit was established in the Department of Justice, Equality, and Law Reform in that same year. A high-level group on trafficking in human beings was also established, and was tasked with presenting to the minister the most effective response for dealing with trafficking in humans. During its participation in the European G6 Human Trafficking Initiative in October 2008, Ireland launched an anti–human trafficking awareness-raising campaign called Blue Blindfold. The Garda Síochana Annual Policing Plan for 2009 identified trafficking in human beings as one of its priorities. The "National Action Plan to Prevent and Combat Trafficking of Human Beings in Ireland 2009–2012" was published in June 2009.

Yet the conceptual confusion around smuggling, trafficking, and illegal immigration continued to shape how trafficking was understood as well as the actions that were undertaken to address it. Proposed solutions continued to emphasize controlling immigration and crime rather than migrants' rights and needs. This emphasis is reflected in the provisions for helping those who are identified as victims of trafficking. In 2008 rules were enacted to allow a sixty-day period of "recovery and reflection" for victims of trafficking.[48] However, many argue that the rules fall short. For example, migrants in severely abusive and exploitative situations often do not meet the official definition of "trafficking" and are not eligible for even this brief period of assistance. The provisions do not cover EU/EEA nationals. And only a garda who holds the rank of superintendent or higher may identify someone as a victim of trafficking. Due to these and other limitations, few migrants have received assistance; according to the Immigrant Council of Ireland (ICI), "at the time [that our 2009] report went to print, only two women who had been officially identified as victims of trafficking in Ireland had been offered protection by the State," while the vast majority of migrants continued to be treated as illegal immigrants and faced deportation.[49] The ICI concluded, "The State response is complicit with the interests of the trafficker and strengthens the position of the trafficker in relation to the woman who is trafficked. This helps to keep trafficking a hidden and clandestine problem."[50]

For the small numbers who are identified as victims of trafficking, there is no route to long-term residency in Ireland after the recovery and reflection period has ended (although the period may be extended if migrants commit to assist the gardaí in the identification and prosecution of traffickers—which many may be unable or unwilling to do).[51] Thus, these migrants face deportation at some point, even when they have been identified as victims of trafficking. According to the ICI, "There is no avenue for granting 'humanitarian leave to remain' to victims of trafficking. Therefore, the only other avenue into safety is through the protection process [i.e., seeking refugee status. But this] is not appropriate because in many cases the persecution occurs not in the country of origin but in the host country," which means that the migrant is not eligible to be considered.[52] Those who have sought to remain through the asylum process appear to have had little success, and the requirement that they remain in the direct provision system while their cases are processed has raised serious concern since that system seems manifestly inappropriate for addressing their needs.

Thus, to return to informants who suspected that some pregnant women were arriving in Ireland as a result of trafficking: we do not know, and we are unlikely to ever know, whether that was the case, but the possibility cannot be ruled out. Given the absolute lack of assistance and protection for abused and exploited migrants, residency through a child may have provided some migrants with opportunities to negotiate the otherwise impenetrable wall of juridical exclusion and criminalization.

Migrants Who Engaged in Flexible and Transnational Citizenship Strategies

There is no doubt that some women did arrange to enter Ireland, whether through smugglers or tourist visas (although these were increasingly difficult to obtain for citizens from the global south), because they wanted their children to have Irish and EU citizenship. Their experiences can be situated through reference to the rich scholarship on transnationalism and transnational families.

Roger Rouse explains that migration is generally "analyzed mainly in *bipolar* terms . . . as a move between essentially autonomous communities and, within this framework, settlement has been treated as a process in which people steadily shift their focus of attention and the locus of their principal social ties from one community to another."[53] A transnational framework, however, conceives communities of origin and settlement as linked; migrants as actively engaged in "build[ing] social fields that link together their country of origin and their country of settlement";

and settlement as a process that may entail continually moving between two often contradictory worlds, rather than erasing the cultural values associated with communities of origin.[54]

Families scattered across different nation-states are central to transnationalization processes. Deborah Bryceson and Ulla Vuorela remind us that "transnational families are not new to Europe. European trade, colonization and out-migration have created circumstances for their proliferation through the centuries."[55] But in recent decades, with global capitalist restructuring and changes in communication and transportation,

> the "transnational family" . . . is becoming more common across a wide spectrum of society. From the more "elite" astronaut families to those of overseas contract workers, transnational informal "networks," remittance "flows" and "circuits" of care and affection—often facilitated by easier mobilities and communications—have emerged to connect geographically dispersed members. . . . The realm of the "family" continues to retain its significance in the face of distance, dispersal and translocality even as the desire to go on being a family under such conditions is occasionally ruptured and continually reworked.[56]

Families become transnational for many reasons. Among the working classes, transnationalism often "represent[s] a new family form born out of the inequality in the global economy and reproduced by means of dependence on a transnational division of labor."[57] Frequently it is tied to economic survival. Among the middle and upper classes, transnationalism may provide a means to enhance "social, cultural and symbolic capital."[58] Nation-states often facilitate transnationalism among the latter group, while treating transnationalism among the working classes as a social, economic, political, and cultural threat that must be disabled. Immigration, residence, and citizenship laws and policies are crafted accordingly.

Much of the recent scholarship on transnational families focuses on women who leave children and other family members behind while they work overseas, and who remit money and engage in "mothering at a distance."[59] Certainly many migrant women employed as domestics, caregivers, and in other jobs in Ireland participate in transnational family ties. However, during the years of fierce controversy over pregnant migrants, it was virtually impossible for these workers to bring over family members, or to use their employment as a route to long-term residency. As Kieran Allen explains, the work permit system that developed in Ireland after 1999 was modeled on the concept of the guest worker: "migrants were only guests and had to be legally treated as such. There was no provision for permanent residence, no automatic assumption of family reunification, and permits could only be applied for from outside Ireland."[60]

In this context, reproductive rather than productive labor provided the means through which families, spread across national borders, could potentially build a base for long-term legal residence and various rights in Ireland. There has been no systematic study of women who may have traveled to Ireland to birth a child for these reasons. But some migrants told me that they had traveled for those reasons, or that they knew of other women who had done so. For example, one upper-middle-class Nigerian woman told me that she knew women who had come to Ireland specifically to ensure that their children would hold Irish/EU citizenship. In her view, their actions reflected "responsible" motherhood. For her, being a responsible mother entailed creating flexible futures for one's children by ensuring access to education, opportunities, and mobility that would enhance the child's life chances.[61] Birth in Ireland opened up these possibilities even while, in this woman's view, such possibilities were increasingly unavailable in many parts of Nigeria where structural adjustment programs, military dictatorship, collapse of the rule of law, and the erosion of traditional means for advancing socially had wrought massive insecurity among all classes.

The woman suggested that primarily women with financial resources were able to create these flexible futures for their children, and that they had been doing so for some time, not only in Ireland but also around the world. However, the Irish state's efforts to criminalize migration by pregnant women was undermining their ability to create flexible futures for their children—even while the need for flexible futures was growing more urgent. Since it was increasingly difficult for Nigerians to get tourist visas to Ireland, some women arranged to be smuggled while pregnant while others got tourist visas to Britain and then traveled informally to Ireland to give birth.[62]

The woman's observations echo Elisabetta Zontini's findings that Moroccan and Filipina migrant women in Europe "often . . . undertake the considerable risks involved in emigration with the citizenship rights of their children in mind. They are not only interested in immediate economic gains but often conceive their moves in order to get access to citizenship rights for themselves and above all for their children."[63] These kinds of transnational family formation strategies trouble the Irish state, which prefers to manage migrants in terms of resolutely bounded nationalist narratives, histories, and future horizons (although it is sometimes willing to deal with overseas Irish citizens using transnational and diasporic frameworks). Moreover, state policies generally do not conceive migrants within a transnational frame; as Zontini explains regarding Filipinos and Moroccans in Southern Europe:

> Reception policies . . . do not seem to recognize the possibility of
> multiple identities and different loyalties, neither do they appreci-
> ate the primary role of women migrants in the settlement process.
> Both Filipinos and Moroccans live transnationally, maintaining
> close links and participating in social and family life in at least
> two countries. This is not necessarily in conflict with their desire
> and efforts to establish themselves in Southern Europe. It may,
> however, be in opposition to reception policies that tend to
> oversimplify migrants as inevitably "excluded" and in need of
> "integration" in the local society.[64]

When policymakers are oblivious to transnationalism, women whose actions unfold within a transnational logic can only register as aberrant or criminal, not as responsible mothers.

Some women's migration may have been motivated by a more specific form of transnationalism. Dianna Shandy and David Power suggest that some women likely came to Ireland to give birth children as part of a transnational flow of medical tourists rather than because they were strategizing how to legally create opportunities around the globe for family members. "Ireland may be sought out specifically for its maternity services. In 2004, Dublin was hailed as 'the safest European city for a woman to have a baby' based on an extremely low maternal mortality rate."[65] They note that an Irish person compared women coming to Ireland for maternity health care services with "Irish women flying to South Africa for 'face lifts,' 'boob jobs,' or other cosmetic procedures."[66] Moreover, as described in chapter 4, Irish women seeking abortions have long engaged in medical tourism because abortion is unavailable in Ireland.[67]

Pregnancy and Asylum Seeking

It is likely that some women were pregnant on arrival because they had been sexually assaulted while migrating, which is a very common occurrence.[68] Or else their pregnancies were connected to the substance of their asylum claims. Unfortunately, rape is a common weapon of war and may be used as a form of persecution that results pregnancy. In the context of a gender-sensitive asylum process, these experiences may provide a legitimate basis for claiming asylum, as Irish law recognizes.[69]

Pregnancy may become connected to the need for protection in other ways, too. For example, Atanada Fatimo, a twenty-one-year-old Nigerian computer student in Cyprus, traveled to Ireland on August 17, 2002. Her student visa had expired, she was seven months pregnant outside of marriage, and she said that she was "terrified" that if returned to Nigeria she might be sentenced to death because of the pregnancy. According to news reports, a Sharia Court in Northern Nigeria had recently upheld a sentence of death by stoning that was imposed on a woman who had a child outside marriage, and Fatimo feared the same fate. According to Deputy Attorney General Petros Clerides of Cyprus, "she chose to go to Ireland because she was told that if her child was born there, it would get Irish citizenship and she would be allowed to stay."[70] However, after discovering that she was traveling on a forged British passport, Irish authorities detained her and sent her back to Cyprus. She was arrested, but the Cypriot authorities decided to not send her back to Nigeria under the circumstances. She did, however, have to answer to charges of traveling on a fake passport.

Another woman whose pregnancy was connected to her need for protection was a student in my English class. Katerina attended classes with her husband, Dimitri, a significantly younger man, and their newborn child. Over time, I came to know Katerina as a tough, strong, and optimistic woman. Eventually she told me that she had been a political activist in her own country (as was Dimitri) and was warned by members of the ruling party to stop her activities. When she became pregnant by Dimitri, she experienced medical complications and was admitted to the hospital for surgery so that she could carry the pregnancy to term. The day after her surgery, a doctor checked that no one else was around and then slipped into her room. He told her that it was best for her to leave the country as she had many enemies. She believed he was trying to help, but his advice chilled her. She realized that she had been unconscious under the scalpels of doctors who knew something about (but did not necessarily agree with) her politics. They could have ended her pregnancy rather than helping her to carry the baby to term. Why did the doctor come to warn her, she wondered. Had he heard that an action against her was being planned?

This experience occurred after Katerina and Dimitri's home had already been broken into, Dimitri had been beaten, and Katerina had been warned once more to stop her activism. It persuaded them that it was time to leave. Friends helped them to hide among sealed wooden crates on a truck that was traveling abroad. They did not know where the truck was going but expected that it was bound for Germany, Belgium, or perhaps France. After lengthy travel, the truck stopped, and Dimitri crept out to look around and try to puzzle out where they were. He saw docks and a sign that said "Dublin." He tried to remember where Dublin was and went back to the truck to ask Katerina. "Dublin? Then we are in Ireland," she told him. It began to sink in, they were in Ireland. He was unhappy and wanted to get back on the truck. But she was too sick from the pregnancy and recent surgery to continue. They had to get off. They had brought two bags, but one fell among the freight in the truck and he could not retrieve it. He lost the passports, too, which slipped unnoticed from his pocket. Together they disembarked in Dublin and began the process of seeking asylum (through what was to become their fifth language, English). Their application was refused on the grounds that they did not meet the Geneva Convention requirements.

Pregnant after Arrival

Women also became pregnant after arrival, and this did not necessarily represent "abuse." Instead, diverse circumstances and various contingencies shaped the interconnections among seeking asylum, becoming pregnant, and gaining residency through a child.

Because childbearing could lead to residency, some asylum seekers felt strongly pressured to engage in sexual relations. Many migrants told me that they knew of no one who had ever been granted asylum in Ireland, no matter how severely they had suffered. Migrants who were desperate to avoid being returned to their countries began to perceive childbearing as the "only option."[71] Yet resorting to this option presented difficult dilemmas for unmarried migrants. In some communities, dating is not permitted, marriages are arranged, and sexual activity is sanctioned only within marriage. Moreover, all families and communities have racial or ethnic, gender, and class expectations about who constitutes a suitable marriage partner as well as norms concerning the proper process for getting married. Communities also have norms concerning the acceptability of childbearing outside of marriage. Migrants as well as citizens judged one another on these bases. Thus, availing of the "baby loophole," even as a last resort, presented practical difficulties, cultural dilemmas, and threats of social censure that often worked through gendered, cultural, and class logics.[72] Some migrants resorted to this alternative even though it did not accord with their personal wishes or with familial and community norms that they deeply valued. Others refused the alternative even when they risked deportation as a result.

Reflecting on asylum seekers who viewed pregnancy as their "only option," one woman reminded me that asylum seekers whose claims failed have sometimes tried to kill themselves or mutilate their bodies rather than being forced onto a plane to return to their country of origin.[73] For asylum seekers, the body may become the only terrain that is left for enacting agency and protest, and sometimes even that is denied— for instance, when hunger strikes are abruptly ended through forced feeding, and physical struggles to avoid boarding a plane for deportation are subdued through injections that render the asylum seeker unconscious. Faced with the prospect of deportation to a situation that seems intolerable, might pregnancy not seem like a reasonable alternative, the woman asked.

Pregnancy might also seem like a better option than deliberately getting incarcerated for committing a crime, which is another route that some asylum seekers have adopted when faced with deportation. Hannah Arendt explains that, for displaced people, commission of a crime may offer more rights and security than if they simply cross a border in search of protection. With some irony, she explains:

> The same man yesterday who was in jail because of his mere
> presence in the world, who had no rights whatsoever and lived

under threat of deportation, or who was dispatched without sentence and without trial to some kind of internment because he had tried to work and make a living, may become an almost full-fledged citizen because of a little theft. Even if he is penniless, he can get a lawyer, complain about his jailers, be listened to respectfully. He is no longer the scum of the earth but important enough to be informed of all of the details of the law under which he will be tried. He will become a respectable person.[74]

Arendt's analysis crossed my mind when I overheard two teenage girls at the drop-in center, both of whom were asylum seekers, seriously discussing someone whose asylum claim was denied. One suggested, and the other agreed, that if they lost their cases and lost all appeals, they would kill themselves rather than go back to their countries. Then the first girl proposed, maybe we can do something so we would be sent to Mountjoy Jail instead? Her friend agreed, good idea, she had heard the food was good there and accommodation and living conditions were not so bad. The first girl said, maybe if we steal something we can be sent there. Her friend said, if we steal a banana, they will send us. But maybe only for a few days. Since I knew one of the girls well and felt strongly that she could not possibly return to her country, I said to her, "You need to steal something bigger so that they will send you to prison for longer."[75]

This is not to suggest that all, or even most, asylum seekers seek incarceration through lawbreaking when their claims are denied.[76] But the girls' conversation reflects the limited, often Kafkaesque, possibilities within which asylum seekers operate. Under such circumstances, becoming pregnant and gaining residency through a child—or resorting to being jailed for a crime—seemed to some women to offer the best (or only) option.[77]

Other migrant women became pregnant and bore children under very different circumstances. For example, they often waited significant lengths of time for their asylum cases to be processed. While they were waiting, migrant women, like anyone else, had sex lives. In some instances they were subjected to sexual violence. Some women were not yet planning to have children, but they did not necessarily have access to birth control methods that were familiar to them, or they did not know how to acquire contraception in Ireland. The result was unplanned pregnancies that caused great distress. Since abortion is unavailable in Ireland, some women sent overseas for herbs and medicines to induce abortions. If these did not have the desired result, the women faced a dilemma.[78] As described in chapter 4, some women received special permission from the Department of Justice to travel to the United Kingdom for abortions; others reportedly sought out "back alley" abortions, with all of their attendant risks.

In other cases, women were of childbearing age and planning to have children anyway. In that context, their pregnancies were not particularly unexpected; more striking were their experiences of being pregnant and giving birth while living in a strange country, often without the support of family and relatives, and in living situations that frequently involved impoverishment, making do, and tremendous uncertainty about their future. Patricia Kennedy and Jo Murphy-Lawless's pioneering study *The Maternity Care Needs of Refugee and Asylum Seeking Women* describes some of these struggles with sensitivity and insight.

Women's pregnancies under conditions of migration and displacement often carried important psychological meanings. For instance, one woman said, "If I had been run out of my country, I'd want to make a line in the sand, settle in, and care for a child. Because if you can't have a loving relationship, what's the purpose of life?" Echoing her, another woman said, "If I was sent to a completely unknown culture, I'd want someone to hold dear, and a baby offers that." These women's remarks centralize not only their love of children but also the importance they attach to a loving relationship more generally, especially in the context of multiple displacements. Kennedy and Murphy-Lawless describe that childbearing for asylum-seeker women may evoke painful memories of children lost or left behind but also hopes and plans for a future. One Nigerian woman "indicated firmly that once her daughter was born, Irish people would have to take her and her daughter seriously, because her daughter would be a citizen here, and she herself would want to live out the rest of her life here."[79]

Migrant women who gave birth in Ireland were generally aware that gaining residency through a child used to take significantly less time than going through the asylum system. Therefore, some opted for residency based on their child so that they could more quickly leave the limbo of the asylum system and its deprivations. Kennedy and Murphy-Lawless remind us that the asylum system requires people to cope with "extreme uncertainties and lack of control over their lives" as well as impoverishment and often poor living conditions.[80] People were eager to escape from that situation. Regularizing their status through childbearing meant being able to get on with their lives, for their own sake as well as for others who were depending on them. Over time, however, as applications for residency based on an Irish child grew, people waited for longer and longer periods. One asylum-seeker couple told me, "The process used to take two to four weeks, then two months, then it got longer and longer." When I interviewed them they had been waiting for more than a year. But residency through a child was still quicker than the asylum process, including appeals.

Seeking residency through a child seemed much simpler and less confusing than navigating the asylum system, too. A Nigerian woman described to me that after the birth of her child, her community welfare officer sent her to the Department of Justice, where a staff person helped her to complete an application and told her that she would get acknowledgment within two to four weeks, and residency shortly thereafter— which is exactly what happened. Her experience was not unusual at that time. By contrast, anyone seeking asylum had to complete a lengthy questionnaire, usually without legal assistance and often without an interpreter, then remain in the direct provision system for an indeterminate amount of time. Applicants never knew when the government might get around to calling them for an interview regarding their case, and the interview process itself was frightening and traumatic. A teenager whose parents were murdered and whose brothers permanently disappeared when antigovernment rebels swept through the village described that she was "seen by a blonde lady at the Department of Justice" who "must think I'm some kind of an angel [because she asked me] which way my brothers went when they fled." I realized that the girl understood angels to have a god's eye view of the world's happenings.[81] The girl concluded, "She asked me so many questions, I was shaking, and I screamed, and then she left me alone." Applicants not only had to describe traumatic experiences but do so in ways that made direct connections to a set of laws that few understood (and that officials interpreted so narrowly that few qualified for refugee status, in any case). Those whose asylum claims were refused—which was the vast majority—could appeal, which was

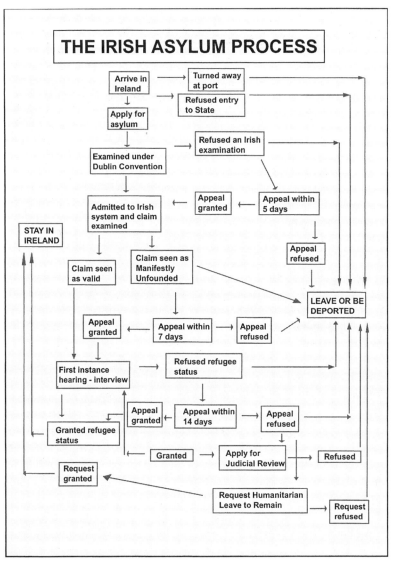

The Irish asylum process in the early years of the millennium. Image from a pamphlet, A Part of Ireland Now.

another lengthy, confusing process that took an indefinite amount of time and offered an uncertain outcome.[82]

Under these circumstances, seeking residency based on the birth of a child often seemed like a better approach. Officials did begin to tighten up the process. Since residency was based on parentage, the applicants had to establish that they were the child's biological parents and that they were each actively involved in raising the child. Women's roles in biological parentage seemed self-evident to most officials, but men's roles were sometimes disputed. In those instances officials could, at their discretion, require measures such as DNA testing—which was the responsibility of the applicant, had to be done through the United Kingdom, and was costly. If the parents were married and living together, officials asked fewer questions, but if they lived separately, then the parent who did not reside with the child had to establish clear involvement in parenting.[83] Yet, compared to the asylum process, acquiring residency through a child was far less difficult and confusing. With residency, the migrant acquired not only the legal right to remain but also the right to engage in paid employment, take FÁS training courses (though not third-level education courses without paying higher fees), be on a housing list, and sign up for regular welfare.[84]

Residency through childbearing involved forms of insecurity too. For instance, those who received residency based on recognition of their asylum claim could apply for citizenship after three years, but parents of Irish citizens had to wait for five years.[85] More importantly, residency gained through asylum was a status that the woman or man acquired for herself or himself. But residency through childbearing was derivative. It depended on the child, needed to be regularly renewed, and could be lost. In several cases I heard about, Irish citizen children died, and their parents suffered not only the terrible loss of their child but also the loss of their right to remain in Ireland. In other cases, parents' relationships broke down, and the person who was no longer actively involved in parenting lost residency rights.[86] Certainly, some who became parents of an Irish citizen child as part of a scam, or without thinking it through, were caught out by these rules and lost their status. But others whose relationships had broken down were caught out too. Moreover, because residency based on a child had to be regularly renewed, parents suffered fear that the department might deny their renewal for random, unclear, or even no reasons, especially when anti-immigrant sentiment ran high. As multiple reports make clear, immigration processes in general were confusing, nontransparent, and regularly changing, which further contributed to migrants' insecurity.[87]

Residency through a child also had potentially significant impacts on family dynamics. Parents depended on the Irish child for their own residency and in some cases for their noncitizen children's residency. This created not only a degree of "role reversal" between parents and child but also distinctions among the children themselves. Irish-born children might feel more valued; they might also have more rights and opportunities than their non-Irish siblings even though they were from the same family and often close in age.[88]

For these and other reasons, some people who dropped their asylum claims in favor of residency through childbearing sometimes came to regret their choices, even though at the time it had seemed like the best way to restart their lives and secure their futures. Women and men made these choices based on advice from friends, other asylum seekers, lawyers, and community workers. Some officials and government workers also recommended to asylum seekers that they should opt for residency based on an Irish child, although officials subsequently strongly denied this. A woman that I interviewed related that upon the birth of her child, "My welfare officer asked me, am I going to stand by the baby? And I said yes, I will stand by my baby," after which the welfare officer sent her to apply for residency on that basis. Many other people insisted that officials and welfare officers had advised them to follow the route of seeking residency based on an Irish child. The *Irish Times* described:

> "Sharon," a Nigerian mother of five children . . . believes she is one of over 100 families in the city who withdrew applications for refugee status under the mistaken impression that an application for residency was the more favourable route.
>
> The Galway Refugee Support Group said yesterday it was very concerned about Sharon and many in her situation who gave birth to children here and who may have been advised by officials to take the residency, rather than the refugee, route on this basis.
>
> "Our evidence is anecdotal, but we know lots of people who dropped their claims for asylum on advice which we believe came

from official sources," Ms. Celine Geoffret, community development worker with the Galway Refugee Support Group, told The
Irish Times yesterday.

    . . . Sharon, who is in her late 20s, says she had to leave Nigeria
when her local Catholic church was burned and several members
of her congregation were killed. She had to leave four children
behind, the oldest 12 and the youngest just one year and four
months, and was pregnant on arrival in Ireland in October 2001.
Her baby boy is now 16 months old.

    "I had applied for refugee status, but then I withdrew it
because I thought that a residency application would be quicker.
But I put in that application over a year ago, and it is still being
dealt with," Sharon said.

    "I realise now I didn't have enough information, and there are
many people like me who didn't understand the system. If I had
known the full implications, or if the refugee process had been
shorter, I would not have looked for residency because of the
birth of my son here."[89]

Clearly, some of the numbers of women who claimed residency through
childbearing, rather than through verification of their asylum claims,
were generated by government officials and workers themselves.

    Some officials explicitly advocated childbearing as a solution to legal
status difficulties. Take the case of one Irish woman I interviewed, who
married a Romanian asylum seeker. She married him despite the fact
that an immigration garda called her in to the Department of Justice and
told her that the man had said he could not love her because she was "too
fat" and he was only marrying her to gain legal status. The woman eventually realized this was not true; rather, the garda was deliberately trying
to block her involvement with the man. The garda's actions were sexist
(no one I spoke to could imagine the reverse situation, in which an Irish
man would be called in and warned that an asylum-seeker woman was
"taking advantage"). The garda may also have acted because the woman's sister had called officials to complain about her involvement with a
Romanian. My interviewee married the Romanian man anyway—
although a "mysterious" bureaucratic snafu cropped up one day before
the scheduled wedding that forced her to postpone, which meant that
she lost significant financial deposits, and her family was furious. After a

smaller, quieter wedding later on, her run-ins with the Department of Justice continued as officials continually "lost" her paperwork and demanded additional documentation. She explained that she had taken days off work to get them the papers, and at this stage they had "everything except my dirty washing." But they still delayed regularizing her husband's status, which not only immobilized him but also constrained his and his children's opportunities. When she complained, the garda suggested contemptuously that she should have a baby with her husband in order to resolve his status difficulties. "It was just like when I wanted bigger council housing and male officials told me to have another baby and I'd be eligible," she commented. "Typical Catholic thinking. But why have a baby when you don't really want it?" She already had a grown son and did not plan more children.

Asylum Seeking, Irish Children: Pursuing Both Routes

Refugee status through the asylum process or residency through birthing an Irish child represented two possible routes to legal status, and people made decisions about which route to pursue in the context of the information that they had and their own personal circumstances. Not all migrants, however, made a choice between these two options; depending on the rules that were in place when they arrived, some migrants pursued both routes.

For instance, a Nigerian couple I interviewed had arrived in stages. He came first, in late 1999. He lost touch with his wife, who left Nigeria in 2001 with the two boys and went initially to the United Kingdom to search for her husband. When she failed to find him there, she traveled to Ireland (through routes that she did not describe, and I did not ask), and they were reunited. Both sought asylum. In Nigeria he was employed as an engineer, and she held a highly ranked position in the banking industry. They had servants and six cars. In Ireland they were not permitted to work while their cases were unresolved. When she gave birth to an Irish child in December 2002 they were allowed to move out of direct provision and into private rented accommodation. But their asylum claims remained unresolved. They applied for residency on the basis of their third child while also keeping their asylum claims under consideration, but at the time when I interviewed them everything remained unsettled.

Pursuing both routes at once was an option only for those who gave birth to a child before February 11, 2003. After that date, the minister refused to accept further applications for residency based on an Irish child, citing the Supreme Court's January 2003 *L&O* decision as a basis for the change. As a result, those who were in the asylum system no longer had the option of opting out upon the birth of a child. Thus, after Katerina and Dimitri arrived in Dublin, they were dispersed to an accommodation center in a remote location in the west of Ireland. When they were called for an interview concerning their asylum claims, she remained pregnant and unwell. Their applications were denied. On the day that they learned of the denial, shock and stress sent Katerina into labor. Indeed, not only did her pregnancy motivate her to flee but she also believes that the grueling asylum process deeply affected her pregnancy, contributing to her baby's small size and low birth weight. After the baby's birth, she spent five days in the hospital. But the system required them to appeal the denial of their claim for refugee status within fifteen working days. So on the day that she got out they began trying to lodge an appeal. Refugee Legal Services, which is tasked with providing legal assistance to asylum seekers, promised to call back to schedule an appointment for them, but five more crucial days passed without any call. Frantic by then, they bundled up the baby, took a public bus to Refugee Legal Services, and got the appeal in by the skin of their teeth and through sheer persistence. They could not, however, seek residency based on the birth of their child (whom Katerina affectionately called "Irish"), since he was born in March 2003.

Multiple Jeopardies, Diverse Circumstances: Contextualizing Migrant Women's Pregnancies

Interviewees challenged many of Minister O'Donoghue's assertions, described in chapter 1, about the connections between childbearing and illegal immigration. According to the minister, pregnant women were deliberately migrating to Ireland so that they could acquire legal residence through birthing a child; then taking advantage of social welfare, educational, and health benefits without contributing to Irish society; and bringing over additional family members who similarly exploited the system. His concerns became condensed into the figure of the "pregnant asylum seeker who is, most likely, really an illegal immigrant."

Interviewees, however, expressed sensitivity to the heterogeneity and diverse circumstances of migrants who acquired residency through their Irish children. These included migrants who left conditions of unrest, uncertainty, and serious violence; migrants seeking employment and business opportunities; participants in transnational family networks; smuggled and trafficked people; and, undoubtedly, migrants motivated by curiosity and adventure. Rather than reducing migrants to a homogenizing stereotype, interviewees indicated the importance of connecting migrants' circumstances to specific families, communities, and nation-states within the global economy, and understanding how these connections shaped their migration to Ireland.

Unlike the minister's characterization of the Irish immigration system as well-functioning but in need of protection from unscrupulous immigrants, interviewees described a reactive, exclusionary, poorly planned, and nontransparent immigration system that drew the line very harshly when determining asylum claims while severely restricting other routes for legal admission. As a result, numerous migrants were set up to become designated as illegal. Particularly for migrants who felt that they could not possibly return to their countries of origin, interviewees suggested, acquiring residency through a child offered a means to negotiate multiple pressures and constraints while avoiding designation as illegal. The pressures included having their asylum claims denied in other EU countries and being pregnant because of circumstances that were directly connected to the substance of their asylum claims or because of sexual assaults that they suffered while migrating. For yet other migrants, pregnancy and childbearing emerged as a means to renegotiate their status only after they had arrived in Ireland and experienced the limitations and jeopardies of the asylum system. These included significant gaps in the provision of protection for those who urgently needed it but whose claims did not meet the strict definitions of the Geneva Convention; the need to find alternative routes to secure their futures if their asylum claims failed; the stress and deprivations of the direct provision system; the nontransparent, changing, and confusing rules governing all aspects of seeking asylum, often combined with asylum seekers' lack of resources to effectively navigate the system; in some instances, the failure of or lack of access to reliable birth control methods, combined with Ireland's ban on abortion; the advice they received from friends, social workers, lawyers, community workers, and government officials; and jeopardies that they experienced as people who were often alone in a strange country, separated from usual forms of support, and dealing with language and cultural difference as well as hostility and racism evoked by their status as asylum seekers.

Migrants quickly learned that seeking asylum was unlikely to lead to legal status. Other routes to long-term legal status were also effectively unavailable. The work visa and work permit systems were not intended to lead to long-term residency, and family-based migration was fraught with difficulty. Effectively, childbearing offered migrants in all kinds of circumstances a mechanism to lawfully acquire secure legal status.

Migrants stressed that they sought secure legal status not so that they could "sponge off" welfare or engage in crime but as a means for becoming productive, contributing members of Irish society while pursuing their own hopes and plans. Like the minister, they expressed concern about "abuse" of the migration system. From their point of view, though, individuals' varied modes of entry or strategies for securing legal residency were not necessarily abusive. Indeed, like undocumented Irish migrants in the United States, migrants viewed creative modes of entry and legalization as expected, given the migration pressures that they faced and the tough, nontransparent, and exclusionary nature of the immigration system. Since birthing a child offered an accessible route to legal status, migrants and many Irish people saw nothing wrong with using that route, which was, after all, institutionalized by the Irish state. Migrant interviewees freely acknowledged that some migrants were troublesome or criminal but insisted that most, including themselves, were worthy and good. Some pointed out that some Irish people were troublesome, criminal, and welfare sponging, too. Therefore, unlike the minister, migrants defined "abuse" as a matter of gaining legal status but then failing to become a productive, contributing member of Irish society. As one woman who acquired residency through her Irish child said, residency was not a license to start misbehaving, but the opposite—a reason to be very good. "After all, if you're not good, [the Department of] Justice will not renew your residency," she pointed out very practically.[90]

Overall, interviewees envisioned diverse situations in which migrants sought to negotiate possibilities for themselves and those who they loved in the context of exclusionary immigration and asylum laws because these intersected with larger structural forces. Childbearing provided one of the ways through which some migrants negotiated new possibilities. The interviewees' remarks challenged the naturalizing and laudatory frameworks that government officials and ministers use to describe asylum and immigration control, raising troubling concerns that still demand to be addressed.

CHAPTER 3

Baby Gives Birth to Parents

Direct Provision and Subject Formation

THIS CHAPTER DESCRIBES the emergence of the direct provision and dispersal systems through which asylum seekers are provided with lodging, food, and health care while waiting for their asylum claims to be decided. Unlike the regular welfare system, direct provision does not seek to produce entrepreneurial, self-governing subjects for the neoliberal nation-state; rather, it seeks to deter asylum seekers from arriving, and to ensure that those who do arrive remain strictly controlled, contained, and effectively incapacitated. In this way, asylum seekers can more readily be made illegal and deportable after their claims are denied, as happens in the vast majority of cases. Yet, because direct provision ensures that asylum seekers' basic bodily needs are met while their claims are being processed, the Irish state cannot be accused of violating human rights. The Irish state is by no means unique in adopting this approach to asylum seekers' welfare; direct provision was introduced in response to and along similar lines as Britain's National Asylum Support Service.

Direct provision never fully achieves the objectives of control, containment, and incapacitation. But by analyzing the direct provision system we can begin to understand some of the material and subjective experiences associated with the status of "asylum seeker" in Ireland at this moment. For "asylum seeker" does not have a transhistorical or essential meaning but instead is constructed and experienced through changing relations of power. Analysis of the direct provision system illuminates some of the relations of power through which "asylum seeker" has come to entail specific material and subjective meanings in Ireland at present. Moreover, such analysis, which reveals the extraordinary challenges of living in direct provision, allows us to begin to grasp the stakes for migrants in securing recognition of their asylum claims (with associated legal right to remain) rather than denial (which removes any legal basis for their continuing presence although this does not mean that they must leave).

The first section of this chapter historicizes the emergence of the direct provision system and the logics of deterrence and control that organize it. The second section critically analyzes the kind of subject that direct provision seeks to produce. By all accounts, this is a demoralized, dependent, and impoverished subject that has been systemically stripped of valued roles and identities—and, as I argue, is racialized, engendered, and heterosexualized. The third section describes that, until May 2003, migrants who gave birth to a child were permitted to exit direct provision and transition into regular welfare. The transition was difficult because direct provision offered no resources to enable it. Nonetheless, migrants overwhelmingly favored the change, as described by Christabel, a Nigerian mother whom I interviewed at length and who transitioned to regular welfare upon the birth of her first child in Ireland. Since May 2003 migrants can no longer leave direct provision upon the birth of a child. But the years during which this was possible illustrates the ways that a dominant heterosexual norm mediated migrants' possibilities for exiting direct provision into better conditions. The conclusion critically discusses what we learn from these experiences about the material and subjective stakes for migrants of gaining long-term legal presence through being recognized as refugees or on other grounds.

Direct Provision: A Departure from the Existing Social Welfare System

Direct provision represented a significant departure from the existing social welfare system. The departure must be placed in political and historical context. Jost Halfmann argues, "The main means by which states won the loyalty of their populations was not only nationalism, but more importantly the welfare state. The welfare state gave the idea of the nation substance."[1] Social welfare offered citizens tangible benefits and opportunities in exchange for their political loyalty. Furthermore, through social welfare systems, states made "legal, political, and financial investments in their populations to transform them into [particular kinds of] citizens."[2] Consequently, national welfare systems became an essential part of nation building and citizenship in the global north until the latter part of the twentieth century.

In the newly independent southern Irish state in the 1920s, social welfare provision "was not high on the agenda of a government struggling to maintain and finance a state."[3] Nonetheless, the role of the state in providing and regulating welfare was acknowledged by the Constitution; Article 45.1 holds that "the State shall strive to promote the welfare of the whole group by securing or protecting as effectively as it may a social order in which justice and charity inform all the institutions of national life." In practice, Ireland has what scholars describe as a "mixed economy" of welfare in which the state and Catholic Church have played dominant roles. According to Bryan Fanning, "social policy was dominated by 'Irish-Ireland' understandings of citizenship.... This advanced a doctrinaire formulation of Irishness grounded in claims about the exclusive authenticity of a Gaelic-Catholic Ireland."[4] The welfare system was organized accordingly, around a heterosexist, nationalist model of a breadwinner male with a dependent wife and children. In the 1960s the state assumed a more dominant role in social welfare provision, while the Church reduced its role, creating gaps that were often filled by "nonreligious voluntary agencies."[5]

Immense changes in the 1990s, including deepening Europeanization, rapid economic growth, and the entry of growing numbers of women into the labor market, resulted in struggles over social values and "an increased emphasis on economic individualism.... Catholic emphasis on the primacy of the family became to some extent subordinated by a neoliberal emphasis on the primacy of the market."[6] Welfare provision increasingly adopted these neoliberal logics. For example, "the Department of Social and Family Affairs ... [moved] from a contingency structured social security regime to one that identifies claimants by reference to their relationship with the labour market—claimants were simply young, old, or 'working age'" and those in receipt of unemployment benefits are "job seekers."[7]

Even while social welfare systems reflected varying levels and strategies of investment in the production of citizen subjects, they have also historically served as a means to transform migrants into long-term residents and possible future citizens. Focusing on Cambodians in California, Aihwa Ong has explored the "complex, ambiguous, and interweaving processes that transform [migrants] ... into citizens."[8] Borrowing

from Foucault, she characterizes the processes as entailing subjectification: "self-making and being-made by power relations that produce consent through schemes of surveillance, discipline, control, and administration."[9] Thus, through interactions with state institutions, civil society,
and the labor market, migrants learn about, engage, and variously inhab-
it "modalities of belonging" that are available and valued in the countries
to which they have moved.[10] According to Ong, these modalities entail
racial, cultural, economic, gender, and, we may add, sexual hierarchies
within which migrants negotiate their belonging, possibilities, and development of their capacities. Welfare systems (involving the state, civil
society, and the religious sector) comprise important locations through
which migrants experience the processes of subjectification that are intended to remake them as particular kinds of citizens.[11]

Yet not all migrants are on track to become subjects and eventual citizens of the states in which they live. In the case of unwanted migrants,
states use these migrants' interactions with social welfare systems as
opportunities not to transform them into desirable citizens but to try to
contain, control, or disable their capacities and possibilities. Ireland's direct provision system, through which asylum seekers receive food, shelter,
and basic services, illustrates these processes.

Significantly, asylum seekers were not at first treated as a distinct and
stigmatized group under the social welfare system (although they were
denied the right to work, which refugees and citizens had). Instead, in
the 1990s their social welfare needs were provided for on the same basis
as homeless Irish people.[12] Thus, upon arrival in Ireland they were usually housed at first in bed-and-breakfast accommodations. Then they either registered at the nearest garda (police) station or waited at the Refugee Centre on Mount Street in Dublin to apply for refugee status. They
were then issued with a card that entitled them to claim social welfare
payments on the same terms as homeless Irish nationals, and to seek accommodation.[13] Serious housing shortages, however, strained the system, and some asylum seekers ended up sleeping rough in public parks.

Beginning in 1997, mainstream media and politicians began to systematically characterize asylum seekers as a distinct and undesirable
group that threatened Irish society, culture, and the economy. The direct
provision system, which was piloted in November 1999 and became
standard and nationwide in April 2000, materially and symbolically institutionalized the idea that asylum seekers were *not* similar to homeless

Irish people after all, nor should such analogies provide the basis for social welfare policies and practices toward them. Instead, direct provision institutionalized the construct of the "asylum seeker" as a distinct, undesirable type of person who must be subjected to relations of governance that were intended to deter, control, and incapacitate him or her.

Under direct provision, asylum seekers are housed for a short period in reception centers in Dublin and then dispersed to accommodation centers around the country.[14] Accommodation centers operate under the auspices of the Department of Justice's Reception and Integration Agency (RIA), rather than the Department of Social and Family Affairs (now the Department of Social Protection), which is normally responsible for welfare matters.[15] The centers significantly vary in quality but are often classed as emergency or transitional accommodation, although people often remain there for years.[16] Moreover, the most centers are run by for-profit private companies.[17] Despite RIA guidelines about minimum standards, "many such companies have . . . cut corners in order to secure greater profits from service provision reducing costs from €38.60 per person per day in 2000 to €28.35 in 2006."[18]

Asylum seekers have no choice about where they are sent and rarely receive information in advance about the accommodation center and regions where they end up.[19] In the accommodation centers, asylum seekers are generally provided with a bed, three meals, and "comfort money" of €19.10 a week for adults and €9.60 a week for children.[20] As of 2012 this sum remains unchanged. They are entitled to a medical card, which ensures medical care. While in direct provision, asylum seekers may not engage in paid employment, attend training, or travel outside the country without the permission of the minister for justice. Children under eighteen are entitled to free primary and secondary schooling.

Asylum seekers' welfare is not administered on the basis of their anticipated relationship to Irish society or the labor market (since the goal is to ensure that most asylum seekers will never have officially sanctioned opportunities for long-term legal presence or employment). Instead, direct provision is administered according to the objectives of deterrence and control. Indeed, the most common rationale offered by the government for implementing direct provision concerned deterring asylum seekers from arriving in the first place.[21] Particularly because Britain planned to implement direct provision, then-minister for justice John O'Donoghue believed that it was urgent for Ireland to follow suit.

Otherwise he feared that increasing numbers of asylum seekers might be drawn to Ireland because of its more generous welfare provisions.

Arguments about deterrence frequently rest on questionable assumptions. As the *Irish Times* reported, "a European Commission survey of asylum seekers in Britain, the Netherlands and Belgium . . . found that the generosity of a state's welfare provision was not a factor in any 'check-list' of host countries that they may have had. Asylum seekers said they were mainly influenced by practical matters such as to where they were physically able to travel or where they had family members, colonial or political ties or language connections."[22] Moreover, the logic of deterrence presumes a strictly economic, rationalist model of migration that is often significantly at odds with the circumstances of people's journeys, including when they were smuggled to unknown destinations.

"Deterrence" as a rationale for implementing direct provision was not accepted without a struggle. As the Free Legal Advice Centre (FLAC) explains:

> The introduction of Direct Provision was a cause of considerable interdepartmental conflict. Records from the period show that much pressure had to be placed on other departments by the DJLER [Department of Justice, Equality and Law Reform] before the necessary personnel were seconded to the newly established directorate with responsibility for enforcing the dual policies of Direct Provision and dispersal. Relations between the DJLER and the then DSFCA [Department of Social, Family, and Community Affairs] were also strained. In January 2000, a senior DJLER official accused the DSFCA of undermining DJLER policy.
>
> More than 550 CWOs [community welfare officers] threatened to boycott Direct Provision, claiming that it was blatantly discriminatory. . . . They saw the role into which they were forced as a policing and not a welfare one. . . . Doubt was expressed as to the authority of DJLER policy in influencing practice in this area.[23]

A 2001 survey of CWOs showed that direct provision "has engendered frustration and disillusionment for those personnel who fundamentally disagree with the system but who are obliged to implement it."[24] According to 17 percent of survey respondents, the greatest challenges facing CWOs are providing services within a system they see as flawed or discriminatory, but within which they are obliged to operate.[25] One CWO wrote, "As a welfare officer, I resent being told how to do my job and take on police-type duties."[26]

But not everyone was opposed. A significant minority of CWOs who responded to the 2001 survey indicated that they shared the mainstream construction of asylum seekers as "bogus" welfare-seeking migrants who should be deterred. Thus, 22 percent indicated that a strength of direct provision is that it "acts as a deterrent," while 18 percent indicated that "controls/monitors asylum seekers" is an important strength.[27]

When outright deterrence fails, direct provision is intended to transform asylum seekers into governable subjects whose biological lives will be sustained, but whose economic, social, and cultural lives will be controlled while their cases are processed. The vast majority will then be issued refusals of their claims for refugee status or subsidiary protection, which renders them deportable or illegal if they remain.[28] Direct provision is indeed a system of subjectification but of a very different nature than that described by Ong, since the goal is not to produce entrepreneurial and self-actualizing subjects that are valorized by the neoliberal state but rather stripped down, disabled, and incapacitated subjects.

Stripped Down, Incapacitated, and Disabled Subjects

Direct provision is part of a larger asylum assemblage that includes experiences of being photographed, fingerprinted, and inscribed into a vast documentary apparatus; negotiating the bureaucracy and dizzying legal codes of the refugee applications commissioner and the refugee appeals tribunal; and in some instances registering with and reporting to the gardaí or other authorities. Direct provision, however, remains the centerpiece of the system for controlling, containing, and incapacitating asylum seekers and is the most extensively studied element of the asylum apparatus. Therefore, I draw on published scholarship and participant ethnography to critically analyze the kinds of subjects that the direct provision produces while acknowledging that the system's effects are never totalizing.

One of the most consistent research findings is that direct provision makes people virtually powerless in nearly every aspect of their lives.

Asylum seekers in direct provision have no choice about where they are sent, with whom they live, and in most cases who shares their room or how many people share their room. Indeed, they have no control over the very food that they eat, which they consistently rate as boring, poor, and unhealthy. They receive little or no information from staff about their rights, or asylum procedures, or available supports in the area. Their powerlessness is constantly underlined: staff may enter their rooms without permission, or may punish or humiliate them for perceived infractions. They rarely get to explain their side of events. In some centers they are required to sign out if they leave and punished if they fail to do so. Some managers relocate them to new centers without advance warning for perceived petty infractions.[29] The existing complaints procedure does not enable migrants to effectively challenge these relations of power; rather, many migrants fear that they will be labeled as troublemakers, or victimized, or have their claims for asylum adversely affected if they complain.[30] Illustrating this, "in one focus group, participants explained that a resident who had complained that expired food was being served in her centre was transferred shortly after the complaint was made."[31] These practices contribute to feelings of "hopelessness" among migrants in direct provision "that they could actually do anything to change their situation for the better."[32]

Migrants' powerlessness is reinforced by their poverty. Barred from working, they subsist on €19.10 per week, a sum that has not changed since 2000, despite inflation. The sum is so low that CWOs and administrators in the Eastern Health Board even voted for strike action in protest.[33] The sum does not begin to meet their needs and often forces difficult choices (e.g., between buying milk for babies or paying for a prescription that is not covered by the medical card). Asylum seekers used to be eligible for additional, modest welfare payments, depending on their needs, but most of these were abolished after the "habitual residence condition" came into effect in 2004 to limit welfare eligibility.[34] Asylum seekers' poverty is reflected in many ways including food insecurity. In 2001, a report called *Beyond the Pale* caused a furor by documenting malnutrition among expectant women, health problems related to diet among children, weight loss by babies, and hunger among adults who prioritized their children's needs for food over their own within the direct provision system.[35] Yet studies continue to uncover food poverty among asylum seekers in direct provision.[36]

Asylum seekers' poverty affects every other sphere of their lives, too. For instance, they can rarely afford to go anywhere unless it is within walking distance or unless transportation is free. They cannot seek out entertainment that entails costs and cannot afford to socialize with others or provide for occasions such as children's birthday parties. They cannot pay for medicine that is not covered by the medical card, or buy clothes or shoes for their children without a so-called exceptional needs payment (even though these are not exceptional but everyday needs). Studies of direct provision consistently conclude that by all measures, asylum seekers are deeply impoverished and experience the attendant effects. As the Irish Refugee Council summarizes, "such an insufficient payment severely restricts the ability of asylum seekers to participate in mainstream Irish society. Many asylum seeker families live in extreme poverty and this is directly attributable to the policy of Direct Provision."[37]

Studies also consistently find that direct provision undermines migrants' health. Certainly, migrants receive a medical card, which ensures access to health care. Yet, as Meave Foreman describes, key barriers to accessing care include language difficulties, lack of understanding about how the Irish health care system works, and lack of information about available services.[38] Moreover, while the Irish health care system is in the midst of transitioning toward a model that addresses "intercultural" dynamics, that process is not yet complete.[39] Health care providers also struggle to offer services within the constraints set by the direct provision system and the immigration and asylum laws that govern it.[40] Studies have also consistently documented the negative impact of the direct provision system on migrants' health. The well-being of migrants in direct provision is greatly affected by the fact that they generally live under very stressful conditions; in overcrowded and noisy accommodation; with strangers; with little support; under conditions of isolation and exclusion; and without possibilities for getting on with their lives as they await a decision from an asylum system that is widely viewed as capricious or discriminatory.[41] The prohibition on work and training offers nothing to take asylum seekers' minds off these conditions, or toward which they can refocus their energies. Some studies argue that direct provision is particularly inappropriate for those who have experienced severe trauma in their countries of origin or during their journeys.[42] Even for those who have not undergone trauma, conditions in direct provision often foster feelings of loss, grief, depression, demoralization, and failure. For example, people who have worked hard all of their lives are suddenly forced to be idle: "Most asylum seekers interviewed had actively worked back home and find it extremely difficult to adjust to a life of relative idleness, extending for months or even years."[43]

Indeed, direct provision challenges and undermines valued identities and roles. These include migrants' identities as workers since the prohibition on paid employment ensures that their existing skills atrophy and new skills for the Irish labor market are not developed. Migrants' identities and roles as family members are also undermined. For example, many asylum seekers have families overseas who depend on them for assistance or survival. Direct provision, however, makes it virtually impossible to fulfill these obligations. Some migrants send every penny of their meager €19.10 a week to family overseas while others feel pressured to earn money in the underground economy even though they risk losing everything (including consideration of their asylum applications) if caught. For example, Salam, from an African country that was devastated by civil war,

> arrived safely in Ireland and lodged his asylum application. . . .
> His major stress at this time was concern about the well-being
> and safety of his family back home. He was under pressure to
> send money back home to feed his family. With an income of
> €19.10 a week, he felt that he had no choice but to work illegally.
> This brought with it the constant fear of being caught and losing
> everything he had been working towards.[44]

Salam was eventually granted refugee status, brought his family to Ireland, and entered the workforce legally. But until that point, he experienced direct provision as enormously stressful, partly because it made it impossible for him to fulfill obligations toward family members about whom he was desperately worried—unless he broke the law that forbids asylum seekers to engage in paid employment.

Asylum seekers describe that their identities as parents, too, are undermined by the direct provision system. In direct provision, they have little capacity to make and enforce choices for their children. They are unable to change conditions that adversely affect their children (e.g., there is no play space, or it is too noisy to do homework, or the child's food needs are not being met). Parents struggle to provide for their children, including books and school supplies. "After-school activities, sports, school trips, computer use—all the things that can enrich a child's life—can often be out of reach for children in the asylum system because of their parents' ongoing poverty."[45] Parents are aware of their children's shame about living in an accommodation center rather than a regular home but can do nothing. They worry about how discrimination affects their children: "Some children in town did not want to play with their children because they were asylum seekers. . . . Some mothers related that their children saw the 'difference between Irish born and African born' and that Irish born children have more rights. Mothers were worried about how this would affect their children's sense of self-worth."[46] Children quickly learn that the power lies with managers and staff of the hostel, not their parents.[47] In these and other ways, parenting as a socially valued role is significantly stripped from asylum seekers in direct provision.

In sum, research consistently describes direct provision as producing dependency, demoralization, institutionalization, hopelessness, helplessness, and incapacity. Such attributes in a citizen are viewed as deeply worrisome or negative. But where asylum seekers are concerned, direct provision systematically produces these outcomes in a questionable effort to deter further arrivals while controlling and containing those who have reached Irish shores.

Direct Provision and Racialization

Many scholars have characterized direct provision as a state apparatus that institutionalizes racism and racialization. They offer diverse arguments and evidence to support their claims, including the fact that only racial and ethnic minorities are subjected to direct provision. Direct provision institutionalizes the treatment of asylum seekers as a separate and distinct class that has fewer rights than other classes, and it ensures that the everyday lives and experiences of asylum seekers are very different than those of everyone else. That difference becomes racialized, and—in an era when welfare use racializes, requiring asylum seekers to be supported at taxpayer expense while denying them opportunities to work—most certainly racializes the asylum seekers.[48] Joe Moran further argues that migration laws racialize asylum seekers by creating geopolitical exclusions and inclusions that become mapped onto constructs of race as visible physical difference. As he explains, EU nationals, by definition, cannot be asylum seekers. After EU enlargement in 2004, "most of those who currently claim asylum from Eastern European states will no longer be in a position to do so, as they will be members of the EU. . . . In such circumstances, [Africans, Asians, and people from the Middle East] will make up the overwhelming majority of asylum seekers in Ireland."[49] The steady production of the asylum seeker as the racialized Other who cannot, by definition, come from an EU state is deeply ironic since, as Dauvergne describes, the initial 1951 Refugee Convention defined only displaced Europeans as possible refugees.[50] But it is also deeply revealing of new ways that racial distinctions are being reproduced through asylum policies and practices—including direct provision.

Not surprisingly, asylum seekers report that they experience high levels of racism and discrimination, not only when compared to Irish citizens but also relative to other migrants. For example, a pioneering 2005 survey of 1,109 migrant workers and asylum seekers discovered that even after controlling for migrants' regional origin, "asylum seekers are more likely to experience discrimination than work permit holders [i.e., migrant workers] in a range of domains—public places, shops and restaurants and institutions."[51] Yet, as Bryan Fanning describes, because of their legal status, asylum seekers are prevented from challenging racism through the state's antiracism apparatus.[52] This situation raises critical questions about the limits and actual functions of state antiracism policies.[53]

No studies have explored how direct provision racializes migrants through mundane, everyday interactions and experiences. But research by Stacey Vandenhurst usefully suggests a starting place for such analysis. Vandenhurst examined whether asylum seekers in a direct provision center, Dun Gibbons in Clifden, County Galway, viewed themselves as members of coherent racial, ethnic, or cultural groups, or if they self-identified as asylum seekers. Her study is significant precisely because she did not presume in advance the kinds of racial, ethnic, or cultural identities or identifications that asylum seekers have, but she instead suggests that we need to inquire into the processes through which these become fashioned and reworked—including through the direct provision system.[54]

Many studies have described significant racial and cultural conflict among migrants in accommodation centers. Vandenhurst implies that rather than naturalizing alliances or conflicts on the basis of essentialized notions of racial or ethnic identities, we should instead inquire how conflicts within direct provision produce racial and ethnic identities or identifications in particular ways. Vandenhurst found that most residents in Dun Gibbons had ties and friendships with people from many countries partly because "the relaxed environment . . . reduce[d] stress and confrontation among the residents."[55] By contrast, Vandenhurst argued, direct provision centers that are less well-run, more tense, more overcrowded, and more stressful generate increased conflict among residents, including along lines that appeared heavily racialized or ethnicized.[56] This suggests, she says, that "resources and management policies can be as important as ethnic differences (if not more important) in predicting social conflicts and divisions."[57] Vandenhurst's findings echo other studies that recommend that direct provision management and staff need to receive information and training about racial and cultural differences, and about responding productively to rather than contributing to conflicts that appear to be racialized and ethnicized.[58]

More importantly, though, Vandenhurst's study opens up questions about how everyday living conditions and practices in direct provision racialize migrants, and how migrants make sense of and negotiate these experiences. The questions merit further analyses that do not naturalize racial or cultural categories in advance but instead inquires into their shifting production through everyday experiences and interactions within the direct provision system.

Engendering and (Hetero)sexualizing

No study has explored how direct provision engenders or (hetero)sexualizes migrants, or how these processes intersect with racialization. Instead studies of direct provision treat gender as a self-evident attribute that people already "have." Yet the best feminist research understands gender as relational, contextual, multiscalar, and power laden rather than as biologically determined and essentially unchanging.[59] Moreover, migration processes not only are thoroughly shaped by gender but also result in the reconfiguration of gender identities, roles, and ideologies. An earlier generation of scholarship assumed that migration was inevitably "empowering" for those who are gendered as women, but more recent research has established that the outcomes are often mixed (improved in some respects, but worse in other respects).[60] Certainly, there is no singular model of how migration reshapes gender.

Asylum seekers in Ireland encounter a deeply gendered and engendering regime that creates significant difficulties. This is despite the fact that Irish law recognizes that migrants may have been persecuted because of their gender, or persecuted in a manner that operated through gender.[61] In general, studies of direct provision fail to address gender as a category of analysis. Most research is ostensibly gender neutral—which means that implicit but unexamined gender norms shape the study. At best, suggestions concerning select categories of women—usually women who are raising children or who have experienced sexual violence—are tacked onto general reports. This represents a positive step, but the next, larger step would be to critically address how direct provision (and the asylum apparatus as a whole) is both gendered and engendering in ways that produce varied contradictions, dilemmas, and perhaps unexpected possibilities for different migrants.

There are some exceptions to the neglect of gender as a category of analysis. A study by the Waterford Area Partnership (WAP), for instance, sought to identify "the issues which male asylum seekers in Waterford face" in Viking House, an all-male accommodation center.[62] Yet the report did not discuss why male asylum seekers might have needs that differ from those of women, or what this suggests about gendering processes within direct provision more generally. The report states that local services tend to target asylum-seeker women, rather than men, which implies that voluntary groups interact with direct provision in a gendered manner. Implicit gender norms are also suggested by the statement, "It was agreed that the direct provision centre in Birchwood, which mainly housed women and children, would be targeted in relation to providing basic courses in budgeting and domestic issues."[63] By contrast, the WAP report recommends the development of activities for men that relate to "sports and health and fitness activities."[64] Are we to assume that men do not need to know about budgeting and domestic issues? And that women do not need sports, health, and fitness activities? What does this suggest about direct provision as a gendered and engendering process, and how do migrants negotiate these norms?

Another exception to the neglect of gender is the 2010 report by AkiDwA, *"Am Only Saying It Now": Experiences of Women Seeking Asylum in Ireland.* AkiDwA (which means "sisterhood" in Swahili) describes itself as "the only ethnic minority led network of African and migrant women living in Ireland."[65] AkiDwA set out to survey the needs of women living in direct provision, and to "empower them to take action to bring about positive change."[66] In many respects the report reproduces female gender in ways that generally conform to the heteronormative image of migrant women as overwhelmingly wives, mothers, or sexually vulnerable people while erasing single women, lesbians, "bad" women, and other kinds of female subjects.[67] Nonetheless, the report is significant because concerns of migrant wives, mothers, and vulnerable women *are* given voice. Moreover, this is the only published report to foreground gender hierarchies—as they interact with racial, cultural, and other inequalities—as a central concern within the asylum system. The report valuably and firmly recommends that asylum and refugee processing must become critically conscious about and responsive to gender issues, and "a mandatory code of conduct, a comprehensive training programme and Garda vetting should be introduced promptly and fully implemented for all personnel, management, accommodation owners and government department officials" working with migrants in the direct provision system.[68]

A 2010 report from the Domestic Violence Advocacy Service (DVAS) clearly suggests ways that gender operates as a site of disenfranchisement for some migrant women in direct provision.[69] According to the report, women self-refer to DVAS, and "to date, women living in direct provision constitute a significant percentage of our service users." The authors describe that direct provision increases women's risk of domestic violence because of overcrowded, communal, stressful living conditions that are poorly monitored and inadequately managed.[70] For instance, women in direct provision must share space with strangers while conducting intimate aspects of their daily lives such as going to the toilet, showering, eating, and parenting. Under these conditions, "all the women DVAS has worked with who live in Direct Provision have disclosed a level of sexual harassment. In most cases this has been perpetrated by male residents, but women have also reported that hostel staff have harassed them. This harassment has included sexualised name-calling, being followed and watched, being touched and sexually propositioned, being accused of being a prostitute and of being 'too loose' with men, and of attempts being made to pimp them. Where women have attempted to challenge or resist such harassment, it has usually escalated."

The direct provision system not only fosters these experiences of harassment and disempowerment; it is also set up to disallow alternatives. For example, in many direct provision centers entire families share one room. As a result, women who are subjected to domestic violence by a husband or partner cannot escape from or avoid the abuser.[71] Moreover, children often witness the abuse. Perpetrators often threaten women who resist with deportation.[72] Women are generally reluctant to seek assistance from the management staff: as described earlier, they perceive that their concerns are unlikely to be addressed, or they may be further victimized, or their asylum claims may be negatively affected.

Women in direct provision also face significant, perhaps insurmountable, barriers to seeking a barring order against an abuser: "In order to apply for a Barring Order, she would probably have to communicate with RIA because her and her husband's access to accommodation is controlled by the state. She would need to seek permission from the state to have him barred. The number of people and number of agencies potentially involved in this takes away her right to privacy, to confidentiality and ultimately to safety. The inequality speaks for itself."[73] A woman facing domestic violence also cannot ask to be moved to a women-only direct provision center, since none of the centers have been designated in this way, despite the need.[74] The woman cannot flee to a women's shelter or refuge in the community where she lives, either, since "women's refuges are not resourced to provide board and lodgings to women who have no recourse to public funds [i.e., asylum seekers]."[75] If the woman stays with friends outside of direct provision, she risks losing her place in the center as well as her meager €19.10 a week, rendering her totally destitute and putting her asylum claim at risk.

Women's disempowerment in these circumstances implicates not just partners or the direct provision system and staff but also the wider community. AkiDwA reports:

Women from several regions reported that while walking in town or picking up their children from school, they were being followed by men, sometimes by men in cars. Women coming from, or going to, accommodation centres have been asked if they want "lifts" in or out of town, or if they want money. Women said they had been approached by local men and asked if they do sex work. Women in one region had been asked by local men, "Do you need money? Do you want to work?" "Women are being harassed here every day. The other day, a man in a car followed me and started shouting, 'Have sex with me!' It doesn't matter—they think everyone black here is an asylum seeker and that they can harass us. They know we live on €19.10."[76]

As this example suggests, pervasive racism, which operates through gendered, sexual, and economic logics, perpetuates this system of disempowerment. DVAS says that when women have raised concerns about harassment or domestic violence with social workers, gardaí, nurses, and others, their concerns are often dismissed using racialized logic. This logic presumes that "gender inequality and domestic violence are an inherent part of African and Asian cultures," so harassment and domestic violence are to be expected (and it is culturally inappropriate to intervene into "their" culture).[77] There is also belief that "certain groups of ethnic minority women—particularly those that wear head scarves or hijabs, are inherently submissive and passive, and culturally not used to mixing with men, and are therefore over-sensitive when it comes to natural male behaviour. . . . [Thus, a woman was told by a garda that] a man touching you might be a crime in your country but it certainly isn't here."[78] What is ignored by these responses is the pervasiveness and acceptability of gender and sexual inequality and harassment in Irish society—and the ways that the system of direct provision, established and mandated by the Irish state, directly contributes to migrant women's disempowerment through gendered, sexualized, racialized harassment and violence. Plainly stated, the perpetrators of gender and sexual harassment are not just other migrants but also Irish workers and community members and the Irish state's system of direct provision. Moreover, gender and sexual harassment and abuse clearly work through and further perpetuate racialized and cultural hierarchies within Irish society. As DVAS describes, institutional responses to women experiencing harassment and domestic violence in direct provision effectively suggest that "Irish women who experience abuse are victims of crime, whilst women of colour, particularly those who live in Direct Provision, are

simply victims of their own cultures" whose predicament has nothing
to do with the violence of the Irish state and society.[79]

Overall, DVAS's report valuably demonstrates that treating gender as
relational, contextual, and multiscalar rather than as essential is vital
when analyzing the direct provision system. Gender is relational not
only in terms of the production of categories of male and female (and
transgender and intersex) but also in terms of racial, ethnic, cultural,
and social class categories. As Yen Le Espiritu says, migrant "minority"
women's genders and sexualities have historically been "systematically
demonized and disparaged by dominant or oppressor groups to justify
and bolster nationalist movements, colonialism, and/or racism."[80] Thus,
gender "is co-constructed with other racial and cultural categories" and
must be analyzed accordingly.[81]

"I've Already Been Accused of Being Gay in Front of Everybody"

Engendering processes invariably normalize certain forms of sexuality
while marking other sexualities as "deviant" and undesirable. Attention
not only to asylum-seeking women who are forced to navigate racialized sexual harassment but also to LGBTQ (lesbian, gay, bisexual,
transgendered, and queer) asylum seekers specifically offers a lens for
understanding how direct provision normalizes a particular version of
heterosexuality.[82]

The Refugee Act 1996 includes sexual orientation, along with gender,
as a legitimate basis for seeking asylum. Although no official statistics
are available and no one has researched their experiences, some numbers of gay men, transgender people, and possibly lesbians have received
asylum in Ireland. An article in the *Irish Times* describes that LGBT migrants, including those who have endured severe persecution because of
their sexualities or gender identities, find that they must hide their
identities (and, effectively, their experiences) within the direct provision system or else risk bullying, ostracism, and the loss of even minimal
support:

> Direct provision centre staff need more intercultural training,
> especially on bullying. I've heard of three cases, one of a Roma-
> nian gay man who left his accommodation centre in Cork due to
> harassment, a Kenyan man in Dublin ostracised because he was

damned if he was going to deny his sexuality after everything he
had been through, and a Kenyan lesbian in accommodation [i.e.,
direct provision] who hides her sexuality to survive.[83]

The risks of disclosure extend beyond bullying; when migrants who are
known to be LGBTQ are returned to their countries of origin, information about their sexualities or gender identities may follow them back,
placing them in danger of grave harm.

   Gay Community News published a short account of the experiences of
Olive Namuddu, a self-identified lesbian asylum seeker from Uganda.[84]
Namuddu's account is likely to have been significantly mediated not
only by language barriers but more importantly by the fact that she was
still in the asylum system, which constrained what she could and could
not tell. Nonetheless, it offers a glimpse into the struggles facing lesbian
asylum applicants as they negotiate the asylum system, including direct
provision. Namuddu first describes experiences of harassment, impris-
onment, and serious abuse in Uganda. After police raided a gay bar
where she was socializing and imprisoned her for the second time:

> Very much against her will my sister came to bail me out.
>   This time my sister decided to get rid of me for good. She sold
> some land and paid a woman to take me away. Initially I refused
> to go. I knew no other life, had no other language, no skills; my
> life was there with [my partner] Grace. Where was the woman
> going to take me, anyway? Was she going to sell me? I'd rather
> die. I was so frightened. Nonetheless, a friend of mine managed
> to convince me that I should travel, that I couldn't go on like this
> in Uganda.
>   This is how I arrived in Ireland in 2007. Someone travelled
> with me and basically dropped me off. Initially I was refused
> asylum as the authorities here could not believe that I was lesbian.
> Miscommunication was the order of the day.
>   I've been put into an asylum seeker's hostel, which feels like
> adding insult to injury. These places are barely humane, and for a
> gay person they turn out to provide further opportunities for
> others to humiliate you. There is no privacy, and as one has
> nothing to do other than sit and think about the past. It works as
> a magnifier of everything one is trying to escape.

I'm sharing a room with a Nigerian woman who is very argumentative. I'm scared of her finding out about my sexuality because I fear the situation could become a lot worse. She might start threatening me and making my life a living hell. I've already been accused of being gay by another woman in front everyone in the hostel, because I'm not dating men. I don't know how long this situation can go on for.

I am seeing a counsellor; I take English classes, do volunteer work and go to the Outhouse,[85] but the things that happened to me still weigh me down something terrible. Sometimes I don't know if I can make it.[86]

Namuddu's account suggests some of the struggles of living as a lesbian asylum seeker in direct provision. She indicates that everyday cultures in direct provision centers are heterosexualizing and heterosexist (for example, the expectation that unmarried women will engage in dating men), and concerns that LGBTQ migrants in direct provision experience bullying, harassment, and fear. The larger asylum apparatus also clearly presents barriers: she courageously explains to authorities that she is a lesbian, and that identity is materially connected to her reasons for fleeing, but asylum authorities cannot believe her. Other barriers facing LGBTQ asylum seekers were identified in the 2011 report *Fleeing Homophobia: Asylum Claims Related to Sexual Orientation and Gender Identity in Europe*. These included inconsistent practices; stereotypical views that affected assessments of LGBTQ applicants' credibility and the outcomes of their cases; and decisions to return applicants to their countries of origin with injunctions to be "discreet" in order to avoid persecution (an argument that was finally invalidated and abolished in the United Kingdom in 2010 but still widely persists elsewhere). The report also raises concerns about housing LGBTQ applicants in accommodation such as direct provision: "Homophobia and transphobic incidents towards LGBTI[87] asylum seekers in reception centres, accommodation centres and in alien detention occur in most EU countries.... Often there is social exclusion, verbal and physical harassment, and sometimes even sexual abuse, mostly by other asylum seekers, in particular people from the same country of origin. Also incidents by staff members and by guards and police officers in detention are reported."[88] In January 2012 the youth organization BeLonGTo launched a pilot program "aimed at giving asylum service providers in Dublin and Meath the skills to deal with LGBT refugees" while also providing support to LGBTQ migrants.[89] Nonetheless, LGBTQ people continue to face extraordinary difficulties while navigating the asylum system—including direct provision. The system operates through and perpetuates heterosexism in ways that severely disenfranchise and disempower migrants.[90]

"I Put All My Life on One Card and I Didn't Win Anything"

Tanya, an asylum seeker from the Former Soviet Union (FSU), describes some of the cumulative effects of direct provision in her life. She explained that, as a visibly different ethnic minority member in her country of origin, she was singled out for constant physical and sexual attack, including rape, and was unable to secure adequate employment. With the assistance of her family, she eventually fled, leaving behind an infant son. She initially worked without authorization in the Irish economy, but after the birth of her second child, she felt she had no option other than to seek asylum. While in direct provision, she sent every possible penny from her meager €19.10 a week to family in the FSU where her son lived, which left her in "extreme loneliness and social isolation."[91] Her experiences were deeply disheartening, and she sums them up this way:

> I'm wasting my time for nothing. I'm not working—not building my social life. It's like living in a prison. It is a prison: I have free accommodation and three meals, but since it is a prison, I can do nothing. The government treats me like a prisoner. I steal their money and accommodation. I'm not wanted here. I have not seen my son [in the FSU] in two and a half years. If I go on with the legal process it may take another two or three years. I haven't gained anything in Ireland. At least back home I had some respect. . . . My brain stopped working here. I put all my life on one card and I didn't win anything.[92]

Her application for asylum was denied, and she was refused the possibility of a judicial review. "Her only remaining possibility is [to be granted] leave to remain on humanitarian grounds, regarding which she holds little hope: 'Nobody gets it.'"[93]

Tanya's experience is an example of many of the ways that life in direct provision profoundly impacts on people's lives. Yet the system's effects are never uniform, predictable, or totalizing. Migrants in direct provision have built ties with one another; sometimes engaged in paid labor in the underground economy; and taken advantage of the opportunities offered by nongovernmental organizations (NGO), church groups, and community groups that try to counter the isolationist and exclusionary structure of the direct provision system. Not insignificant numbers have engaged in unpaid volunteer work. Migrants in direct provision have also periodically engaged in hunger striking, a tactic that reflects the state's reduction of them to bare lives that are permitted only bodily existence, and their redeployment of bodily existence as a means for protest. In May 2006 Afghan asylum seekers occupied St. Patrick's Cathedral in Dublin for nearly a week to protest their treatment and the asylum and direct provision system generally.[94] More recently, in July 2010 asylum seekers who were housed in Mosney, County Meath, protested when RIA tried to summarily relocate them to Hatch Hall in Dublin. Many of the migrants had lived in Mosney for years while waiting for the government to process their claims, and had formed close ties with one another. More than forty were receiving medical treatment or monitoring, and their transfer raised concern about their continued access to medical care. But the government was adamant that the migrants had to be moved:

> "There is severe financial pressure on the government and the
> Department of Justice has a duty to act in the best interests of
> taxpayers," said a spokesman for Minister for Justice Dermot
> Ahern. A value-for-money audit found savings could be made by
> transferring some of the 800 people living at Mosney to direct
> provision hostels, mainly in Dublin. In a letter to The Irish Times,
> a group of academics argued that this move was "a further
> instance of the profit-before-people mentality that is rehearsed
> every time the government seeks to remove or reduce social
> provision."[95]

The Mosney protestors generated significant support among NGOs, academics, and the public, but the government continued to pressure them until they complied. Their treatment disturbed the Irish Refugee Council so deeply that it concluded there was "no alternative but to publish information regarding the events," and in so doing, "we would hope to shine a light on the courageous action of the residents of the Mosney Accommodation Centre, past and present. They have opened up debate about the asylum system in Ireland, not least the system of Direct Provision."[96] The resulting report detailed internal dynamics of the struggle that were not otherwise widely known.

Despite the Mosney protests and other challenges, direct provision remains organized so as to produce passive, dependent, demoralized, stripped down, isolated, impoverished, controllable subjects whose biological life is sustained while they go through the asylum review process. Moreover, Roland Bank argues that the system reduces protest when asylum seekers are issued with deportation orders: "By excluding asylum seekers as far as possible from participation in normal life of the host society, states attempt to ensure law enforcement against rejected asylum seekers is not impaired by the development of strong social ties."[97] As I have argued, these processes work through logics of race, culture, gender, and sexuality that demand further analysis.

To reinforce direct provision's multiple forms of control, asylum seekers are discouraged from leaving the system. According to the Citizens' Information website, "you are required to reside or remain at the accommodation centre allocated to you by the Reception and Integration Agency. You can only move from this accommodation with the permission of the Reception and Integration Agency and only in circumstances where the Reception and Integration Agency is in a position to offer you alternative accommodation." The Reception and Integration Agency is less direct: their website says, "There is no obligation placed upon asylum seekers to avail of the accommodation offered by RIA. Some choose to live with relatives or friends, or make use of their own resources to source accommodation." However, asylum seekers who do not reside in direct provision are disqualified from any form of government social support or assistance, and forbidden from engaging in paid employment, which renders options other than direct provision effectively unavailable to most people. The confinement of asylum seekers to direct provision is reinforced through petty rules; for example, if an asylum seeker is absent for three or more days, her or his bed is deemed "abandoned" and he or she loses even the meager social support that is currently available for asylum seekers.[98] Such an absence can potentially be used to raise questions about the validity of an asylum claim, too. Thus, an asylum seeker who takes a lover or makes a friend who lives outside direct provision cannot resort to staying informally with the lover or friend on a regular basis as an alternative to living in the system. Containment and control are exercised over all without exception.

Baby Gives Birth to Parents

Until 2003 giving birth to a child offered migrants a basis on which to leave direct provision and enter into the regular welfare system.[99] Effectively, giving birth enabled migrants to shift from living conditions that controlled, contained, and incapacitated them into conditions that were intended to transform them into entrepreneurial, self-sufficient legal residents and possible future citizens of the neoliberal state. That childbearing was the basis on which such a shift was allowed is truly extraordinary, and ultimately deeply contradictory.

Women who birthed children were not the only group to exit direct provision, but they were the largest. Liam Thornton explains: "DFSC Ministerial Circular 05/00 made a number of exceptions to the general policy of direct provision. Heavily pregnant women, nursing mothers, and families were to be catered for within the traditional welfare state apparatus."[100] FLAC clarifies that "families" meant "a newly arrived asylum seeker having a spouse/partner who arrived in the State some time earlier and was now in private rented accommodation."[101] These exceptions applied to male/female couples, not same-gender couples. Some people were permitted to exit direct provision for health and medical reasons, too. According to CWOs who were surveyed in 2001, the two most common reasons for authorizing departure of asylum seekers from direct provision were pregnancy and physical health.[102] Those who exited direct provision were entitled to rent supplement, which enabled them to rent private accommodation, and to regular welfare benefits.

Making the transition from direct provision to regular welfare was deeply challenging. Indeed, direct provision, with its focus on containment and control, was never intended to facilitate such a transition, and migrants' time in direct provision militated against it. For instance, migrants who moved from direct provision to rental housing were unable to save toward the first month's rent, or to purchase necessities such as dishes, furniture, or bed linens.[103] They had no experience with the costs of everyday living in Ireland, or with budgeting accordingly.[104] The prohibition on working and training meant that most lacked any Irish credentials, experiences, or references.

Regular welfare was not intended as an end in itself but instead as preparation for self-sufficiency in Irish society. Yet the welfare system was not adequately prepared to address the complex needs of migrants who were making a transition from direct provision. Migrants faced numerous hurdles to accessing housing, education, and employment, including because of systemic racism, (hetero)sexism, cultural and language barriers, and lack of social support. In terms of housing, for example, a primary difficulty was even finding rental possibilities in what was then a very tight market; this was compounded by landlord racism and landlord reluctance to accept tenants who paid rent through supplemental welfare allowance or tenants who had children.[105] Migrants also faced systemic discrimination in the job market. Many women remained primarily responsible for children, and significant numbers of them were lone parents; consequently, they faced additional barriers including lack of child care; or child care that cost so much that they could not afford to work or take training classes; or the fact that working part-time left them poorer than if they relied solely on welfare assistance.[106] Moreover, migrants faced language difficulties, lack of support with aspects of everyday life, racism on the streets and in shops, and incomplete knowledge about life in Ireland. The social welfare system, which enabled them to transition out of direct provision, was in many respects not structured to respond to these intersecting needs.

Nonetheless, migrants "overwhelmingly favoured living in private rented accommodation to living in hostels. They described a 'sense of freedom' and improved quality of life," even with all these barriers.[107] Effectively, for those who left direct provision through childbearing, their babies gave birth to them as subjects who could suddenly negotiate complex form of participation and imagined futures in Irish society.[108]

The experiences of Christabel, a Nigerian mother who arrived during the period when migrants could secure residency through a child, illuminate these transformations and some of what it meant, materially and subjectively, to get on track toward becoming a long-term resident and possible citizen (rather than someone who was in danger of being deemed as illegal and deportable if her asylum claim was denied). I was referred to Christabel by an Irish priest who had worked for many years in Nigeria before he returned to Dublin and began working at the center where I volunteered. The priest had come to know Christabel through her involvement in the center's many activities. I rang Christabel from the Talk Shop on O'Connell Street, which is one of the busiest call centers in the city. After I explained my research project, who had referred me, and my connection with the center, she agreed to be interviewed if I could come to her house on the outskirts of Dublin. She gave directions and information about bus schedules. It was a journey of more than an hour and a half by public bus.

When I rang the bell, Christabel answered with a sleeping baby in her arms and a boy at her heels. He was the child through whom she acquired her Irish residency and her ability to exit direct provision. Christabel wore dark jeans, a flower-burst top, and no makeup. She thanked me for coming, and for the packets of tea and biscuits that I brought. I thanked her for inviting me to her home. She was very direct and friendly. I was shown into the living room, and she sent the boy to play while we started the interview.

Christabel: A Reflexive, Responsible Subject

Christabel is an Ibo from one of the southern states of Nigeria. Middle class without being rich, her parents prioritized education for their children over material goods for themselves. Christabel and all of her siblings attended university and hold an impressive array of qualifications among them. Christabel's qualification is in teaching English. She married a man with a good job at a petroleum company, and she ran her own small business for many years. But in her seventh month of pregnancy, she arranged to be smuggled to Ireland while her husband remained in Nigeria. Christabel describes that her journey was impelled by a strong desire to keep herself and her unborn child safe in the context of ongoing violence and struggle in the region where she lived. In accordance with the rules of the center where I volunteered, I did not ask for further details about why or how she came.

Direct provision, followed by the welfare system, framed the horizon within which Christabel negotiated her initial belonging in Irish society. Contrary to the mainstream image, however, her account suggests that she was never simply a "user" or "sponger" who had first to be controlled by direct provision and then instructed in norms of responsibility and self-reliance through regular welfare. Equally, she was never a "premodern" subject who required instruction in the norms of "modern" (or postmodern) Irish living. Instead, Christabel's account suggests that she was already a postmodern, reflexive, and responsible subject when she arrived in Ireland.[109]

Within the confines of direct provision and welfare, she not only grasped the modalities of being that were proposed but also deliberately used these logics as a means to resignify herself. In particular, by learning and engaging in the practices that the Irish government prescribed for asylum seekers and long-term residents, she sought to resignify herself away from an image of sponger, user, and dependent, and toward the image of a responsible, trustworthy, active member of society. Her efforts clearly show that direct provision practices are not only technologies for organizing and distributing material resources while establishing governing relationships with populations but also technologies for refashioning the self.[110]

Negotiating belonging from within the direct provision and welfare systems was complex. On the one hand, asylum seekers are stigmatized as spongers and users for being in direct provision even though they are required by the state to do so. Echoing mainstream views, Christabel criticized the government's mandate that asylum seekers should languish in direct provision rather than going to work. For instance, she told a group of trainee recruits at the police academy, "Stop giving people money. Giving people money is not the best thing. Let them work for their money." She also echoed arguments that government support transforms able-bodied, energetic newcomers into passive dependents: "Your government makes people sit in the house for two or three years while they process their cases, and is making them lazy through this process—and then expects them to go out and get a job." She believed that work makes people more realistic in assessing their life choices and options, which translates into promoting a culture of individual responsibility: "You begin to think straight, think better, like 'what can I afford? What can I do with my life?'"

Her views on government support, however, raised concerns beyond those of the mainstream, to address the situation of asylum seekers. For instance, she suggested that denying asylum seekers work when they are in a strange country, generally separated from family and friends and often fleeing severe trauma, was cruel because it left them with nothing to take their minds off their difficulties. Illustrating this, she described meeting a Nigerian woman from her tribe, who, like Christabel, entered Ireland through claiming asylum, having an Irish citizen child, and staying in Dublin. But unlike Christabel, this woman did not receive residency based on her Irish child. She also withdrew her asylum claim, which meant that she no longer had any legal basis for being in Ireland. She was desperately worried about her future. Christabel's advice was, "Thinking about it is not going to solve anything. Find something to do. Start doing something for yourself." Since paid work was not allowed, she advised the woman to find volunteer work. Through a regular system of volunteer work, "you tend to go out, come back, and you're tired, so you just sleep" instead of worrying. Christabel's advice was based on her own experience, which included extensive volunteer work in Ireland.[111] Her advice also illustrated how the rise of volunteerism as a critical architecture for neoliberal subject formation connects with the control of asylum seekers.[112]

Christabel suggested that asylum seekers should be allowed to work after three to six months in Ireland (a proposal that has been put forth by many groups and organizations but consistently rebuffed by successive ministers for justice on the grounds that it would "attract" asylum seekers). Asylum seekers should be allowed to work, she argued, because it would not only cut costs to the Irish government but also challenge the pervasive imagery that constructs all asylum seekers, but especially African ones, as "abusers" of the asylum system who live at Irish taxpayer expense. As we will see in the following, Christabel herself had her status denigrated on that basis in a way that made her ability to engage in active citizenship quite problematic.

Being Responsible, Making Sacrifices

Although she was very critical of forcing all asylum seekers, including able-bodied single people, into dependency within direct provision, Christabel nonetheless decided that if this was what the Irish government required, then she would abide by those rules. This was a practical decision because asylum seekers risk having their asylum claims invalidated if they do not follow the rules, as described earlier. But Christabel's strategy extended beyond mere pragmatism; she also used rule-following as an opportunity to try to symbolize to all those who met and dealt with her that she was capable of being a responsible, credible, legitimate, trustworthy person who could become a valuable legal resident and active future citizen of Ireland.[113] Within the confines of her situation, scrupulous adherence to the rules offered one of the few avenues within which she could try to resignify her status and worth, and she seized that opportunity.

Illustrating the process, she recounted the following experience when she was in direct provision:

> I remember that when I had my baby—before I had my baby they gave me a maternity allowance, it was like £60.[114] After I had my baby, the community welfare officer came and brought the cheque for £60 again. I was asking him what the money was for. And he said, "Oh, it's the maternity money that you were supposed to get." And I said to him, "But it was paid to me." He said, "Are you sure?" He checked the system and it wasn't [recorded] there. But I told him that I collected the money, I was paid the money [already]. And I said, "I can't have the money. Unless you want to give it to me." And he said, "Okay, if you are sure, I will take back the cheque and I will have to destroy the cheque." The people in the hostel were like, "You're silly, why didn't you take the money? Why were you telling him you already got it?" And I said, "Why would I want to take the money twice?" I mean, why would I want to do that?

In this narrative, the direct provision system—rather than those forced by asylum law to use it—emerges as a problem that needs to be addressed. Christabel subtly criticizes the system for inefficiency and inaccuracy, issuing a payment twice without keeping a proper record of the first disbursement. She also differentiates her style of engagement with the system from that of others in the hostel, who felt she should have kept the money. Moreover, the story shows that Christabel made sure that her practices of being good, honest, and responsible were recognized and acknowledged by an official in the system (and by me, the interviewer). In that way, she challenged presumptions that asylum seekers cannot be honest, reliable members of society—even when they are forced to negotiate their positions from within direct provision.

After her baby's birth, Christabel became eligible to leave direct provision, move into regular rented accommodation and receive regular welfare. Eleven months later, after she officially acquired leave to remain, she became eligible to leave welfare and enter the paid labor force if she wanted. But she faced a series of obstacles to doing do. These included the fact that she was effectively the single mother of a newborn child, surviving without family support in a foreign country and culture. Moreover, her university degree from Nigeria was not recognized as a valuable credential in Ireland.

Accepting this devaluation of her educational credentials was surely painful; the achievement of a university education by herself and by her siblings was a point of pride and identity for her. Christabel's husband indicated that he was unwilling to join her in Ireland, in part because he realized through Christabel's experience that his own educational credentials and ten years of work experience would not translate into an equivalent job and status. Yet although Christabel worked hard to acquire her degree, only to be told that it did not count in Ireland, she merely told her husband, "Well, this is their system, it's what their system is, you don't blame them." Christabel's acceptance that her degree does not count signaled that she was willing to learn and abide by, rather than challenge, the rules of the Irish system. In other words, contrary to the mainstream construction of asylum seekers as merely spongers, she signaled her willingness and ability to act as a good citizen—even when this demanded significant sacrifice.[115]

Not only did she resign herself to the painful stripping of much of the value of her university degree; she also decided to pursue retraining to develop a new career path for herself. This further demonstrated her active citizenship—her assumption not only of rights but also of responsibilities. She became eligible for government-sponsored retraining after her residency was granted. Thus, she enrolled in a FÁS (the Irish national training and employment authority) program in computers.[116]

The construct of asylum seekers (especially pregnant Nigerian women) as spongers and scammers continued to dog her, though. For example, she described a run-in with a welfare officer over her participation in the FÁS training program. Participants in the program receive a stipend, and Christabel was careful to inquire from FÁS staff about whether she was entitled to the stipend and if it would affect her social welfare payments. She was assured there was no problem. She also believed that since both social welfare and training stipends came from the government, the government would have a record of all payments that were being disbursed to her; therefore, welfare staff would know that she was receiving an FÁS stipend. But this turned out to not be true. When her welfare officer realized that she was receiving an FÁS stipend as well as regular welfare payments, he severely upbraided her in terms suggesting that she was taking advantage of the system. These are the very terms in which asylum seekers' unworthiness tends to be cast, in a distinctly racialized and gendered manner. Christabel took great exception to the welfare officer's remarks. Emphasizing her honesty and sincerity, and the problems of a government system that seemed incapable of tracking money that it was disbursing, she asked angrily, "Do you want people to ever do anything for ourselves? Do you want us to really be useful to the system?" Her angry response further maddened the welfare officer, but Christabel retorted, "There are Irish people who do funny things too. You should be able to check your system and know what people are doing. Because if you don't do it, people will take advantage. It's not just people who are coming in [who take advantage]. There are a lot of people who take advantage of it. There are Irish people who are working but social welfare does not know that they are working. Some of them are not even paying taxes, and all that. It's so amazing, you should be checking. I think it's your job to check."

While enrolled in the FÁS training course, Christabel was pregnant with her second child (her husband had visited her by then but left). "I used to go to the hospital in the morning, then the crèche [to leave off my son], come for lectures, then go back home." Some friendly acquaintances asked how she managed to do all that, as a lone mother who was expecting again. "I'd say to them, sometimes you have to stress yourself to get what you want." Two weeks after the course finished, she gave birth to her daughter. At the time I interviewed Christabel, her daughter was one month old. When she reached three months old, Christabel planned to place her in a crèche and continue with her training. If possible, she wanted to save money, return to university, and be trained in computer programming. "If I can do it, I will be very, very happy. It would be a very big achievement for me. I'd love to do it and I'm hoping I can do it." She wanted to achieve this not only for herself, and as further evidence of being a worthy legal resident and possible future citizen of Ireland, but also for the sake of her children. Through her accomplishments, she wanted to model achievement for her children, just as her parents modeled achievement for her.

She faced significant barriers in realizing her dreams, however. Not least was the fact that she was still effectively a lone parent, without family support. She tried to get a visa for her mother to come to Ireland for three months to help with the baby but was denied by the Irish government. She planned to reapply because, with her mother's support, she could make progress on her own education while ensuring her children's well-being. Her husband had no plans to join her in Ireland, and she did not discuss whether he provided financial support (or what the value of remittances from Nigeria to Ireland would amount to in real terms). Moreover, Christabel regularly encountered others who treated the fact that she was African, in the welfare system, and had been an asylum seeker as evidence that she did not have what it took to be or become a "good citizen." The encounters made clear that her efforts to resignify herself were critical to securing her own and her children's futures—yet the racializing, engendering, and classist structures of the welfare system, combined with multiple structural barriers in Irish society, continued to limit her possibilities despite her efforts.[117]

Conclusion

This chapter further contributed to the argument about why it is critical to differentiate migrants from their legal status. When we conflate migrants with their status, we participate in and reinforce the violence of the state while erasing critical questions about the power relations through which these statuses have emerged and acquired meaning. We also lose sight of the ways that legal statuses such as "asylum seeker" mean different things at different times and places. Yet, although migrants should never be equated with their status, we also cannot overlook how legal status profoundly shapes people's possibilities and conditions their interactions with social welfare, employment, and community structures. This chapter has sought to navigate these imperatives and, in the process, to illuminate "asylum seeker" as a category to which extraordinarily burdensome conditions of living are attached—and that is variously inhabited, challenged, and remade by people from all walks of life. In so doing, I have suggested the value of historicizing rather than naturalizing the category "asylum seeker."

In focusing on asylum seekers' interaction with the direct provision system, I built on and extended the rich scholarship about how social

welfare under neoliberalism seeks to produce particular kinds of entrepreneurial subjects for neoliberal capitalism.[118] Where asylum seekers
are concerned, social welfare in the form of direct provision is not intended to generate that outcome. On the contrary, it is intended to deter
asylum seekers from arriving, and to control and incapacitate those who
do manage to arrive. In that sense, migrants' experiences in direct provision may be better apprehended through the scholarship on populations
who are perpetually being controlled and contained, rather than being
made ready for participation in neoliberal citizenship.[119] Yet, as noncitizens whose presence is temporarily permitted because they invoke international human rights through their asylum claims, asylum seekers also
differ in some important ways from populations targeted for perpetual
control such as long-term citizen prisoners and undocumented migrants
who do not claim asylum.

Drawing on Giorgio Agamben's argument that the refugee camp
serves as a model and means for reducing human beings to bare lives that
can be killed with impunity, scholars have written rich and insightful
analyses of asylum seeker lives.[120] Agamben's framework captures critical aspects of the power relationship through which "asylum seeker" is
produced, policed, and deployed for statecraft and global dominance.[121]
Yet scholarship sometimes overlooks the fact that asylum seekers and
refugees are not the same, legally speaking, and the difference matters.
Precisely what asylum seekers want is official recognition as "refugees"
because that will release them from direct provision and provide them
with various rights, including to legally remain. If refugee status is not
available, then asylum seekers hope to gain some other status that allows
them to remain. Yet "refugee" is the designation that the state seeks to
withhold from the vast majority of the asylum seekers.

Direct provision intervenes into the struggle over legal status by
seeking to position asylum seekers, subjectively and materially, for a future in which their right to remain has been refused and they are on
track to becoming illegal and deportable. That outcome does not necessarily mean that they will leave; rather, some will leave while others will
remain as subaltern, dispossessed, rightless laborers for capital now that
the asylum system has refused them. Yet, as Christabel's experiences
show, until 2003 adherence to heterosexual reproduction was one of the
ways that migrants could create different and better futures than those
for which direct provision sought to position them. Giving birth to a

child allowed migrants to exit direct provision and become regular subjects of social welfare who were introduced to modalities of Irish living. The modalities remain deeply shaped by hierarchies of gender, sexuality, race, class, culture, and geopolitics, which migrants at once negotiated and helped to transform. Nonetheless, regular social welfare offered life possibilities that were utterly unavailable in direct provision. The fact that childbearing could effect this transformation in migrants' life possibilities shows the extraordinary value that was attached to a particular narrative of family and heterosexual reproduction in Irish culture. Following Agamben, one could argue that direct provision is structured to produce death in every way except biologically; as a result, childbearing, which enabled migrants to exit direct provision, provided a route back into social, cultural, economic, and political life. In that sense, Irish born children gave birth to their parents.[122]

Admittedly, the presence of a newborn child deeply conditioned these migrants' entry into mainstream Irish life. They negotiated the housing market, the welfare system, and the labor market as parents (often lone parents) with a newborn child, which is very different from doing so as a single migrant, or as a migrant in a same-sex relationship. Despite the Irish state's official valorization of children and childbearing, adequate support for those trying to negotiate parenting and other roles is not in place. As a result, childbearing migrants' entry into Irish life was very challenging. At the same time, the fact that childbearing enabled them to exit direct provision highlights ways that the immigration, asylum, and welfare systems privileged and reproduced the dominant sexual order, albeit in messy and contradictory ways. Those who could not match that dominant order remained relegated to direct provision.

The Irish government, however, was intent on steadily eroding even these possibilities. In January 2003 the Supreme Court issued its *L&O* decision, which ended migrants' entitlement to residency based on the birth of a child. Until May 27, 2003, asylum seekers with newborns were still entitled to move out of direct provision even though they could no longer gain residency through their child. On May 27, however, section 13 of the Social Welfare (Miscellaneous Provisions) Act 2003 came into effect, rendering anyone who was unlawfully in the state or who had applied for asylum ineligible for rent assistance. Without rent assistance, it was virtually impossible to move out of direct provision.[123] The *Irish*

Times explained, "Since direct provision was introduced more than three years ago, some 10,000 people have left it and claimed ordinary welfare benefits, according to the Department of Justice.... The new measures are aimed at ensuring that all asylum seekers remain instead in the 'direct provision' system."[124] The welfare rules underwent an important further revision in May 2004, when the government introduced a "habitual residence condition" (HRC) that had to be satisfied in order to receive welfare. Newly arrived asylum seekers were unlikely to be able to meet the HRC standard; this effectively reinforced their ban from regular welfare and their confinement within the direct provision system.[125]

Direct provision continues to be challenged by a wide range of individuals and groups, but without success. The challenges usually adopt one or both of two major arguments: that direct provision produces social exclusion, which is contrary to the government's stated social policies; and that direct provision violates human rights.[126] Detailed analysis of these arguments is beyond the scope of this chapter. Although these discourses help to make legible the severe conditions under which migrants live, their inability to generate significant transformation suggests that "progress" and "economic development," framed in nationalist terms under neoliberalism, fundamentally require the creation and maintenance of classes of subordinated, dispossessed people. Thus, asylum seekers' exclusion from the state's social inclusion remit, and from the ambit of human rights understood broadly, is no aberration. Rather, it is deeply revealing of the contradictions and limitations of a social inclusion and human rights agendas under neoliberalism.

In 2007 Nasc concluded, "Despite the overwhelming consensus in research available that direct provision and dispersal should be abolished, almost eight years after it was implemented, the system remains in place."[127] Ministers for justice continue to claim that direct provision meets "the best standards in terms of transparency, consistency, and justice."[128] RIA's 2010 report, *Value for Money and Policy Review*, concluded, "The RIA has done very commendable work in challenging circumstances to ensure that the primary objective of the programme is achieved."[129] The report also argued that direct provision provides "the best choice" when compared with regular social welfare, self-catering, or reliance on local housing authorities as possible alternatives for asylum seekers.[130] Migrants, however, regularly describe direct provision as "an open prison."[131]

Poster from a public protest on June 16, 2001, against the government's treatment of asylum seekers.

Birthing a child no longer offers the possibility of exiting the direct provision system. This change shows how direct provision was restructured to more thoroughly contain, control, and dispossess migrants. The other possible route for restructuring, which was not taken, would have been to further open the doors that had already opened for childbearing asylum seekers by welcoming a broader spectrum of people, families, intimacies, and affiliations and considering how to facilitate their lives to the fullest. Until we reach that point, efforts to not just improve but to totally abolish direct provision and the current asylum system must continue.

CHAPTER 4

The "Right to Life of the Unborn" and Migration Controls

IN JANUARY 2002 Ms. I.A.O., a thirty-two-year-old Nigerian citizen, made headlines in Ireland when she appealed to the High Court to prevent her deportation to Nigeria on the ground that she was pregnant. Her solicitor, deploying pro-life rhetoric, claimed that her deportation contravened Article 40.3.3 of the Irish Constitution, which guarantees that the Irish State will "defend and vindicate" the "right to life of the unborn."[1] Ms. O had entered Ireland in December 1999, claiming asylum on the basis that she feared her life would be in danger if she returned to Nigeria. An official who interviewed her judged her claim to be "manifestly unfounded" and that she had deliberately made false or misleading representations about her case.[2] Ms. O appealed the decision, lost, and was issued a deportation order. She sought and received permission to institute a judicial review of the deportation order, which did not succeed, and a second deportation order was issued against her on October 26, 2001. Ms. O then sought the services of a firm of private solicitors, who appealed her deportation on several grounds including the fact that she had become pregnant. Building on the Irish Constitution's guarantee of the "right to life of the unborn," her solicitor argued that deporting her to "Nigeria, where the mortality rate was 90 per thousand births, compared with seven in the Irish Republic," amounted to jeopardizing the life of the unborn child.[3]

Other arguments against Ms. O's deportation were also marshaled, but it was her solicitor's deployment of claims concerning "the unborn" that captured the public imagination.[4] When her case went to the Supreme Court, the *Irish Times'* headline announced, "Status of the Unborn at the Centre of a Plea against Deportation."[5] Unfortunately for Ms. O, the Supreme Court, like the High Court, affirmed that her deportation was legal.

Drawing on Ms. O's case, this chapter explores how pro-life discourses are invoked to try to challenge and redraw the Irish state's differentiation between legal and illegal migration. I address both women's migration out of Ireland and women's migration into Ireland as these are mediated through discourses and practices concerning abortion. Thus, I connect Ms. O's Supreme Court case to the long history of Irish women's travel across international borders for purposes of abortion. In 1992 the X case, which involved a raped, pregnant teenager who sought an abortion in Britain, forced the Supreme Court to consider whether the Irish state had the power to prevent Irish women's abortion migration, given the state's constitutional commitment to defend and vindicate the right to life of the "unborn." Reading the X and O cases side by side therefore makes clear that the state's pro-life position has shaped its approach to managing migration into and out of the territory. The two cases' divergent outcomes, however, reveal that the state's power over migration and abortion has been interpreted so as to widen the gap between citizen versus migrant women's possibilities for legally authorized travel across borders, and their possibilities for giving birth to children who are recognized as Irish citizens.

To explore these arguments, the chapter first describes how the celebration of women's reproduction (and the consequent ban on abortion) became a means to articulate a distinction between Britishness and Irishness, as well as among the hierarchies within the category of "Irish" itself. Next, I describe how the ban on abortion gave rise to a distinct history of migration by Irish women. In the 1992 X case, however, citizen women's right to travel overseas for abortions came into question. That same year, the Irish public was asked to ratify the Maastricht Treaty. Although the treaty was intended to further facilitate migration by EU/EEA citizens, it fueled growing concern about Irish women's ability to travel for abortions without state interference. The concern was resolved in a manner that cleared the way for C, another raped and pregnant teenager, to seek an abortion in Britain in 1997. Unlike X, however, C was a Traveller, which is a community that has historically born much of the brunt of systemic racism and discrimination in Ireland. Her case therefore allows us to understand how racial discourses intersect with pro-life and pro-choice arguments. The following section returns to Ms. O's case, and analyzes the arguments about whether the state's commitment to defend and vindicate the right to life of the unborn had relevance for the state's power to deport migrants. I conclude that these cases show how abortion politics serve as a site of racializing, nationalizing struggles over where and how to draw the line between legal and illegal migrant, which in turn affects who may give birth to children who are Irish citizens.

Women's Reproduction: Marking External and Internal Boundaries

Abortion has been illegal in Ireland since the Offenses against the Person Act, which passed in 1861 while Ireland was under British rule.[6] As described earlier, in 1921 Ireland became partitioned into a Free State (composed of the southern twenty-six counties that would eventually become a republic) and the North, which remained under British rule. In this post-colonial context, "the overwhelming push to define Ireland as 'not-England' lead to a search for distinguishing marks of identity," of which women's reproductive sexuality became key.[7] The 1937 constitution constructed women as mothers and child-bearers located within the private home.[8] Women's dedication to reproducing the next generation of Irish people became elevated as a symbol of Ireland's moral and cultural distinctiveness over the former colonial master, Britain.[9] This symbolism intertwined with the direct regulation of women's sexuality, not only channeling it into childbearing within marriage but also banning abortion and the sale of contraceptives.[10]

Women's childbearing was not only burdened by the weight of the Irish/British distinction. In addition, as described in the introduction to this book, a particular vision and version of Irishness as race/ethnicity was enshrined in the constitution, which conceived Irish women as settled, Catholic, and "white."[11] Thus, reproductive politics would become a site for struggle over who was included on racial and cultural grounds within definitions of Irishness. As Laury Oaks summarizes, "In Ireland, reproduction is a medium through which competing national origin stories that focus on Irish national identity and cultural self-determination, indeed versions of 'Irishness' itself, are imagined and expressed."[12]

Struggles over abortion reflected these dynamics. For example, in 1974 the Supreme Court recognized the right to marital privacy (including in terms of accessing contraception).[13] The Right feared that this decision might open the door to legalized abortion, as had happened in the

United States.[14] Thus, they organized to introduce a constitutional ban on abortion, using powerfully nationalist imagery that equated a pro-life stance with a restrictive vision of Irish cultural identity and values, and with the protection of important national resources—people—who might not otherwise be born.[15] Moreover, they portrayed abortion as "a British practice that threatens the Irish race," and "as a 'violent colonial tool' threatening the integrity of the Irish nation."[16] Pro-choice groups often responded in similarly nationalist terms that were also exclusionary, for example, by portraying abortion as an indigenous Irish practice that could be linked to such figures as St. Brigid.[17]

The resulting bitter campaign has been described as "the second partitioning of Ireland," a phrase that evokes the independence struggle that left the island divided into a British-ruled North and an independent South.[18] In the end, the Right was successful, and in 1983, Article 40.3.3 was added to the constitution. It states: "The State acknowledges the right to life of the unborn and, with due regard to the equal right to life of the mother, guarantees in its laws to respect, and, as far as practicable, by its laws to defend and vindicate that right."[19] This article would become central in the Baby O case. The Right began working to limit access to information about abortion abroad and women's right to travel outside the country for abortions.

Abortion Restriction and International Migration

Because abortion is banned in Ireland, women have been forced to travel abroad to access such services. Their travel is part of the larger migration history that has significantly constructed the ideological and material boundaries of the nation-state. As M. A. G. O'Tuathaigh describes, emigration was the single most important fact of Irish life for nearly two centuries.[20] High rates of emigration have "long been linked to the process of class formation and capitalist development in Ireland" and, indeed, enabled the consolidation of a nationalist bourgeoisie that would eventually seize the state from British hands.[21] After independence, sustained emigration continued.

As described in chapter 1, emigration has centrally shaped, and subsequently sustained, the modern Irish sexual order. For example, those who violated or were violated by the strict sexual codes of independent Ireland often resorted to emigration on either a temporary or permanent basis.[22] These "sexiles" included people in same-sex relationships or flee-ing incest.[23] Women who were pregnant but unmarried also "emigrated to Britain in significant numbers during the twentieth century."[24] This form of emigration was widely recognized and critically debated, but the state generally turned a blind eye.[25] According to Lindsey Earner-Byrne, emigration by pregnant unmarried women "forms a vital part of what has become known as 'the abortion trail.' "[26]

The abortion trail concerns Irish women facing unwanted pregnan-cies who have traveled to England and elsewhere for abortions. The prac-tice is so extensive that it has left a recognizable "abortion migration" history.[27] Many scholars suggest that abortion migration dates from 1967, when abortion was legalized in Britain. Pauline Jackson, however, argues that Irish abortion migration to England dates from around 1937, when the United Kingdom's *Rex v. Bourne* case opened the door to abor-tion under certain circumstances.[28] With the passage of the British Abortion Act of 1967, Irish women's migration to Britain for abortions became more thoroughly institutionalized, even though "for many women [such travel] is a huge hurdle, involving financial strain, distress and fear, [and] unknown places in an unknown country."[29]

Having to travel overseas underscores that abortion remains deemed "un-Irish," and forces women to question their relationship to national identity. For example, Ellen was an Irish woman who had been living in Germany, became pregnant, sought an abortion, and returned to Ire-land. She describes:

> I was faced with the fact that I had done something which divided the country. . . . In Ireland I became one of those questionable women who'd had an abortion, in Germany I had been a respon-sible young woman who had dealt with a difficult situation. In Ireland it was something which could hurt others, make others ashamed of me, it was something upon which I would be judged and found wanting. It felt strange to have done something which was so condemned and considered so wrong but which was so right for me.[30]

Irish women's abortion migration continues today. No one knows the full extent, but the Irish Family Planning Association suggests that "be-tween January 1980 and December 2010, at least 147,881 women travelled from the Republic of Ireland for safe abortion services abroad," primarily in Britain.[31] These practices contribute to the continued association of abortion with Britishness, not Irishness. At the same time, they ironically reveal the Irish state's thorough dependence on British abortion services in order to sustain the Irish/British sexual dichotomy.[32] Women traveled to other countries, too, although in far fewer numbers.[33]

The X Case: Questioning Women's Right to Travel for Abortions

The complicated relationship between official nationalism and women's abortion migration came into crisis in 1992 during the X case. X was a fourteen-year-old Irish girl, pregnant through rape, whose parents brought her to Britain for an abortion. The attorney general of Ireland issued an injunction against them, and they returned to Ireland without X having procured an abortion. The injunction prohibited X from leaving the state for nine months. A tremendous public outcry resulted. Even "people who had voted for the 1983 amendment reacted as if this were their daughter and added their voices of protest."[34] "Coverage of women's right to travel repeatedly drew an analogy with internment. . . . The parallel with internment implied that the Irish State had, implicitly, become indistinguishable from the British State, whose policy of internment without trial for the nationalist population in the North of Ireland only led to an intensification of violence."[35] A famous cartoon showed a little girl (X) clutching a teddy bear and interned within the national territory. The fact that X and her family were white, settled, middle-class, and law-abiding significantly contributed to the public response.[36] The X case was also widely covered in the international media in a manner that generally condemned Ireland. "The international media reported Ireland to be 'backward,' 'barbarous,' 'punitive,' 'priest-ridden'—a portrayal that did not sit well with the modernizing image of an emerging Celtic Tiger economy."[37] The portrayal threatened to have economic repercussions. "Embarrassed by the potentially damaging attention, the government undertook to pay all legal expenses arising from X's appeal to the Supreme Court."[38] In March 1992 the Supreme Court ruled that X could procure an abortion, given that she was suicidal, which represented a threat to her life.[39]

But in the Supreme Court decision, "the right of a pregnant woman to travel outside the country was contested 3–2 and was not seen as an inalienable right."[40] Moreover, travel by a pregnant woman seeking an abortion "had never been thought illegal before in Ireland, as [Irish law that criminalizes abortion] does not normally have effect outside the jurisdiction."[41] Three of the five Supreme Court justices ruled in X, however, "that the implicit right to travel which the Irish Constitution confers on citizens was subordinate to the courts' duty to protect the right to life of the foetus."[42] Even the invocation of the Treaty of Rome, which allows EU citizens to travel freely to avail of services, including abortion services, was not sufficient to persuade the majority of the court that women had the right to travel for abortions.[43]

The possible consequences of the X decision were serious: "the potential restriction on a woman's freedom of movement, and with it, the spectre of anti-abortion groups seeking injunctions to restrain pregnant women from traveling abroad, provoked widespread protests."[44] These included a pro-abortion protest at Dublin airport "where an 'X-ray machine' was used to screen female 'passengers' to England. Those found to be pregnant were not allowed to board the planes and were 'taken into State custody."[45] This demonstration dramatized the question of whether and how the state could inquire into women's reproductive status and adjudicate their migration accordingly. Feminist concerns about women's ability to travel were not unfounded; Angela, who found herself unexpectedly pregnant and who decided to seek an abortion in England, describes that "those were the days when anti-abortion protestors were doing everything to stop women from getting to England. I had nightmares that somehow they would stop me before I got to England and force me to continue the pregnancy."[46]

Concerns about women's ability to travel outside the state for an abortion became more urgent after the Irish government asked the public to ratify the Maastricht Treaty. The treaty was another step in the process, initiated by the Treaty of Rome, to open up migration by EU citizens by introducing EU citizenship.[47] Of course, even while Maastricht further opened up migration for EU nationals, it contributed to further restricting and criminalizing migration for non-EU/EEA nationals.[48] For Irish citizen women, however, Maastricht's ability to further facilitate their migration came into question after it emerged that in 1991 the Irish government had secretly appended a protocol to the treaty, stating that "no act or amendment at European level could supersede the 1983 Amendment to the Irish Constitution. In other words, this protocol

denied Irish women recourse to European Community law" in their efforts to challenge abortion restrictions.[49] This included in regard to their
ability to travel overseas for abortions. Maastricht's promise of enhanced
international mobility therefore coexisted uneasily with the potential
for increased restriction on women's travel because of the protocol and
the X decision.

Some women's groups urged a "no" vote because they argued that
Maastricht with the protocol was not in the best interests of women. Antiabortion groups also urged a "no" vote but on the grounds that Europeanization allowed EU institutions (especially courts) to interfere in Irish
affairs, including on matters of morality and sexuality, in ways that eroded Irish national sovereignty and distinctiveness.[50] As Oaks summarizes, "The extreme publicity of the interrelationship between abortion
politics and the meanings of Irish membership within the European
Union created a different space for the presentation of competing sorts
of Irishness at a time when 'nation' itself is being transformed within the
New Europe."[51]

The Irish government, eager for the public to ratify Maastricht and
concerned that the X case and revelations of the protocol might derail
that process, "made a Solemn Declaration to try to mitigate the effects
of their own Protocol. They promised a separate referendum on abortion travel and information, and the Treaty was passed."[52] In November
1992 the promised referendum on abortion took place, and it involved
three different issues. "Two proposed constitutional amendments—
guaranteeing pregnant women's freedom to travel abroad and limited
rights to the circulation of information about abortion services—were
voted into the Constitution in this referendum. A third amendment,
proposing a more limited right to abortion than that already allowed by
the Supreme Court, was rejected."[53] Therefore, citizen women who remain subjected to the state's antiabortion laws at least secured a guarantee that the state would not prevent them from traveling abroad to procure abortions, should they decide to do so and should they have the
means.[54]

The C Case: Racialization and the Pro-Life State

These events demonstrate that abortion discourses remain deeply intertwined with an Irish/British (and Irish/EU) binary. Moreover, they

make clear that the Irish state's pro-life stance has generated abortion migration, which prompted questions about whether the state has the power to regulate women's travel out of Ireland, given the constitution's guarantee to "defend and vindicate" the "right to life of the unborn." In this section I turn to the 1997 C case, which shows how racialization within the category of "Irish" also shapes abortion discourses and migration possibilities.

C was a thirteen-year-old Traveller, who, like X, sought an abortion after she had been raped and made pregnant. Her Traveller status, however, significantly affected how the mainstream media and public constructed her circumstances. Travellers are a distinct cultural group that has experienced systemic racism, discrimination, and exclusion in Ireland.[55] As Steve Garner describes, "They record the highest frequency of physical and verbal attacks among [all] minorities in the (2001) Amnesty International survey [of racism in Ireland], and experience discrimination principally in the areas of accommodation, leisure, health services, and education. Mortality levels are well in excess of the settled population and life expectancy far lower."[56] Nevertheless, there is "strong resistance by policy makers and others" to the idea that Travellers' poor living conditions have a causal connection with systemic racism.[57] Instead, Travellers' bodies and cultures are simultaneously exoticized and denigrated, such that poor living conditions frequently become blamed on Travellers themselves.

Claims about gender and sexuality are integral to the racialization of Travellers. For example, Jane Helleiner describes that Traveller women are constructed by settled people as alternately sexualized and exotic, overly masculinized, or victims of Traveller men.[58] Some government studies approvingly commented on Traveller girls' and women's great modesty "in dress and demeanor" and expressed concern that "the 'high standards' of sexual morality among Travellers might 'be imperilled' through exposure to 'the less desirable incidents of life in the settled community.'"[59] But Sinéad Ní Shúineár suggests the existence of a far less positive view that constructs Traveller sexuality and childbearing as the means to reproduce "pathological" Traveller bodies: as Ní Shúineár describes, metabolic disorders among Travellers are ascribed to "inbreeding"; a video on the supposed dangers of consanguineous marriage is "required viewing" during "compulsory 'marriage preparation courses' for Traveller couples"; and "everyone—including the Catholic Church, normally opposed to such practices—urges Travellers to seek genetic counseling" before marriage.[60] Ní Shúineár characterizes these as examples of "the late 20th century version of scientific racism" that is directed at Travellers, and she concludes that "Travellers are thus physiologically othered within the parameters of 'pure Irish' racial status."[61] Ní Shúineár's analysis suggests the existence of a racist mainstream narrative about biologically distinct Traveller bodies that are reproduced through marriage, sex, and childbearing. Traveller child-rearing practices are frequently impugned for perpetuating "undesirable" Traveller culture; for example, Traveller parents have been described as "no credit to the nation."[62] As recently as 1996, "TD [member of parliament] Austin Deasy created considerable controversy . . . when he commented that the Traveller 'problem' could be solved by containing their numbers through birth control."[63]

Against this backdrop, the C case unfolded. C lived with her parents and eleven siblings in a caravan. After a family friend raped her, she was taken into care by the Eastern Health Board. When she learned that she was pregnant, she wanted an abortion, which her parents initially supported but then they changed their minds after the antichoice Youth Defense League approached them. The Eastern Health Board applied to the District Court for an order that would allow them to bring C to England for an abortion, given that she was suicidal, which represented a threat to her life (as with X). The order was granted. Her parents then applied to the High Court for judicial review of the District Court's order, with Youth Defense funding their legal team. The High Court refused to quash the order, plans for an appeal to the Supreme Court were abandoned, and C traveled to England for an abortion.

As Ruth Fletcher observes, from a feminist perspective, the outcome was positive. Yet Fletcher also provides a valuable analysis of the troubling racial and economic aspects of the case. For example, "photographs of C's family caravan were published in the press, exposing C and her family to intrusive public scrutiny in a manner that was not shared by the settled, middle class family of X. The Irish Travellers' Movement (ITM) held a press conference objecting to the racism that it saw in the media treatment of the case."[64] While the public was clearly sympathetic, this was nonetheless "tainted by the assumption that Travellers were their own worst enemy" and that Traveller culture had somehow brought this on C.[65] Moreover, "C's poverty, her membership in the Travelling community, and her membership in a family of twelve children provided justification for an emerging public view that C *ought* to get an abortion."[66]

Antichoice groups, for their part, claimed that Travellers were particularly likely to stigmatize C if she had an abortion, implying that Traveller culture was more intolerant than the mainstream. Both prochoice and pro-life groups thus converged in celebrating the modernity of settled white Irish people by contrasting it with their images of Traveller culture, including in gender and sexual terms. While abortion appears to have been the right decision, given C's expressed wishes, public discourses effectively implied that "while X was to be spared motherhood because of her innocence, C was to be spared motherhood because she was unfit for it."[67] Fletcher concludes that these events show how "a young Traveller woman was represented as a less worthy bearer of Irishness."[68]

Fletcher importantly insists that these racialized representations are neither new nor caused by the arrival of migrants, as is commonly claimed. Instead, they are a contemporary rearticulation of long-standing beliefs about who is "really" Irish, and about whose childbearing therefore most closely reproduces a desired version of Irishness.

Contesting Deportation through the "Right to Life of the Unborn"

The troubled intersections among the state's pro-life stance, the regulation of women's mobility across international borders, and heterosexualized racialization emerged in new form during the *Baby O* case. In the case, Ms. O's solicitors sought to prevent her deportation by invoking the state's commitment to "defend and vindicate" the "right to life of the unborn."

Modern deportation has its roots in historical practices of forced transportation, exile, and banishment.[69] Matthew Gibney characterizes deportation as "'a cruel power,' one that is sometimes seen as incompatible with the modern liberal state. . . . Deportation tears individuals from families and cruelly uproots people from communities . . . sometimes banishing them to places where they have few ties or connections."[70] A U.S. judge famously described deportation as a punishment "that may deprive a man and his family of everything that makes life worth living."[71]

Until recently, deportation was "a secondary instrument of migration control," used with caution because it presents practical difficulties (locating people, forcing them to onto planes and boats, forcing countries of origin to take their migrants back) as well as moral issues.[72] But in recent years the deportation of non-EU/EEA migrants has become a centerpiece for European-wide immigration controls. Indeed, this has become the twin face of the expansion of freedom of movement for EU/ EEA nationals. In Ireland, deportation was significantly codified by one of the first major pieces of immigration legislation, the Immigration Act 1999, and recodified in 2004 and subsequent legislation. The minister for justice is vested with the authority to deport migrants on behalf of the state. Typically, migrants receive written notification that the minister plans to deport them.[73] By law they then have three choices: within fifteen days, submit a written explanation of any grounds on which the minister should consider allowing them to remain;[74] leave voluntarily (the benefit is that they will not be barred from returning to the state in future); or consent to be deported.[75] For the latter, Emma Quinn and Gerard Hughes blandly describe what is often a terrifying and traumatic process: "deportees may be escorted by Garda officers or may travel unescorted. Escorts are required in cases where carriers do not accept unaccompanied deportees or when individuals are considered potentially violent."[76] This description normalizes and bureaucratizes the practical difficulties, moral issues, and emotional anguish associated with deportation, and understates the degree of state coercion that may be required. Across Europe deportations have sometimes resulted in death, "mainly from suffocation," as officials seek to subdue struggling deportees.[77] Consequently, human rights groups have called for states to abide by human rights standards in their treatment of deportees, and have expressed concern about the fate of some deportees who have been imprisoned or executed upon return to their home countries.[78] But because "the national security of powerful states takes precedence over human rights," a significantly unfettered EU-wide deportation regime has taken shape.[79] Ireland's willing participation in the process is suggested by the fact that the minister for justice approvingly drew attention to an EU statement that described joint "repatriation" flights "as a means of '... demonstrating solidarity among member states.'"[80] Deportation, it seems, has become a route through which EU states express support of one another.[81]

Deportation represents an endpoint for migrants who attempt to challenge where and how the state draws the line between legal and illegal presence. Matthew Gibney points out that the presence of asylum seekers, rather than "illegal immigrants," has significantly legitimized the expansion of deportation in many countries. The fact that asylum seekers are singled out to play this role is partly because, as Gibney describes, asylum seekers are countable and trackable. The state is aware of their presence, keeps track of their movements, and knows when their applications and appeals fail—which is the point when they become deportable. By contrast, migrants who enter without the state's knowledge, or enter legally but whose visas have expired, are not as easily countable and trackable. Moreover, stricter interpretation of "noncompliance" with administrative rules, truncated or expedited processing for many including those from countries designated as "safe," and reduced judicial safeguards have made increasing numbers of asylum seekers available for deportation. Therefore, as deportation numbers become a crucial measure for showing a government's "success" in managing migration, the deportation of refused asylum seekers, particularly, provides the best opportunity for demonstrating "effective" government.

Gibney's analysis illuminates developments in the Irish deportation system. Major immigration laws each included provisions to ramp up the surveillance of and introduce new restrictions on asylum seekers, making it easier to dismiss their cases and designate them as deportable.[82] The 2002 Program for Government identified increasing the rate of "repatriation" of failed asylum seekers as its top priority in the area of immigration control.[83] In January 2005 the minister introduced measures to speed up the processing of "prioritized" asylum cases including those from so-called safe countries of origin: "The aim is to reduce the duration of the initial application and appeal to three weeks for each process. Applicants may be housed in dedicated accommodation centres. . . . Unsuccessful asylum applicants will, therefore, be more readily available to Immigration Authorities/Garda National Immigration Bureau . . . for removal from the state."[84] The proposed and revised Immigration Residence Protection Bill, which failed to become law when the parliament was dissolved in February 2011 but will likely be reintroduced, further expanded the state's deportation powers, including over asylum seekers, while reducing an individual's ability to challenge these powers.[85] In all these ways, an expanding deportation regime has been significantly piloted and implemented on the backs of asylum seekers, who are particularly vulnerable.[86] Indeed, Emma Quinn explains, "the majority of people who are deported from Ireland are unsuccessful asylum seekers."[87]

Ms. O experienced and challenged these developments. When her claim for asylum was deemed to be manifestly unfounded, she appealed; when this failed and the minister issued a deportation order against her, her solicitors sought and received permission for a judicial review of the deportation order. A High Court decision on a similar case, however, "effectively disposed of the only ground" on which Ms. O's solicitors had sought the review.[88] A second deportation order was issued against her, but by then she was pregnant. Ms. O sought the services of a new firm of solicitors, who appealed the second deportation order on several grounds—including the fact that she was pregnant; therefore, they argued, her deportation contravened Article 40.3.3 of the constitution, which guaranteed to defend and vindicate the right to life of the unborn. As Fletcher summarizes, in the O case, "the legal arguments . . . revolved around the nature and degree of the state's obligation to the 'unborn' in the context of an order to deport a pregnant woman."[89] The ways that sexual regimes may mediate where the line is drawn between legal and illegal migrant could not have been posed more starkly.

If O's solicitors were successful, they would not only prevent her immediate deportation but her baby would also have been born in Ireland, making it an Irish citizen who was entitled to parental care and company. The baby's entitlement would then have provided Ms. O with a basis for continuing residency rather than the prospect of deportation. A positive decision, moreover, potentially offered relief to many *other* migrant women facing deportation. Paradoxically, however, O's case heavily relied on arguments about the right to life of the unborn, which have oppressive consequences for any woman who is or may become pregnant.[90]

The paradoxical implications of Ms. O's challenge were clear to everyone. For example, in its submission to the High Court, the state pointed out that if Ms. O's case succeeded, the implication was that "no woman of childbearing age who could assert that she was pregnant could ever be deported."[91] In the Supreme Court, Ms. O's counsel "conceded that, if his submission was well-founded it would necessarily follow that every woman or girl of childbearing age would have to submit to pregnancy testing before she was deported or extradited to a country with less developed pre- or ante-natal services than are available in this country."[92]

Chief Justice Keane argued indignantly, "No such gross violation of the privacy of women and girls would possibly have been intended by the enactment of Article 40.3.3. of the Constitution."[93] Yet, as chapters in this book describe, asylum-seeking women and girls *were* continually subjected to intensive violation of their privacy where their reproductive status was concerned, as reflected in government statistics about the numbers who were pregnant on arrival and the ways that those numbers circulated and performed ideological work. Moreover, some women may have prioritized avoiding deportation over protecting their privacy— especially since privacy was effectively unavailable anyway because of their migrant status. In short, balancing the state's power to deport against Article 40.3.3's guarantee to protect and vindicate the right to life of the "unborn" raised very complex questions.

The Right to Life, the Right to Deport

At the Supreme Court, counsel for Ms. O argued that Article 40.3.3 directly impacted on the state's power to deport her, since she was now pregnant. According to the *Irish Times,* counsel claimed that an "unborn" is a person under Irish law; therefore, a separate deportation order should have been made against Baby O; although Baby O was a person, she or he did not (yet) have a nationality, and only nonnationals can be deported; and finally, the state had a duty to defend and vindicate Baby O's right to life. Since infant mortality in Nigeria was 90 per 1,000, compared with 7 per 1,000 in Ireland, deporting Ms. O amounted to jeopardizing Baby O's right to life.

In response, the state initially denied that Baby O was a person or had a right to legal personality, including under the Immigration Act. This stand was quickly revised to an assertion that "in the context of these proceedings the rights of the unborn are not distinguishable" from those of the pregnant woman.[94] As Ruth Fletcher notes, this claim stands in marked contrast to other instances when the state has treated the rights of the "unborn" as distinct from those of pregnant women.[95] Overall, the state's strategy was to deny that the constitutional commitment to "defend and vindicate" the "right to life of the unborn" had any application to Ms. O's situation. Instead, they painted her as simply another failed asylum seeker trying to find ways to remain in Ireland so as to scrounge off public services. In the High Court, the state's counsel argued this "is not a case where the right to life is being put at risk. Instead, however it's dressed up, this is about a person who comes here, puts in a claim for asylum, loses at all stages and says, while the claim is being processed, 'I've become pregnant and because the health service here is superior to that in my country of origin, I claim the right to have my baby here.'"[96] Adopting a narrow interpretation of Article 40.3.3 that reduced it to a matter of preventing abortion, the High Court concurred that "the right to life of the unborn, as enshrined in Article 40.3.3, was not an issue in the case."[97]

The Supreme Court affirmed the High Court's narrow reading:

> The passage from Article 40.3.3 on which Counsel relied . . . was intended to prevent the legalisation of abortion either by legislation or by judicial decision within the State, except when there was a real and substantial risk to the life of the mother which could only be avoided by the termination of the pregnancy. In this case, neither the State nor any of its organs was seeking to terminate [Ms. O.]'s pregnancy, and the fact that the standard of ante or post natal care available to her in Nigeria was less than would be available to her in this country was entirely irrelevant to the legality of her deportation. . . . If the State's right to deport persons who have been refused refugee status and who have no legal right to remain in this country were thus circumscribed, it would be, in a great range of cases, virtually negated. It is obvious that the rights of the born, in this context, cannot be less than those of the unborn.[98]

These comments suggest that the state's commitment to defending and vindicating the right to life of the unborn involves a very circumscribed realm.[99] Article 40.3.3 could have been interpreted as entailing a positive duty on the part of the state to enable women with wanted pregnancies to carry the pregnancies to term, and to give birth to a healthy baby. Yet, at least in Baby O's case, "the threat posed by higher infant mortality rates could not invoke the protection of Article 40(3)(3). The state's duty to defend and vindicate the right to life of the unborn did not extend to ensuring the health and well-being of Baby O, or even to ensuring a safe delivery."[100] The court's comments therefore exclude "reproductive health care issues from consideration in this deportation case."[101] But they do so without explaining why there is no positive duty on the state "to ensure a minimum standard of care in pregnancy or at least a negative duty to prevent infringements of a right to basic care."[102] Nor do they explain why the rights of the "unborn" should be limited in this way. Ultimately Fletcher suggests that the case "unveils the racialized stratification of foetal protection."[103]

The court's narrow interpretation of Article 40.3.3 provides grounds for the chief justice to argue that the state's power to deport cannot be constrained by this pro-life provision. Yet, as Fletcher indicates, Article 40.3.3 has historically been used to trump other rights and powers. Therefore, she argues, it is not "obvious" that Article 40.3.3 has no bearing on deportation, and instead, this claim needs to be explained. Overall, as Fletcher tartly observes, "the chief justice appears to find it unthinkable that the state should be fettered in its right to deport non-citizens. Yet the whole point of guaranteeing rights constitutionally or legislatively is to fetter the state."[104] The justice's conclusion that the rights of the unborn cannot trump the rights of the born are at best bitterly ironic when we recall that pregnant women suffering life-threatening illnesses have sometimes been left without medical treatment because it was feared that their treatment might jeopardize the foetus.[105] In Ms. O's case, however, "the born" likely refers to Irish citizens, in whose name and on whose behalf the state implements immigration controls, including deportation orders directed against pregnant women such as Ms. O.[106]

With the Supreme Court's denial that Article 40.3.3 had any relevance to, or might in any way constrain, the state's deportation powers, Ms. O's efforts to challenge where and how the state drew the line between legal and illegal immigrant status reached their limit. Based on the court's ruling, she was deported before her baby could be born—thereby ensuring that the baby was not an Irish citizen, which foreclosed another basis on which Ms. O could have sought legal status. But her challenge importantly forced public consideration of the relationship between state's guarantee to defend and vindicate the right to life of the "unborn" on one hand and its deportation powers on the other.

Regulating Migration, Regulating Abortion

The X and O cases were important in clarifying the relationship between Irish state policies for governing migration across international borders and the state's pro-life policies. In terms of migration, until the 1990s the state's migration concerns focused primarily on those who were leaving the country while relatively little attention was given to those who were entering. The Maastricht Treaty, however, was a crucial element in creating an integrated European Union through which mobile capital and mobile European bodies could move with relative ease. Since the Irish government embraced the project of Europeanization as a means for economic growth, it made concerted efforts to ensure that the electorate approved the Maastricht Treaty.

Yet in the post-Maastricht era the growing numbers of migrants seeking to cross the borders into Ireland—especially those from outside the EU/EEA or who were seeking asylum—were systematically problematized, increasingly restricted, and steadily criminalized. Growing restrictions, particularly on asylum seekers' possibilities to enter the state and have their claims considered, were complemented by deportation—a form of forced removal that expels them from the nation-state. Despite these restrictions, European integration and transnational capital have also called into being mobile subjects such as Ms. O, for whom new migration possibilities both emerge and become newly necessary, regardless of official Irish or European restrictions.

Therefore, reading the X and O cases side by side makes clear that state regimes for regulating mobility in the post-Maastricht era position women such as Ms. O versus women holding Irish and EU/EEA citizenship very differently. This differential positioning is relational in the sense that mobility for one is thoroughly implicated in growing criminalization and immobilization for the other. Thus, state regimes for governing mobility reiterate national origin as a source of hierarchy and inequality—despite Europeanization and globalization processes.[107]

These points, of course, also hold true for men. So the X and O cases are additionally important because they highlight how state regimes that reduce women's sexualities to heterosexualized childbearing, which is controlled through the denial of abortion, factored into these developments. In both X and O, the question arose as to whether the Irish government could or should inquire into women's pregnancy status and regulate their mobility accordingly. In both cases, the answer was eventually negative. But that common answer emerged through quite different considerations. With X, concerns about the global—especially about the possible impact of negative international opinion on economic development—shaped the final resolution to the case. Other important factors were feminist mobilizations and concern that the international community might see Ireland as less than rather than equal to the rich and powerful nations.

In the O case, it was also decided that the government should not inquire into women's reproductive status and regulate their mobility accordingly. But that decision emerged through a very different set of concerns. Unlike in X's case, Ms. O solicitors actually argued that her mobility *should* be mediated through government consideration of her pregnancy. This troubling claim was couched in the powerful language of the pro-life state, and ironically, if accepted, the result could have been *positive,* not only for Ms. O but also for potentially thousands of migrant women. The government's and courts' rejection of Ms. O's claim was couched within a very narrow reading of what constitutes a pro-life position, and in terms respecting women's "privacy," both of which were harnessed to state discourses and practices of immigration control. In particular, the court dismissed the suggestion that Article 40.3.3 should force a reconsideration of the state's power to deport by painting Ms. O as an untrustworthy migrant who intended to sponge off Irish health and other services; juridically separating her and her fetus, although in other cases such a separation was not made; and refusing to consider how her deportation would impact her child both before and after its birth.

Through Ms. O's pregnant body, the state and courts thus redrew and restabilized the line between national and nonnational women and, within the latter group, the line between supposedly "bogus" asylum seekers who should be deported and "genuine" asylum seekers who should be permitted to legally remain. Effectively, they harnessed women's (hetero)sexualities as tools for racialized strategies of immigration control that rebounded the Irish nation-state in the context of Europeanization and globalization. They foreclosed opportunities and possibilities for migrant women to legalize their presence in the state while further legitimizing the state's deportation regime. At the same time Irish citizen women remained unable to access abortion services unless they traveled abroad, which kept them harnessed to reproducing the next generation of the Irish population, now defined in ever more narrow terms.[108]

Coda: Reproductive Politics at the Intersections between the X and O Cases

The experiences of migrant women who face unplanned pregnancies suggest the urgency of revisioning reproductive politics in order to address how gender, race, class, sexuality, legal status, and the global governance of migration converge.

Travel overseas for abortion presents significant difficulties for migrant women—especially those women who are from outside the EU/EEA or whose legal status is not finalized, as is the case for asylum seekers.[109] For example, when *Women on Waves,* a Dutch ship that planned to provide on-board reproductive health services including abortions, sailed for Ireland on June 11, 2001, they were contacted by three hundred women seeking abortions, including "political refugees [i.e., asylum seekers] who did not have the papers to travel."[110] Asylum seekers whose cases are still undecided cannot leave the state unless they receive special permission from the Department of Justice. Remarkably in an officially antiabortion state, there is in fact a process through which asylum seekers may seek special permission for abortion travel. The Department of Justice has justified giving permission for travel by noting that the constitution guarantees freedom to travel for abortion; this, combined with advice from the attorney general that "under the Geneva Convention the Department had to 'give sympathetic consideration to requests from asylum-seekers for a travel document'" meant that asylum-seeker women could seek documents to travel for abortions.[111] The minister made clear, however, that "the State was not involved in any expenditure relating to those journeys."[112] Moreover, the Department of Justice "was unwilling to come up with a policy to [generally cover cases where asylum seekers need travel visas for abortions] and persisted in treating each application as a new and separate case," which adds to the delay, uncertainty, and stress.[113]

Many asylum-seeking women are likely unaware of the process for securing permission to travel to Britain for abortions.[114] Those who are aware face significant barriers:

> In order to legally access an abortion abroad, a migrant woman has to make an appointment with the Department of Justice to acquire temporary travel documents. She has to give reasons and

prove evidence. Some women will say that they need to travel for an abortion, others will say they are applying to travel for a medical procedure. . . . The woman needs to have confirmation of a positive pregnancy test, confirmation of a clinic booking abroad, usually, in England, a letter from her doctor or counsellor, and a copy of an identification card. She has to take the application form, together with two passport photos and the supporting evidence, to a Garda (Irish police) station and ask a guard to stamp the form, and, hence, the guards come to know her personal business. She then has to send the stamped form and photos to the Department of Justice and await processing of her permission to leave . . . which can take from a few days to a couple of weeks.[115]

Women also have to apply for a British visa so they can legally enter the state, even if only for an abortion.[116]

The whole process involves submitting one's request for abortion to scrutiny by officials and guards; negotiating multiple bureaucratic hurdles; accessing fax machines and phones; and seeking translation services. Moreover, the costs are often insurmountable, especially for asylum seekers who are living on €19.10 a week and prohibited from paid employment.[117] For women with small children, child care arrangements must be made. In some cases, the process is so lengthy that women miss their clinic appointments and have to reschedule. In the worst case scenarios, "they end up passing the 24 week limit that applies to British abortion services" and cannot get abortions even if the paperwork comes through.[118] All of these hurdles make abortion effectively inaccessible to the vast majority of asylum-seeking women.[119]

Some women negotiate these difficulties in ways that put them at considerable risk. For example, Human Rights Watch describes the experiences of Mary, "a young woman from an African country" who became pregnant while she was in the asylum process.[120] "Struggling to raise the costs of travel and the abortion, 'it took six weeks to get the money together,' Mary couldn't afford a further delay or additional costs. She decided to 'borrow' a passport from a friend, fully aware that if she was caught she would face immediate deportation."[121]

Women whose claims for asylum have been denied and who have subsequently applied for humanitarian leave to remain face even greater hurdles. A policy officer with the Irish Refugee Council explained that "women who had failed in their asylum applications and had applied for humanitarian leave to remain had lost the protection of the State. 'While they are free to leave the State they will almost certainly not get back in. Also, they won't gain entry to Britain without a visa and they won't get a visa if they don't have travel documents to get back into Ireland.'"[122] One such case involved an Eastern European woman who was married with children and living in Cork. Although she did "not want to go through with her pregnancy under any circumstances," she had to cancel her appointment for an abortion in Britain because she could not get the necessary travel documents. A supporter described her as devastated.[123]

Some women have opted to "'sneak' out of the State" without permission, which meant they risked being denied reentry if they were caught. Or they were refused entry to Britain and forcibly returned to Ireland where they ended up having the baby against their wishes.[124] Others turned to whatever resources are at hand, including trying to obtain herbs and medicines to induce abortion through personal contacts or the Internet.[125]

Migrant women of all legal statuses confront considerable difficulties when faced with an unplanned pregnancy. The Migrant Rights Centre Ireland (MRCI) describes the experiences of one migrant worker who became pregnant: "Her employers exerted tremendous pressure on her; they threatened to write to her parents to inform them of the pregnancy (which was unplanned) and to report her to immigration." She was subsequently dismissed and suffered a miscarriage the following day.[126] Other pregnant workers have faced equally harrowing circumstances. Depending on the rules in force at the time, immigrant workers who are fired for being pregnant may lose their legal status.

Facing unplanned pregnancies, some women have sought back-street abortions. The media reported in 2004 on a Moldovan woman who offered "gynecological services" in Dublin for €500, performed abortions on a Romanian and a Filipina woman, and had fled the state.[127] In 2008 the media reported that a Filipina woman who worked as a part-time child-minder had "aborted her own child" using tablets and "an instrument" that she inserted into her uterus. When the gardaí began an investigation, the woman fled to the Philippines.[128]

Planned pregnancies, too, present risks and dangers that are multiplied when women need to travel outside the country for abortions. In

2010, in the *A, B, and C case,* the European Court of Human Rights found that the Irish state was in violation of the European Convention on Human Rights because there were no provisions for abortion in cases where a woman's life was at risk.[129] The Irish government delayed responding to the judgment until the tragic death of Savita Halappanavar, a thirty-one-year-old Indian citizen who worked as a dentist in Ireland. Ms. Halappanavar presented at University Hospital, Galway, in October 2012, with severe back pain. She was seventeen weeks pregnant and found to be miscarrying. Ms. Halappanavar died of septicemia and *E. coli* one week after her admission to the hospital. Local, national, and international demonstrations protested Ms. Halappanavar's death and called for changes to Ireland's abortion laws.

Reproductive politics are centrally implicated in nation-formation, including, as I have shown, in state strategies for affirming and further extending differentiations between citizens and noncitizens—as well as efforts to contest and renegotiate these lines. Yet these issues usually fall outside the remit of even the most progressive reproductive politics. How may we extend antisexist, antiracist, and antipoor reproductive politics so we can better address the anticolonial and transnational dimensions of reproductive struggles? What kinds of activism, coalition-building, and social transformation are needed to enable both migrant women (who confront global, regional, and national migration controls) and diverse citizen women to exercise control over their bodies?

CHAPTER 5

Reproductive Futurism and the Temporality of Migration Control

I N MARCH 2004 the minister for justice announced that voters would be asked to amend the constitution by removing the automatic entitlement to citizenship for any child born in Ireland, north or south. Newborn children who did not have at least one parent who was an Irish citizen, who was entitled to Irish citizenship, or who had resided legally in Ireland for three of the last four years would no longer acquire citizenship at birth. The targets of the proposed amendment were migrants, although their children were most directly affected. Migrants were targeted because "there has been no significant diminution in the numbers of non-nationals arriving heavily pregnant."[1] By denying citizenship to children who were born to recently arrived migrants, the government hoped to discourage unwanted migration.

This chapter critically analyzes the citizenship referendum, showing how government claims that migrant pregnancy reflected and enabled illegal immigration were again mobilized to further redraw the line around who was, or could become, legally present. Because children were most directly affected, however, the referendum also highlights the temporal dimensions of migration control. Effectively, the referendum rendered not migrants but migrants' children and their children's children vulnerable to becoming designated as illegal and deportable.

My description of the referendum's outcome deliberately evokes the heteronormative temporality of generational reproduction and succession through which states strive to create particular kinds of national futures. Lee Edelman has analyzed how these heteronormative cultural logics saturate social meanings, possibilities, and politics by invoking an imaginary child on whose behalf a better future is to be struggled for. According to Edelman, such "reproductive futurism" venerates normative heterosexuality while figuring gay men as narcissistic, culturally unintelligible, socially dead, and incapable of working toward the future.[2] I suggest that populations in addition to gay men are abjected through reproductive futurism, though not in exactly the same way. For the imperative to realize a particular kind of national future often justifies state interference in the sexualities, childbearing opportunities, and parenting by women of color, poor or disabled women, lesbians, migrant women, and others.

The controversies over pregnant migrants evoke these other subaltern populations. But the controversies also foreground the fact that states seek to govern reproduction in ways that, over time, maintain differentiations between citizens and noncitizens that correlates with inequitable access to resources and opportunities.[3] Indeed, the Irish government claimed that migrant women's childbearing threatened the state's ability to produce a desirable future for "properly" Irish citizens in part because the births offered a means to steadily erase the distinction, thereby opening the door to expanding claims on resources that are normally reserved for citizens. By withholding automatic citizenship from migrants' children, however, the referendum promised to restabilize the citizen/migrant distinction and its associated inequalities. If children were not citizens at birth, then migrant parents could not eventually become citizens through their children (although some could become citizens on other grounds). At the same time, by designating many migrants' children as noncitizens, the referendum would not only limit their future entitlements but also render them vulnerable to becoming designated as "illegal" and deportable in their own right. In these ways, the referendum harnessed heteronormative logics to ensure that not just migrants but also migrants' children and their children's children would remain largely excluded from a range of resources, possibilities, and futures.

To develop these arguments, the chapter first provides an overview of the history of Irish citizenship eligibility, including how this intersected with the state's revalorization of the diaspora in the 1990s. Yet, even while elements of the Irish diaspora were being revalorized through heterosexist logics, pregnant migrants in Ireland were increasingly being constructed not as bearers of the next generation of Irish children but as illegal migrants.[4] Thus, the second section of the chapter explores exactly how governmental justifications for the referendum again constructed pregnancy as evidence of migrant illegality that supposedly necessitated changes to citizenship law in order to avert an undesirable national future. The conclusion argues that resulting changes in citizenship law, which effectively rendered many migrants illegal to the second generation and beyond, highlights not only the importance of laws and politics in making people illegal but also the temporal dimensions of immigration control that operates through heteronormative reproductive futurism.

Redefining the Boundaries of Irish Citizenship: Historical Context

The grant of birthright citizenship to anyone born in Ireland became included in Article 2 of the constitution in 1998 as a result of the Northern Ireland Peace Accords. Effectively, during the peace process the Irish state had relinquished its territorial claim on Northern Ireland but added a constitutional provision stating that anyone born anywhere on the island of Ireland was entitled to Irish citizenship.[5] Yet birthright citizenship had been the rule since the establishment of the independent Irish state, even though it was not included in the constitution but was written into law.[6] Thus, the government's proposal to end the automatic grant of citizenship to anyone born on Irish territory would alter what had been a long-standing approach to allocating citizenship.[7]

Irish citizenship has not been based only on birthright, however. The Irish Nationality and Citizenship Act 1956 made citizenship through descent available to the children and grandchildren of Irish emigrants. The provision for citizenship through descent was made in a time of emigration, depopulation, and fears that the Irish were a "dying race."[8] The revised Article 2 of the constitution, which refers to "cherish[ing] . . . special affinity with people of Irish ancestry living abroad who share [Irish] cultural identity and heritage," reflects this history of citizenship through descent. But it also highlights the new importance that came to be attached to the Irish "diaspora" in the 1990s, including through the efforts of President Mary Robinson. As Breda Gray describes, Robinson's embrace of the diaspora importantly resignified Irishness along more plural lines that were intended to ease nationalist tensions in Northern Ireland while forging a new relationship with Ireland's emigrant history.[9] Yet, the diaspora also provided what Gray describes as a technology "of integration into the global economy."[10] For example,

Catherine Nash relates that "diasporic identifications with Irish ancestral origins were being fostered to encourage inward investment and tourist revenue," not to mention "labor flexibility."[11] Moreover, hundreds of thousands of people who had emigrated from Ireland during the bleak decade of the 1980s were recruited to return as labor for the Celtic Tiger's economy. As Katy Hayward and Kevin Howard describe, recruitment of diasporic labor relied on a discourse of "ethnic consanguinity," suggestions that "the time of exile was over and the dream of returning home could at last be realised," and appeals to "think with the blood and return to Ireland as a patriotic duty."[12] This accords with Gray's analysis that the Irish diaspora was imagined around a model of heteronormative family, with Irishness understood as "pseudo-biological property" that was transmitted through heterosexual reproduction with culturally appropriate partners.[13] Moreover, Irish diaspora was normed as white (as is very evident in accounts by Irish people of color or, alternatively, when we consider that "the identification with Irish heritage by African Americans with Irish ancestors has to be asserted against the assumptions that blackness determines identity and that Irishness is fundamentally and naturally white"[14]).

The proposed constitutional amendment, however, promised to further reconfigure the conjunctions among migration, diaspora, and constructs of Irishness as pseudo-biological property that is transmitted through heterosexual reproduction.

Expanding Migrant Parents' Routes into Illegal Status: The *L&O* Decision

Government publications and speeches consistently situated the need for the referendum in terms of the Supreme Court's decision in the 2003 *Lobe and Osayande* case (known as the *L&O* case). As chapter 1 explained, the minister for justice had sought to unfetter his immigration control powers from the Supreme Court's 1990 *Fajujonu* decision that allowed migrants to gain residency through their Irish citizen children. Two asylum-seeking families, the Lobes from the Czech Republic and the Osayandes from Nigeria, provided the minister with that opportunity. The Supreme Court ruled on the *L&O* case in January 2003.[15]

As one of the Supreme Court justices described, the *L&O* case required balancing two competing claims: on one hand, the rights of the heteronormative family as the fundamental building block of the Irish nation-state, and on the other hand, the state's right to control immigration as a central dimension of the exercise of national sovereignty. What was striking was that these two rights were no longer in alignment, and the figure of the pregnant migrant had supposedly brought them into disjuncture.

The majority of the justices reflected mainstream discourses by identifying pregnancy and childbearing as a route for illegal and unwanted immigration. For example, Chief Justice Keane decided:

> The executive are entitled to take the view . . . that the orderly system in place for dealing with immigration and asylum applications should not be undermined by persons seeking to take advantage of the period of time which necessarily elapses between their arrival in the State and the complete processing of their applications for asylum by relying on the birth of a child to one of them . . . as a reason for permitting them to reside in the State indefinitely.[16]

Justice Murray reached a similar conclusion:

> It was argued on behalf of the Minister that if non-nationals who came to this country for the purpose of seeking asylum or refugee status could claim an automatic right to remain in the State independent of the outcome of their application for asylum by reason of the "fortuity" that a child was born to them while awaiting a final decision on their application, the Immigration and Asylum System would be distorted. It is also self-evident that in such a situation a substantial number of non-nationals could come to the State for the ostensible reason of seeking asylum with the intent of circumventing the controls which the State has imposed on immigration in the interests of the common good. That certainly seems to me to be at least a possibility against which the State is entitled to protect itself.[17]

Ultimately, five of the seven justices ruled that the need "to maintain the integrity" of the immigration and asylum systems took priority over the rights of citizen children. Yet one could strongly dispute the claim that an "orderly" immigration system imbued with "integrity" was already in place. Instead, I would suggest that the majority's ruling significantly contributed to creating a system in which "order" depended on denying citizen children the company and care of their migrant parents on Irish soil.

These important changes to children's citizenship rights were made in the name of enabling the minister to control illegal immigration. Yet they reinforced the equation of migrant women's pregnancy with illegal immigration, thereby ensuring that migrant women's bodies continued to be targeted as sites through which to achieve immigration control. The L&O decision ended an important basis on which migrant parents had been able to get legal residency. Beginning in February 2003, the government stopped accepting further applications for residency from migrant parents with Irish citizen children, and froze nearly 11,500 such applications that had been submitted but not processed, leaving these migrants in limbo. After that date migrants had to find grounds other than parentage of an Irish citizen child if they wished to remain—yet this was often difficult or impossible. Effectively, the L&O decision expanded migrants' routes into becoming designated as illegal.[18]

In June 2003 the grassroots organization Residents Against Racism assisted migrant parents, whose applications for residency had been frozen, to organize a demonstration to publicize their situation. This event marked a shift in the struggle over immigration control, from imagery dominated by pregnant migrant women's bodies to one that highlighted vulnerable Irish children who risked being deported when their migrant parents were ordered to leave.[19] Organizers strategized dressing the children in ways that underlined their Irishness, especially through the use of shamrocks and the color green. Black-and-white posters announcing the demonstration were wheatpasted onto walls and attached to lampposts around Dublin. The posters showed images of a "Black" child's face side by side with a "white" child's face and read, "Let my parents stay. Stop deportations. Demonstrate against the deportations of families of Irish born children. Thursday, 3 July, 12 noon, Central Bank, Dame Street. Organized by Residents Against Racism."[20] Posters were also left off at immigrant-serving organizations.

Organizers hoped for a demonstration where parents with babies in prams and small children provided a striking image and point of political mobilization. They were aware, however, that many migrant parents were fearful of demonstrating because their participation might be used against them when the minister for justice decided their cases. The *Irish Examiner* reported on the demonstration: "They came with a sea of push chairs and prams, as unlikely a protest as Leinster House [i.e., parliament] has ever seen. More than 500 immigrants and asylum seekers who have applied for residency here on the basis of an Irish born child assembled to call on Justice Minister Michael McDowell to not deport them. Yesterday was the first public protest involving so many of the 11,000 families living in limbo since January's Supreme Court ruling."[21] Migrants and supporters had gathered at the Central Bank, where signs were distributed, including to toddlers, bearing slogans such as "I am an Irish child, let me stay," "Don't deport Irish children," "Protect the children's rights," and "This is my home." After speeches condemning government immigration policies as racist, producing two-tier citizenship, and causing fear and dispossession among migrants, the demonstrators moved into the streets. Chanting "Michael McDowell, hear us say, Irish children are here to say," and "Big Mac [i.e., McDowell], Big Mac, don't send Irish children back," the marchers ended up opposite the Dáil, where police marshaled everyone into a tidy group.[22] Rows of parents patiently jounced babies and toddlers in buggies while listening to speeches by supportive politicians, even when the speeches were difficult to hear or fully understand. Organizers estimated that Eastern Europeans turned out in far greater numbers than Africans, but as Ronit Lentin observed, in a continuation of the racializing politics that dominated media representations of migration, the *Irish Times* and *Irish Examiner* centrally featured African families in their photographs of the demonstration.[23]

On July 18, migrant parents and their supporters received the minister's response to their demonstration. A "Notice to Non-National Parents of Irish Born Children" was printed in that day's newspapers. The notice explained that following *L&O*, the procedure that allowed migrants to apply to reside in Ireland based on being the parent of an Irish child had ended. It continued:

2. In relation to outstanding claims to reside in the State on the basis of parentage of an Irish born child and the implications for the effectiveness and integrity of the State's immigration and asylum systems, the Government has decided that every such case shall be examined and decided individually. 3. In any case

Young demonstrator at a protest against the deportation of families of Irish children, July 3, 2003. Image by author.

where the Minister proposes to deport a person affected, that person will be given an opportunity to make representations in relation to the proposal, and the range of factors relevant under existing law to the Minister's determination will be taken into account when making a decision in every such case. Those factors include the person's individual family and domestic circumstances and humanitarian considerations, in the context of the matters mentioned at paragraph two above. 4. Where any person other-

Mothers and children at a protest against the deportation of families of Irish children, July 3, 2003. Image by author.

wise liable to deportation wishes to leave the State voluntarily, the Minister will provide assistance. 5. Any person who wishes to make enquiries in relation to this notice or to discuss the possibility of voluntary return to their country of origin is invited to telephone the Immigration and Citizenship division.[24]

This notice made clear that each case would be handled individually—but that one could apply for leave to remain as the parent of an Irish citizen *only* in the context of responding to a deportation order. An Irish child would be just one factor among many to consider when the minister weighed whether to proceed with the deportation order. The stakes could not have been made higher, nor could the chances of a successful outcome been smaller.

The Department of Justice immediately began issuing deportation notices, also called Section 3 letters, which read:

> Dear X:
>
> I am directed by the Minister for Justice, Equality and Law Reform to notify you that the Minister proposes to make a deportation order in respect to you under the power given him by Section 3 of the Immigration Act 1999, as amended by the Illegal Immigrants (Trafficking) Act 2000.
>
> The reasons for the Minister's proposal are as follows:
>
> You are a person to whom permission to remain in the State was granted for the purpose of having an asylum claim determined. You subsequently withdrew that claim and thus your entitlement to remain temporarily in the State in accordance with section 9(2) of the Refugee Act 1996 thereupon ceased. You have since remained in the State without the permission of the Minister.
>
> Accordingly, you are a person whose deportation would, in the opinion of the Minister, be in accordance with the common good.
>
> In accordance with the aforementioned provision, the following alternatives are open to you:
>
> (a) you may make representations in writing to the Minister within 15 working days of the sending to you of the notification,
>
> (b) you may leave the State before the Minister decides whether to make the order and, if you decide to do this, you are required to so inform the Minister in writing and to furnish him with information concerning your arrangements for leaving,
>
> (c) you may consent to the making of the deportation order within 15 working days of the sending of this letter and, if you do this, the Minister shall arrange for your removal from the state as soon as practicable. . . . [25]

Among those who received such letters, there was "absolute panic."[26] Although the Irish government paid the costs associated with voluntary departure, it did not provide legal aid for those who wanted to appeal a Section 3 letter. Private solicitors charged as much as €2,000–€4,000 to prepare an appeal letter, which most migrants could not afford.[27] Moreover, it was unclear what information needed to be included in a response to a Section 3 letter.

AkiDwA, the network of African and migrant women, "provided the motivating force" for the formation of the Coalition against the Deportation of Irish Children (CADIC), which was a broad coalition of groups that intended to address the rights of the Irish children who were being threatened with deportation, and to prevent the parents' deportation.[28] CADIC decided to seek clarification from the Department of Justice about policies and procedures concerning migrant parents (e.g., what needed to be included in a representation to challenge a Section 3 letter, what was the process for reactivating an asylum claim), to bring test cases to challenge the policy, and to organize support and a public campaign. They also organized town halls to give information to migrants.

At the same time, the Irish government passed and signed into law the Immigration Act 2003. *Metro Eireann,* an immigrant-serving newspaper, wrote that "the Immigration Act 2003 is primarily concerned with speeding up the asylum process and expelling from the procedure asylum seekers who exhibit no interest in pursuing their asylum applications. A higher duty is placed on asylum applicants to cooperate, the burden of proving entitlement to refugee status has shifted significantly to asylum seekers, and faster processing times are planned."[29]

The minister had predicted that the *L&O* decision, combined with the other measures described earlier, would end what he considered to be a significant "incentive" for illegal immigration. But by November of 2003 he had reversed himself and suggested that illegal immigrants were still traveling to Ireland to give birth. Even though they could no longer get residency for themselves through their child, the minister suggested that they were doing so in order that the child would be an Irish citizen, which conferred opportunities and benefits (including because Irish citizenship was also EU citizenship). Thus, he argued, a referendum was needed to change the rules so that migrants' children could no longer automatically acquire Irish citizenship at birth.

Framing the Debate: Pregnant Asylum Seekers, Illegality, and the Future

Multiple materials and discourses about the referendum were produced. The materials that framed the debate, however, came from the government in the form of an information note that was published in March 2004. This was followed several days later by an article in the *Sunday Independent*, written by Minister for Justice Michael McDowell. Using these two materials we can track how pregnancy and illegality again become equated. Moreover, we can see how the government constructed images of a dystopian national future that could be avoided only by controlling migrant women's childbearing bodies in the present.[30]

The government's information note explained that the government had hoped that the *L&O* decision would deter asylum seekers from entering Ireland. Other measures that had been taken to reduce opportunities for asylum seeking were also described. The information note rhetorically inquires, "What effect has the strategy had in reducing the attraction for illegal migration?," which leads to a discussion about pregnancy rates among asylum-seeking women since the *L&O* decision.[31] This framing thus inaccurately treats pregnancy rates among asylum seekers as a direct measure for rates of illegal immigration.[32] The information note claims that although absolute numbers of asylum seekers have been reduced, "the proportion of women who are pregnant remains very high. The rate of pregnancy is largely unchanged, averaging 57% of women aged over 16 years for the 6-month period."[33] The information note concludes: "The Supreme Court judgement in the cases of *L&O* . . . [and] the actions undertaken on foot of it have had some effect in lessening the attraction of illegal migration to Ireland. However, expectations that the number of non-national births in Ireland would drop significantly after *L&O* have not been fulfilled."[34]

The information note creates a narrative (unsupported by evidence) about why women continue to deliberately migrate to Ireland to birth children: "The fact remains that a non-national becoming the parent of a child born in Ireland attracts greater entitlements than would be the case if they were present in any other Member State of the European Union—in terms of that child's entitlement to Irish and European citizenship and the perceived benefits of this for the parents now or in the future."[35] Thus, migrant women are portrayed as trying to create desirable futures for themselves and their children through strategic childbearing. (Chapter 2 in this book attempted to place that claim into a historical and social context.) Yet, according to the government, migrant women's childbearing threatens the possibility of creating a desirable future for Ireland and "legitimate" Irish people.[36] For example, their ac-

tions are "placing strains on our hospital services, attracting illegal immigration, and creating long-term commitments for the State."[37] Moreover, their childbearing has "broader, and indeed profound, implications
for health and social policy . . . —both in terms of short-term pressures
on maternity services and medical services generally and in medium- and
long-term patterns of social provision and expenditure. There are also very
obvious implications for the future of Irish immigration policy and for the
maintenance of the integrity of Irish law on immigration and residence."[38]
In these ways, the information note paints a scenario of competing futures in which pregnant migrant women's alleged efforts to realize positive futures for themselves and their families threaten Irish state's efforts
to create bright futures for Irish people. The possibility of creating bright
futures for everyone, both migrant and citizen, is not considered.

In order to realize the government's vision for the future, the information note argues that women's migration to Ireland to give birth to
children must be prevented. But in the minister's view, "we cannot rely on
immigration controls; to require non-national women of child-bearing
age to make declarations of pregnancy or otherwise when arriving in the
State is clearly unworkable."[39] Rather, "we must address the incentive
that induces them to make the journey in the first place."[40] That supposed
"incentive" is Irish citizenship for the child.[41]

The referendum proposed to sever the link that the Irish state has created between being born and being inscribed into the political community of citizens.[42] Without inscription at birth as a citizen, a newborn
child would become subject to immigration law with all its contingencies, exclusions, and modes of subjectification—and its capacity to designate people as "illegal." Effectively, severing the link between birth
and inscription as a citizen would allow for the production and expansion of migrant—including "illegal migrant"—status, not for migrant
parents but for *children and future generations* (to employ language and
logics of reproductive futurism once more). This is what the Irish state
proposed to accomplish through the citizenship referendum.[43]

The Russians Are Coming: "Citizenship Tourists," Childbearing, and the National Future

The government's proposed referendum and the rationale provided were
not accepted uncritically. For example, despite the minister's strong

emphasis on the "strain" placed on maternity hospitals by migrant pregnancies, the masters of the maternity hospitals immediately distanced themselves from any suggestion that they had asked the minister to take action.[44] The minister was also swiftly accused by opposition parties of "playing the race card" by proposing the referendum (further addressed later). Reports such as that by Dervla King for the Children's Rights Alliance, a coalition of more than seventy child welfare groups, also raised important questions about the minister's framing of the issue and the data on which he built his claims.[45] As King describes, Dublin's maternity hospitals did not in fact collect data on the legal status of women who presented to give birth. Nor did they collect information about the legal status of newborns' fathers. In regard to nonnational women who gave birth in Ireland, the government provided no information about "the number of non-national mothers who are legally resident in the state on the basis of possessing a work permit or work visa/authorisation. There is no mention of the exact number of mothers who are here as students, as the non-national spouses or partners of Irish citizens, or as people who have been given permission to reside in Ireland under family reunification programs."[46] King concludes, "The government has not demonstrated that the increase in the number of births to non-nationals is substantially attributable to the fact that their children are entitled to Irish and EU citizenship. When immigration patterns are examined in closer detail, it can be seen that state policy is a main causal factor in the increase in the number of non-nationals in Ireland."[47] This includes the state's aggressive recruitment of migrant labor to fuel the Celtic Tiger economy.

In response to these and other criticisms, the minister and other leaders began to reframe their arguments away from pregnant asylum seekers, instead emphasizing concerns about "citizenship tourist" women "who had come on holiday visas, given birth, collected the birth certificate and the passport for the child and returned home."[48] The figure of the citizenship tourist had been evoked by the information note and in interviews with the minister. For example, the information note describes that "the scale of the problem is even greater outside of the asylum framework, with very large numbers of non-EEA nationals now coming to Ireland to give birth. . . . The Dublin maternity hospitals estimate that two thirds of the births to non-nationals last year will have been to persons other than asylum seekers, many of whom follow the pattern of a very late arrival in the State to give birth."[49] The implication was that illegal immigration, figured by the pregnant asylum seeker, was "spreading" to other categories of migrant.[50] Yet, as the National Consultative Committee on Racism and Interculturalism describes, the term "citizenship tourism" was "derogatory and has its origin in the similarly pejorative term 'benefit tourism.' It should be recalled that the term benefit tourism emerged as part of a xenophobic and unfounded scare campaign by British tabloids in the run up to the enlargement of the EU on 1 May 2004."[51]

Late or last-minute booking at maternity hospitals was described by the government as an important measure of the prevalence of "citizenship tourism." But this measure became significantly challenged, including through the minister's own materials. In late April 2004 he released documentation of meetings with the masters of the maternity hospitals that seemed to support his earlier contention that the masters had expressed concern about "citizenship tourism." However, the documents also showed that the masters expressed concerns about another issue—the arrival at hospitals of asylum-seeking women who had been dispersed throughout the country within the state's direct provision system but, upon receipt of maternity benefits at thirty-two weeks, had relocated to Dublin where they booked late or at the last minute into hospitals to give birth. "The Masters' letter suggests that this, and not the 'citizenship tourism' phenomenon talked about by the Minister, was their prime concern in January 2003. In August 2003 a memo from an official in the Department of Justice's Reception and Integration Agency, Mr. Frank Edwards, to its director, Mr. Noel Waters, backed up the suggestion that 'dispersed' asylum seekers arriving at Dublin hospitals in or near labour were a significant contributor to the problem."[52] Irish citizen women were also acknowledged to arrive at late stages at maternity hospitals, for various reasons, which further complicated any simple equation between late arrival and so-called citizenship tourism.

The masters did express concern about "citizenship tourism" involving women who arrived at the last minute from the United Kingdom and Europe, sometimes with medical records in hand, to birth a child and then leave.[53] Nonetheless, their reframing of the possible meaning of "late arrival," and diversification in understanding of who was arriving late in their pregnancies at maternity hospitals, led the *Irish Times* to conclude that "the statistics and documents published yesterday indicate there is a phenomenon on 'citizenship tourism,' as Mr. McDowell has insisted, but that it appears to be very small," apparently in the hundreds per year.[54] The leader of the Green Party, Michael Gormley, placed the statistics in perspective by suggesting that it would take a century before those estimated to be citizenship tourists would fill the stadium at Lansdowne Road (since replaced by the Aviva Stadium) in Dublin.[55]

Overall, there was never abandonment of one image of the pregnant migrant in favor of another one; rather, several images coexisted and were variously invoked. For example, Taoiseach (Prime Minister) Ahern asserted that Ireland's citizenship regime was being "rampantly abused," as was evident when 60 percent of all asylum-seeker women were supposedly pregnant when they made their application—but equally when women entered the country late in pregnancy "solely for the purposes of getting Irish citizenship and then leaving as quickly as they came." He added that he never envisioned that "Russians, Moldovans, and Ukrainians would be coming to this country for two or three weeks simply for the benefit of Irish citizenship."[56] A subsequent opinion piece mocked the taoiseach for invoking the Cold War trope that "the Russians are coming."[57]

Okay, Then the Chinese Are Coming: Pregnancy, Illegality, and Citizenship Again

In the context of these struggles to persuade the electorate to abolish automatic birthright citizenship for children of migrants, the *Chen* case proved a godsend for the government. Ms. Chen and her husband worked for a large China-based company that produced and exported chemicals, including to the United Kingdom and the European Union.[58] Ms. Chen's husband was one of the company's directors, and traveled often to the United Kingdom and other parts of the European Union in connection with company business.[59] The couple had one child, a son born in the People's Republic of China in 1998. They decided to have a second child, but because of China's one-child policy, "Ms Chen decided to give birth abroad and for that purpose travelled to the United Kingdom."[60] British legal counsel advised Ms. Chen to travel to Ireland since birth there would confer Irish citizenship on the child, whereas birth in Britain would not result in British citizenship.[61] Accordingly, Ms. Chen traveled to Belfast, Northern Ireland, and gave birth to a daughter, Kunquian Catherine Zhu, on September 16, 2000. Northern Ireland occupies the distinctive position of being at once part of the United Kingdom (so that travel to Belfast kept Ms. Chen within the jurisdiction of the United Kingdom) yet also part of the island of Ireland, to which birthright citizenship applied regardless of north/south divisions.[62] Catherine (as court documents refer to her) therefore acquired Irish citizenship at birth, after which Ms. Chen returned to the British mainland. She settled in Cardiff, Wales, and applied to U.K. authorities for permission to reside in the United Kingdom. The U.K. authorities denied Ms. Chen's application, which was eventually appealed to the European Court of Justice. The *Irish Times* captures the significance of the case: "The mother's legal team argues that the child, who is an Irish citizen, is entitled to U.K. residence under EU law, and that the mother is 'dependent' on the child for immigration status. If Ms Chen wins her case, it would mean that having a child born anywhere in Ireland, including Northern Ireland, would provide a basis for non-EU nationals to establish a right to reside in any other EU state."[63] Ms. Chen became a valuable example for the Irish government of the "threat" of citizenship tourism.

On May 18, 2004, the advocate general of the European Court of Justice issued his preliminary opinion on the *Chen* case, finding that under EU law, Catherine, an Irish citizen, had a right to reside in Britain, which was also a member state of the EU, and that Ms. Chen acquired the right to reside there too. The right was not unqualified; the opinion significantly hinged on the fact that Ms. Chen had sufficient resources to support herself and her child, including private health insurance, without becoming a burden on the British state. This element of the finding was consistently underplayed by mainstream representations, however.

In general, the *Chen* case was treated as illustrating why a "yes" vote was needed on the referendum: it showed how parents could use a child's Irish citizenship to secure residency for themselves in *other* EU countries. Thus, according to the minister for justice, the Chen decision confirmed that Ireland's citizenship regime "constitutes a significant loophole with significant European dimensions";[64] Ms. Coughlin, the minister for social and family affairs who was in charge of Fianna Fail's pro-referendum campaign, argued that the Chen decision "would be seen as a back door into the EU";[65] Mr. Martin stated that "the loophole in our citizenship law has been used to circumvent immigration controls in other EU states";[66] and Minister for Foreign Affairs Brian Cowen stated that the Chen decision "raises the prospect of Ireland becoming 'the destination of choice' for migrants seeking the benefits of EU citizenship."[67] Fanning the flames, the minister for justice suggested, "There is now an obvious case of urgency. We have to face up to the issue. It can only get worse from now. The Chen decision will go out right across Europe: if I want to resist being sent home, all I have to do is go to either part of Ireland and have a child there."[68] Politicians and pundits further expanded these themes, suggesting that the use of Ireland as a "back door" for illegal entry to the EU needed to be considered in terms of Irish obligations toward the EU.[69]

Critics questioned this argument. For example, "the Labour Party has questioned the need to bring Ireland's citizenship laws into line with the rest of the EU when harmony does not exist in other areas. Mr. Michael D. Higgins, the party's foreign affairs spokesman, said that 'we are not harmonizing ourselves with Europe on taxation policy, neutrality, or a raft of other issues, and those being asked to vote may reasonably ask how this argument got started.' . . . Mr. Higgins said the 'number of people who have abused state companies and who are now tax exiles certainly exceeds the numbers of non-national women who are giving birth in the State.' "[70]

The prospect of Ireland's citizenship regime providing a "back door" to EU residence for illegal immigrants was repeatedly described as "devaluing" Irish citizenship. For example, according to Mary Hanafin, the government chief whip, "the exploitation of Irish citizenship by non-EU nationals seeking residency rights has undermined the value and integrity of Irish citizenship in Europe."[71] But what was meant by "the value and integrity of Irish citizenship" often remained vague and undefined. A commonly articulated theme was that only those with some "connection" to Ireland should be able to hold citizenship. Taoiseach "Mr. Ahern said the Government 'considers it appropriate that Irish citizenship for a child born to non-national parents should not derive solely from the circumstances of birth in Ireland and that there should be a stronger connection with Ireland on the part of at least one of the parents for the privilege of Irish citizenship to be available to their children born here.' "[72] According to Minister Brian Lenihan, "The reality is that people with no connection to Ireland, and even with no intention to live here, have arranged for their children to be born in Ireland so as to have Irish citizenship."[73] Yet there was little discussion of what was meant by "connection" or why a connection was desirable.

The idea that Irish citizenship entails duties and responsibilities, not simply "rights," was also discussed. For example, according to Minister McDowell, "Citizenship is important. It is not something which is just given out as a little token, or a useful thing to people with no connection with our State. It imposes on people who are Irish citizens duties of loyalty and fidelity to the nation-state."[74] Several weeks later, he expanded on this theme: "This [referendum] is a rational measure which will enhance the standing of Irish citizenship in the eyes of those of us who already hold it and who recognise, as Article 9 of the Constitution requires us to, that fidelity to the State and loyalty to the nation are indeed fundamental political duties of every Irish citizen."[75] Citizenship tourists, deemed to be opportunistically seeking advantage without having contributed or shown commitment, were constructed as the antithesis of this model of the good citizen.[76] (See chapters 2 and 3 for discussion of how migrants often understand legal status and citizenship as entailing significant responsibilities that they strive to meet.)[77]

The fact that most migrants who were deemed to be citizenship tourists had broken no laws and their actions were not illegal was consistently brushed aside. The European Court of Justice had strongly rejected claims by the British government that Ms. Chen's actions constituted "abuse" of the law.[78] The attorney general suggested appropriate standards by which to evaluate whether laws were being abused and argued that Ms. Chen did not meet these standards.[79] He concluded, "I repeat, there is certainly no basis for criticising Catherine or her mother for legitimately taking advantage of the opportunities and rights available to them under Community law."[80] He warned that "if the United Kingdom's argument were accepted, suspicions of abuse could be raised in almost all cases of intentional acquisition of nationality of a Member State."[81] Yet the attorney general's defense of Ms. Chen received no publicity among pro-referendum forces, who instead followed the path against which he had warned: claiming that any nonnational who gave birth in Ireland was likely engaged in "abuse" of the law.

Opponents continued to counter the arguments put forth by the pro-referendum side, but on the day of the vote, 80 percent of those who cast ballots endorsed the government's proposal, and Irish citizenship rules were transformed accordingly.

Making Migrants Illegal to the Second Generation and Beyond

The referendum process shows how competing narratives about the national future, organized through heterosexual reproduction and generational succession, are produced and contested. According to the government, pregnant women were intentionally migrating to Ireland to birth children. Their purpose was supposedly to ensure that their children were Irish (and EU) citizens at birth since this would confer entitlements and opportunities that could be valuable in the future.[82] The women's reproductive futurism was described as threatening the Irish government's efforts to create a bright future for Ireland and Irish people (a claim that produces a specific construct of who is and is not legitimately Irish). Moreover, their actions supposedly threatened other EU countries because migrant parents with Irish citizen children could legally reside elsewhere in the EU. The L&O decision had been expected to stem pregnant women's migration, but when it did not, a referendum to remove automatic birthright citizenship was proposed.

Pregnant women were regularly described as engaging in "illegal" migration. "Illegal," however, assumed a flexible cast. It encompassed not just those who entered outside the scrutiny of state officials but also those who used legal means to enter—including asylum seekers, tourists, students, and workers. But when these legal entrants became pregnant, they were viewed as "illegal" because they did not use their entry status for the ends that the government had intended. The idea that migration statuses should be used only for ends that the government intends represents a fantasy of sovereign omnipotence that is unrealizable.[83] Nonetheless, as "illegal" became unmoored from technicalities of law and instead came to mean "migrants who acted in ways that the government did not intend," the government used this opportunity to redefine the law.

The citizenship referendum was presented as the best way to curtail pregnant women's migration because, according to the government, it would remove the "incentive" that motivated them. In reality, the referendum could not prevent migration, whether authorized or not, since it did not address the dynamics that drive migration. The referendum also could not prevent women from having sex under varied conditions that ranged from consent to force, including sex that resulted in pregnancy and childbearing. Instead, what the referendum accomplished was to disenfranchise significant numbers of children who were born to migrant parents by severing the link between their birth and their automatic political inscription into the community as citizens. That link remains highly naturalized within the heteronormative logics of family, kinship and nation, yet, as Jacqueline Stevens reminds us, states actually determine which family and kinship forms receive official recognition. This means that these forms not particularly "natural," but they are crucial for and harnessed to nation building. The referendum laid bare the ways that state power had linked birth to political inscription as part of nation building, and how that link may become contested and reworked.

Importantly, the referendum process did not completely abolish the link between birth and political inscription as a citizen where migrants' children were concerned. Instead the referendum produced differentiations where none had previously existed. After the referendum, children born to migrants who had resided "lawfully" in Ireland for three of the last four years were eligible for citizenship at birth. John Harrington suggests that the referendum thus served as a carrot to secure some migrants' compliance with immigration law, since compliant long-term migrants were rewarded with citizenship for their Irish born children.[84] Children born to migrants who had resided for fewer than three of the last four years, however, were not eligible for citizenship at birth. In their cases, the referendum made "the temporary workforce *more temporary* by severing emotional and legal ties—the birth of a citizen child—that might make a temporary worker feel a 'connection' to Ireland."[85] Time spent as an asylum seeker or an international student also did not count toward the required three years, thereby ensuring that these migrants and their children were made more temporary too.

The referendum did not just produce and institutionalize a distinction between the children of productive, hardworking, long-term labor migrants versus the children of other migrants (such that one group of children will be citizens at birth while the others will not). The referendum also institutionalized distinctions by allowing children and grandchildren born abroad to Irish citizens to continue to acquire citizenship through descent, even when they had never set foot in Ireland. These children and grandchildren, however, were eligible for citizenship only if they could trace their descent through heteronormative rather than queer forms of family.[86] Yet their eligibility was very striking because one major argument against automatic birthright citizenship for children born to newly arrived migrants in Ireland was that the migrants (and their children) lacked a sufficient connection to Ireland. Critics therefore wondered about the nature of the connection that children and grandchildren of the Irish diaspora were imagined to have that justified their continued access to citizenship through descent, especially among those who had never been to Ireland or had no active ties.

This question was addressed in part through competing discourses about race and racism. The minister for justice and the government consistently insisted that the referendum was not racist; on the contrary, they argued that it would *prevent* racism by ensuring that only those who properly followed immigration and asylum rules were rewarded. These claims conveniently ignore that the state regularly changes the rules, often without migrants being informed; underplays the pervasiveness and functioning of racism; and blames *migrants* for racism in Ireland.[87] A related government strategy entailed portraying the referendum as a simple, commonsense measure that did not require intensive deliberation and debate. For instance, the *Irish Times* reported, "Fianna Fail has launched its campaign for a Yes vote on the citizenship referendum, insisting that the Government's proposal is 'simple and balanced' and that it has nothing to do with race."[88] Silvia Brandi characterizes this approach as entailing "ideological naturalization."[89] Exemplifying the naturalization approach, officials frequently characterized the referendum as simply fixing a "legal loophole" that allowed newly arrived migrants to acquire citizenship for their children and benefits for themselves.[90] Yet this claim did not acknowledge that even if birthright citizenship (the supposed "loophole") had become included in the constitution only in 1998, birthright citizenship itself was not new; it had been provided for by law since the inception of the state. Thus, the proposed citizenship referendum was no mere "tweak" of a technicality. As Oran Doyle suggests, "the government's proposal cannot plausibly claim to be the mere pragmatic closing of a loophole. Rather, the proposal amounts to a fundamental alteration" in the state's manner of determining who may be a citizen.[91]

Another government strategy for countering charges of racism was to construct those who raised concerns about racism as extremists who were, through intimidation, trying to prevent government officials and ordinary Irish people from making a necessary, commonsense change. In this situation, the government insisted that it was exercising moral courage and leadership by insisting on the referendum.[92] A variant on this argument suggested that Irish people (imagined as white) were overwhelmed or uncomfortable by the diversification of Ireland but felt unable to express their concerns, and brave spokespeople therefore spoke for them. For example, Dr. Paul Byrne, a consultant gynecologist at the Rotunda maternity hospital, "claimed that Irish patients were avoiding his hospital out of fear that 'they would be in the minority compared to African patients.' A desire not to be labelled racists prevented them from speaking out."[93] As Brandi describes, these arguments suggest that "not only were McDowell, the government, and the vast majority of supporters [of the referendum] decent people, but they were also anti-racist. Indeed, opponents of the referendum were rather constructed as the real racists, since they offered the 'would-be racists the opportunity to exploit public perceptions that our law is being exploited.' "[94]

The minister for justice and other government members also countered charges of racism by proclaiming that the referendum "most certainly [will] not be racist; it will apply even-handedly to the children of all non-nationals, irrespective of colour, ethnicity, or any other criterion on which racism is based."[95] This argument understands racism simply as a matter of differential treatment that is motivated by prejudice. The systemic, institutionalized nature of racism, whether intentional or not, is thereby dismissed. Moreover, the ways that racialization operates through cultural discourses about morality—as was manifestly evident throughout the referendum process—was also dismissed.[96] Although all migrants were deemed by the state as theoretically capable of exercising morality, in practice, as Anwen Tormey argues, immorality became "configured upon, and therefore experienced as a [particular] type of body" throughout the referendum process.[97] That body was the racialized, heterosexualized body of the pregnant Black migrant woman. "Irish anxieties were laminated upon black bodies with such an effect that a significant alteration to the Irish constitution could be passed. . . . The Irish case is illustrative of new ways in which the old story of race continues to be told."[98] It is also illustrative of the critical role played by sexual and moral regimes in racialization processes.[99]

Claims that the proposed citizenship rules would operate "even-handedly" also ignored the fact that the larger social and economic fields in which the rules operated were already structured inequitably, and the proposed change would further reinforce that inequity. Those holding

EU citizenship already had the right to migrate legally and therefore had no need to seek Irish citizenship, so the changed rules would primarily impact on non-EU migrants. In that sense, the rules further institutionalized a line between Europe and its Others. For these and other reasons, critics viewed the referendum as institutionalizing a racist definition of "connection" and Irishness that depended on blood—and, we should add, heteronormative kinship genealogy. Indeed, Lentin and McVeigh characterize the referendum as a crucial turning point that transformed Ireland from a racist state to a racial state by making "blood and heredity the cornerstone of Irish citizenship."[100]

Since the referendum provided for citizenship through descent for members of the Irish diaspora, this racist definition of Irishness was institutionalized not only nationally but also globally. "The global" however, is unequally scaled because of the violent histories of colonialism and global capitalism from which today's nation-state system has emerged.[101] Thus, Irish people were diasporicized as a result of colonization, displacement, and peripheralization, and they migrated along routes that largely followed in the tracks of colonial settler formations created by the British Empire. In these settler societies, they negotiated between white British settlers' racialization of Irishness and Irish communities' racialization of other colonized and indigenous peoples.[102] These histories of racial, colonial, and geopolitical inequality were rearticulated in the present through the citizenship referendum, which granted citizenship to children of the Irish diaspora but not to children born in Ireland to migrants. The inequalities were further reinforced by the Irish government's economic strategy that actively works through location-specific, "white" versions of diaspora to reposition the state within global capitalism.[103]

Material resources were at stake in these processes. The referendum made clear that important entitlements and opportunities were at stake in holding Irish citizenship. Non-EU/EEA migrant women were described as wanting Irish and EU citizenship because these citizenship statuses offered more entitlements and opportunities than citizenship status in their own nation states. This argument makes very clear that citizenship status is tied to material resources, including what Aristide Zolberg describes as "bundles of collective goods," and that not all citizenship statuses are equal.[104] If they were equal, there would be no need for women to migrate to ensure that their babies acquired Irish/EU citizenship at birth.[105] The inequalities associated with citizenship statuses are rooted in histories of colonialism, global capitalism, and the nation-state system that emerged as a result. Citizenship status in global northern states have crucial "wealth-preserving" functions that perpetuate these inequalities.[106] Moreover, since citizenship status designates who is subject to the violence of immigration control and who is not, it further perpetuates these inequalities. Yet the ways that states naturalize the link between being born and the acquisition of citizenship status has insulated these inequalities from critical scrutiny. Aylet Shachar suggests that "it is . . . vital that we sever the Gordian knot that has long obscured the connections between birthright, political membership, and differential access to the wealth of nations."[107] The Irish citizenship referendum, however, further tightened the knot.

The referendum tightened the knot by ensuring that many migrants' children, and their children's children, into the indefinite future, not only lack access to the material opportunities associated with Irish citizenship but also are subjected to immigration law and thus are vulnerable to becoming designated as illegal and deportable. Such outcomes importantly shows that immigration controls entail not just spatial dimensions ("protecting the borders") but also temporal dimensions ("protecting the future") that are articulated through the state's mobilization of heteronormative logics: in this case, a model of *competing* reproductive futurism.

The fact that the referendum (and the *L&O* decision before that) actively constructed new routes into illegal status challenges the commonly held assumption that illegal status reflects inherent, undesirable qualities that are already present within migrants' bodies, and shows instead that illegal status is actively produced and imposed on particular bodies by state regimes. The importance of temporal logics in ensuring these outcomes is evident not only through the state's deployment of arguments about about the likely future impact of current migrants' childbearing but also through the fact that many migrants who were characterized as "illegal" in public debates (because they had given birth to children) were actually present in compliance with the law. Claims about their putative illegality, however, legitimized changes in law that ensured they or their children would *become* illegal in the future. A reproductive futurism framework, when transported to the realm of migration scholarship, therefore significantly opens up our understanding of the connections between violent state heteronormativity and processes for making migrants illegal. At the same time, foregrounding histories of migration, diaspora, and displacement shows the importance of addressing colonialism, global capitalism, geopolitical inequalities, racism, and gender violence as interlinked within the struggles over reproductive futurism.[108]

CHAPTER 6

From Childbearing to Multiple Sexuality and Migration Struggles

THIS BOOK HAS TRACKED how pregnancy and migrant status became interwoven through panics over illegal immigration that expanded the numbers of migrants who would become designated as illegal while at the same time refashioning social, economic, and geopolitical hierarchies. This chapter argues that struggles over migrant pregnancies were part of a wider constellation of conflicts over migrant sexualities and intimacies that, although distinct in important ways, were nonetheless linked through their antagonistic relationship to nationalist heteronormativity. First I describe what happened to migrant parents with citizen children after the passage of the citizenship referendum. Next I briefly discuss other conflicts over sexuality and migration that occurred, including over heterosexual marriage migration, same-sex couples' migration, sex work, and domestic workers. I conclude that these struggles must be treated as interlinked through multiple inequalities that demand transformation.

"To Take Away Your Right of Being Married and Your Child": Migrants, Children, and Legal Status since the Citizenship Referendum

Days after Irish voters overwhelmingly approved the citizenship referendum, the *Irish Times* reported that, "welcoming the outcome of the citizenship referendum, [Minister for Justice Michael McDowell] said that without the change in the Constitution it was likely that the *L & O* decision would be challenged in Europe if the Chen decision was upheld by the full European Court of Justice."[1] In other words, the approval of the referendum, especially in light of the *Chen* case, reinforced the *L&O* decision while further extending the illegalization of migrants.[2] Conversely, failure to approve the referendum would not only have left the existing citizenship law intact but also might have contributed to undoing *L&O*. The minister's statement therefore makes clear that the logics and technologies of migration control are never unassailable or inevitable. Rather, they emerge through political struggles, individual decision-making, and contingencies, and they remain susceptible to challenge.[3]

The referendum particularly strengthened the emerging migration control system because it ensured that the population of citizen children with migrant parents would no longer continue to grow by much. In the months leading up to the referendum, the government's deportation of Irish citizen children and babies with their migrant parents had generated strong public criticism. Moreover, as the Irish Refugee Council argued, "The Government was 'storing up trouble for the future' by deporting Irish-born children. Chief Executive Peter O'Mahony said: 'It will come back to haunt them in the long term. In around 15 years time, you will have an 18-year-old returning from Nigeria with an Irish passport, claiming to have suffered as a result of the deportation.'"[4] The referendum resolved concerns about "storing up trouble for the future" *not* by addressing critics' arguments about the impact of deportation on citizen children and babies or by criticizing immigration and asylum policy but rather by restricting citizenship eligibility so that after January 1, 2005, most children and babies who were deported would not hold citizenship status anyway.

After the success of the referendum, the minster focused on the next elements of his plan: a revised citizenship and nationality act; comprehensive immigration legislation in the form of an immigration and residence bill; and a plan for "dealing with the situation of the estimated 11,000 parents of Irish-born children" whose application for residency on that basis had been frozen in the wake of the *L&O* decision.[5] Once these parents' situation had been addressed, the existing migration controls, which wove together rules concerning pregnancy, childbearing, and birthright citizenship in a battle against supposed illegal migration, were unlikely to be seriously challenged.

The minister's plan for parents was unveiled on January 15, 2005, when the Department of Justice announced a new scheme whereby migrant parents of Irish citizen children who were born before January 1, 2005, could apply for residency.[6] This was the so-called IBC/05 scheme, with an application deadline of March 31, 2005. Eligibility depended on several conditions, the most important of which were "not to become in-volved in criminal activity; to make every effort to become economical-ly viable; to take steps that would lead to employment; and to accept that the status 'did not confer any entitlement or legitimate expectation of family reunification.' "[7] The last condition "proved most problematic, causing hardship and sadness to many."[8]

Effectively, the scheme legally striped away many of the migrants' es-tablished family ties as a condition for receiving legal status. Thus, it underlined again that family ties are never simply "natural" but instead mediated through relations of power, including state power over migra-tion. As migrants described, the rules threatened to transform them into lone (i.e., single) parents, even when they had partners and spouses: "You can't tell somebody . . . that like if you have your husband in Nigeria or Ghana or Asia or whatever, that your husband should divorce you, and that he can't join you."[9] The rules also asked them to relinquish at-tachments to children and others who were still overseas. If migrants did not sign away their right to family reunification, including with partners, spouses, children, and other relatives who were still overseas, their appli-cations would not be processed. But if they did sign, they relinquished the possibility of future reunification.

The requirement to relinquish their right to family reunification thus presented migrants with painful dilemmas.[10] Advocates and NGOs understood migrants' dilemma and generally advised them to secure their own status first and then contest the restriction on their right to family reunification later. Many eventually opted for that route. Nonetheless, migrants described the situation as akin to being caught between the devil and the deep blue sea, and completing the application as "like sign-ing with a gun at your head."[11] One migrant suggested, "Even U.K. and America would never do this. These people are tougher people but they will never ask you to do this. To take away your right of being married and to take away your right of your child that you left behind when we are running from one thing to the other, never to join you again, I think that is a madness. That is absolute madness."[12]

In the end, more than eighteen thousand applications for residency were submitted—by migrants whose applications had been frozen in the wake of *L&O* and by migrants who had given birth to a child in Ire-land before January 1, 2005.[13] Nearly seventeen thousand applications were approved. The largest number of denials was on the grounds that applicants could not prove continuous residency in Ireland since the births of their Irish citizen children. Other grounds for denial included having a criminal conviction; being unable to prove one's identity; and having no apparent role in parenting the Irish child.[14] Those who received recognition under the ICB/05 scheme had to register with the immigration authorities and receive a Stamp 4, which entitled them to paid employment and social welfare. The entitlements were certainly welcome and allowed migrants to begin regularizing aspects of their lives.

IBC/05 status was valid for two years, after which migrants had to apply for renewal. To successfully renew, they had to show continuous residence in Ireland; either residence with the Irish child or active involvement in the child's upbringing; a continued absence of any criminal record; and efforts to become economically viable.[15] The contingent nature of IBC status created apprehension and insecurity for some migrants, including one who said, "I am living in a contract" that felt dehumanizing.[16] As Coakley and Healy describe, the scheme significantly "define[d] the degree to which those it accepts as residents are allowed to orient themselves towards Irish society," and in what ways.[17]

The fact that they were not allowed to bring in other family members for reunification continued to cause practical difficulties and emotional distress. Family members were generally not permitted to enter Ireland even for brief visits. The policy was so entrenched that the website for the Irish Naturalisation and Immigration Services included an "explanation of reasons for refusal of a visa." Refusal code "GP" states that "it is not general policy to permit any person, whether related or not, to join any persons who have been granted residency in the State under the IBC 05 scheme. Your case has been fully examined, and you have not shown any compelling grounds as to why an exception to this policy should be made in your case."[18] When the policy has been challenged, the results have been erratic and confusing: "some families are still separated, others have been allowed to live together in Ireland though some spouses are forbidden from working having been given a stamp 3, while others have been given a stamp 4 permit . . . to reside and work in Ireland. There doesn't appear to be any consistency in procedure for the granting of stamps [i.e., entry, residency, and various rights] to partners of IBC/05 parents."[19]

Coakley and Healy argue that migrants' inability to reunite with family contributes to significant structural disadvantages, including economically:

Individuals resident in Ireland with this status are by definition parents with dependent children. The conditions attaching to their legal residency mean that they are often operating as single parents. These parents are then required to engage in waged labour on a number of levels. They work primarily because they have to earn a living and support themselves and their dependents but also because another set of legislative hurdles attaching to their status require them to do so. These parents, who inevitably are channelled into work at the lower levels of a vertically segregated waged labour force by virtue of the multiple discriminatory practices that they encounter thus find themselves to be doubly disadvantaged by their status. Reasonably low wages are earned and a significant expense is incurred by the need to employ child-minders or enroll children in crèches.[20]

Moreover, as Coakley argues, the situation locks migrants "into a transnational economic field that they can scarcely afford" as they struggle to support two households that span borders:

Sean states, "I send money home all the time. All the time. It is very very difficult. I am always in debt. I cannot make up. Here if we cook a pot of soup everybody could share in it but now if we cook a pot of soup, I have to cook another there to pay for the rent there. Pay for my rent here. It is not easy." This difficulty has become more acute over the past few years as a result of the current economically difficult climate in Ireland.[21]

In 2010 those with IBC/05 residency were required to renew their status again. In 2011 another important development affected migrant parents with citizen children: the European Court of Justice ruled in the *Zambrano* case "that an EU member state may not refuse the non-EU parents of a dependent child who is a citizen of, and resident in, an EU member state the right to live and work in that member state."[22] Accordingly, the Department of Justice began reviewing the cases of children with non-EU parents who might meet the *Zambrano* criteria. Because of the 2004 Citizenship Referendum, as well as the IBC/05 scheme, the pool of children whose migrant parents were eligible was smaller than it might otherwise have been. The *Irish Times* reported on January 24, 2012, that more than 850 non-EU parents of Irish citizen children had received residency based on *Zambrano*, including six people who had previously been deported. A further 700 cases were pending.[23]

The Supreme Court characterized the IBC/05 scheme as "generous."[24] A more plausible interpretation is that the scheme was intended to head off future lawsuits and other repercussions for exiling or deporting citizen children while allowing the Department of Justice to further consolidate a restrictive architecture of migration control.[25] Moreover, the IBC/05 requirement for migrants to relinquish their rights to family reunification reflects a broader pattern whereby Irish policies make family reunification extremely difficult, and often impossible, even for legal migrants who fit within narrowly recognized definitions of "family." Not surprisingly, the Migrant Integration Index rated Ireland as having the least favorable family reunification policies among thirty-one countries in Europe and North America in 2010.[26]

Sexualities and Migrations: Dispersing and Diversifying the Conflicts

Controversies over childbearing asylum seekers have died down, but new struggles over the connections between sexual regimes and legal migration possibilities have emerged. The following sections briefly address struggles over heterosexual marriage, same-sex couples, sex workers, and domestic workers. The struggles not only revealed competing perspectives about which sexual norms should provide a basis for legal status but also contributed to refashioning the dominant norms.

Heterosexual Marriage

As might be expected from heteronormative nationalism, heterosexual marriage has historically been a privileged means for legally entering the country and for gaining residence and citizenship. Until November 29, 2005, non-EU spouses of Irish citizens could acquire citizenship simply by making a postnuptial declaration. Since then heterosexual marriage has become an important arena through which the government began attempting to police against illegal migration. This development was foreshadowed in a report written for the government by the International Organization for Migration.[27] Vividly illustrating connections between different struggles, the report not only identified the practice of granting legal status to nonnational parents of Irish children as a possible basis for "potential exploitation of the law" but also suggested that "another area of potential immigration abuse has been the question of spousal entitlement to acquire either permanent residence or even citizenship or nationality by the act of marriage."[28] Successive ministers for justice regularly expressed concerns that heterosexual marriage might provide a means "to thwart and bypass the immigration laws of this country" and characterized such marriages as "shams."[29] Yet, as with the discourses about pregnant migrants as illegal immigrants, factual information to support these claims proved elusive, and efforts to police heterosexual marriage based on fears of illegal immigration have become fraught with difficulty.[30]

The ways that heterosexual marriage has become an important locus of struggle over where to draw the line between legal and illegal migration (and, in the process, produce new configurations of legality and illegality) was especially evident in a 2008 case known as *Metock*. The *Metock* case involved four couples, each composed of an EU (but not Irish) citizen wife and a non-EU citizen husband who had been denied asylum in Ireland. Each couple married in Ireland, and each husband subsequently received a deportation order. The deportation orders were based on the Irish government's interpretation and implementation of the European Free Movement Directive 2004, which, according to the Department of Justice, required that non-EU family members of an EU citizen must have resided lawfully in another EU state before being allowed to live and work in Ireland.[31] Effectively, the government's interpretation of the Directive treated lack of prior legal residence in another EU country as grounds for suspicion that the marriages were entered into primarily to facilitate otherwise illegal immigration—a leap of logic that merits scrutiny. Yet, based on this assumption, more than one thousand non-EU migrant men were refused residency despite their marriages to EU citizen women who were living in Ireland.[32] Once again, governmental fears of illegal migration directly led to the creation of more illegal migrants (i.e., migrants without the legal status that they had expected to receive based on their marriages). Meanwhile, the EU citizen spouses found that the supposed sanctity of their marriages was subordinated to the exigencies of "the common good," especially the government's authority to prevent illegal migration.

When the *Metock* case was appealed to the European Court of Justice (ECJ), the ECJ ruled that one's prior immigration status in another EU country was a separate matter from the validity, sincerity, and legality of the marriage.[33] Thus, they challenged the department's conflation of these two issues. The one-thousand-plus non-EU migrants who had been denied residency based on their marriages then became entitled to have their cases reopened and, in many cases, to have their statuses switched again, this time from unauthorized to authorized and legally resident.

These events vividly illustrate ways that the line between legal and illegal status was negotiated through heterosexual marriage, and furthermore, that possibilities for such negotiation changed in response to government directives and court rulings.[34] The case also highlighted that the policing of heterosexual marriage often operates through gendered, racialized, regionalized, and economic logics. For even as migration policies generally "place heterosexual marriage at the centre of the discourse of entitlement to rights and entry," migrants whose heterosexual marriages provide a basis of entitlement have further depended on these other factors, as well as on adherence to norms of "proper" intimacy and sexuality.[35] In *Metock,* all of the wives were EU citizens and all of the husbands were not, which suggests that claims about marriage as a route to illegal migration may be most effective when they were represented as a matter of European wives being "taken advantage of" by non-European husbands rather than vice versa. Moreover, the stereotype of the asylum seeker as a likely illegal immigrant was redeployed in the case, through the construction of asylum seeking men whose claims were refused but who married EU wives as illegal and deportable.[36]

Although the Irish government lost the *Metock* battle, officials' certainty that "sham" marriage was being used to enable otherwise "illegal" migration has continued. Marriages that offer a means to extend the duration of a migrant's legal presence—including for asylum seekers whose cases have been refused, and for students "from Asia and Africa" whose visas have expired—are frequently seen as likely "illegal."[37] The logical conundrum, of course, is that when marriage makes migration or continued residence legally possible, such migration or residence is not in fact illegal. For the government, the question of legality or illegality apparently inheres in the intentions and motivations that guided the marriage on which the migrant's residence is based. Quite simply, marriages that are viewed as having been entered into primarily or completely for purposes of gaining legal migration status (called "sham" marriages) cause great concern. Officials suggest that these marriages are not entered into in the right spirit or with the right intentions—which underlines that marriages are normatively expected to entail particular kinds of feelings, intentions, and aspirations that are expected produce socially valued outcomes. Historically, arguments about the lack of particular feelings, intentions, and intimacies within marriage have been used to create racial, cultural, and geopolitical distinctions.[38] But in this instance they have become a basis to produce and circulate constructions of migrant illegality—that are also manifestly racializing, engendering, and neocolonial.

The argument that migrants were entering into marriages not for the "right" reasons but mainly to avoid deportation and gain legal residence eventually presented difficulties for state policing efforts. In 2011 the High Court ruled that marriages entered into for purposes of gaining immigration benefits were not, in fact, illegal: "The validity of a marriage is largely a matter of form and there is no 'abuse of rights doctrine' in respect of marriage. In other words, the motive for the marriage is irrelevant. . . . A marriage of convenience can be a valid marriage, as long as both parties consent to it and as long as none of the impediments to marriage (affinity, capacity, age, marital status, gender) enumerated in the Civil Registration Act, 2004 are present."[39] This ruling raised concerns about the Garda National Immigration Bureau's "Operation Charity," which attempted to prevent marriages that officials believed were motivated primarily by a desire for immigration benefits. I argue that it also raises questions about the basis on which the state describes certain marriages as entailing "illegal immigration." It might be more accurate to describe the marriages as generating "unwanted" migration that is not illegal, although the state continues to seek ways to eventually make it illegal.

The continued description of certain marriages as "sham" reveals investments in a particular norm of marriage as well as concerns about what happens when that norm becomes detached from its usual ends or is monetized for profit, including by third parties. Government efforts to police against "sham" marriages have particularly drawn legitimacy from instances when women have been tricked or forced into marriage through situations that include sexual activity against their will. In particular, Latvian women (and EU women from Eastern Europe generally) have been described as being lured to Ireland with promises of jobs and then forced into marriage with non-EU men. Men from Pakistan, but also Nigeria, India, the Ukraine, and sometimes Brazil, have been publicly identified as particularly likely to engage in marriage for immigration status.[40] In some cases it was reported that the women were raped before being forcibly married.

These situations most certainly cannot be ignored. They evoke concerns about sex trafficking rather than ideals of heterosexual marriage. Yet we must be very cautious about the responses that they inspire and the policing that they legitimize. As chapter 2 describes, government responses to the disparate phenomena that get characterized as sex trafficking often primarily reproduce a binary of innocent victim/criminal whore, rather than addressing women's complex needs and circumstances. Moreover, government interventions involving marriages across geopolitical and legal status lines have historically often extended rather than undone gendered, sexual, racial, class, and geopolitical hierarchies.[41] Today's context, where global capitalism has thoroughly transformed marriage as an institution in ways that states have not necessarily caught up with, further adds to the complexity of crafting an appropriate response.

All of these struggles reveal that the sexualities and intimacies of heterosexual marriage have become governmentalized in troubling ways because of marriage's presumed capacity to generate "illegal" migration. Of course, it would be more precise to say that heterosexual marriage generates some migration that is unwanted, which the government is seeking to make "illegal," especially because it fears that this unwanted migration could grow. Government efforts in that regard have been stumbling and uncertain (one blogger calls them "ham fisted"). But that does not mean the efforts do not have consequences. On the contrary, officials increasingly inquire into sexualities and intimacies within marriages that involve a non-EU migrant based on their concerns about the supposed misuse of marriage as a route to illegal immigration. Everyone is affected, including migrants whose possibilities for legal entry, residence, and eventual citizenship are redirected and curtailed, and also citizens, whose marriages emerge as the supposed "weak point" in border control, generating scrutiny and surveillance that is engendering, racializing, neocolonial, and neoliberalizing.[42]

Same-Sex Couples

The centrality of heterosexual marriage as a model for migration control has deeply affected those in same-sex couple relationships. Historically, same-sex relationships were not recognized as a basis for legal migration. Effectively, same-sex migrant partners were always already the illegal migrants, meaning that legal status was unavailable through their relationships and had to be sought instead through the work permit or work visa system. This situation dovetailed with a history of casting lesbianism or gayness as "un-Irish," including in ways that generated significant migration from Ireland by lesbian and gay citizens.[43] Yet lesbian and gay citizens' status began to change, as reflected by the decriminalization of homosexuality (1993), the passage of the Employment Equality Act (1998) and the Equal Status Act (2000), the establishment of the Equality Authority (2000), and, most recently, the passage of the Civil Partnership Act (2010). Moreover, "many key voices within the queer movement in Ireland in the early 1990s sought to counter the positioning of homosexuality as intrinsically anti-Irish."[44]

Since migration rules did not recognize same-sex relationships, migrants had to find other grounds to construct themselves as legal, which was particularly challenging for those from outside the EU/EEA. As GLEN (Gay and Lesbian Equality Network) describes, "lack of recognition has meant that relationships established between lesbian and gay Irish people and non-EU nationals [were] dependent on the capacity of the latter to obtain and sustain their employment and residency status in Ireland in their own right," including through the work permit system.[45] Dil Wickremasinghe from Sri Lanka described:

> I met my [Irish] partner when I was living in the Middle East, and she brought me here [five years ago]. Although I have a work permit, I should point out that the work permit system is flawed in that one has to apply for a new permit on an annual basis. I decided to apply for residency on the basis of my relationship with an Irish woman. The Department of Justice, Equality and Law Reform kept my partner and I waiting for two years, before sending us a letter stating that I did not need residency because I had a work permit. It suggested that I give up my work permit and reapply for residency. I could not do such a thing because, like

everyone else, I have bills to pay. I would not be allowed to work
in the absence of a work permit.[46]

Dil's account, which was written in 2005, reflects the lack of guaranteed
rights for same-sex couples and the particular difficulties this presented
for non-EU migrants; the tenuous nature of life under the work permit
system, which required annual renewal and thus held couples hostage to
continual uncertainty and inability to plan for a future; and the convo-
luted logic through which the Department of Justice considered her case.

Dil, through her leadership in GLUE (Gays and Lesbians United
Eire), along with GLEN and other allies, struggled to ensure that the
Irish state recognized same-sex relationships for purposes of legal migration. Eventually an informal process was established that allowed migrants in same-sex relationships to seek residency based on the relationship. However, both partners already had to be living in Ireland, and the
grant of residency remained at the minister's discretion; it was not provided for in law. Ministerial decisions often seemed to be arbitrary. Stories circulated about the minister granting residency to one migrant in a
same-sex partnership but denying it to another whose circumstances
seemed virtually identical. Or freely granting one residency application
but attaching conditions to another one that were difficult to meet. As
with married heterosexuals, race, gender, economics, and region of origin seemed to shape possibilities for residency for migrants in same-sex
relationships. Informal interviews I conducted suggested that those who
were well off and socially well positioned had an easier time getting status; those from countries such as the United States, Canada, and Austra-
lia also tended to have an easier time. Conversely, migrants who were
from the global south, who were visibly people of color, or who had limited English skills experienced greater barriers—though interviewees
also noted there were shifting trends regarding which nationalities were
singled out as most liable to suspicion and refusal. Income remained a
decisive factor in shaping possibilities.

The government then institutionalized an administrative process for
handling "de facto relationships," which applied to both same-gender
and male/female couples. Nonetheless, according to Marriage Equality,
these couples had to prove they had a durable, cohabiting relationship that
had been in existence for a defined number of years (whereas heterosexual married couples did not have to prove this), which meant that they

were not treated equally and remained vulnerable to refusal. Effectively, suspicion about the nature and durability of intimate ties, and difficulties establishing them to the satisfaction of officials remained at issue.

The rules were further changed after passage of the Civil Partnership and Certain Rights of Cohabitants Act of 2010, which came into effect in January 2011. Based on the act, GLEN declared, "there is now equal treatment between same-sex civil partners and opposite-sex married spouses, and equal treatment between *de facto* same-sex and *de facto* opposite-sex couples."[47]

Same-sex couple relationships now do provide a basis for legal status, but this requires couples to submit their sexualities and intimacies to evaluation by officials and, indeed, as GLEN notes, allow themselves to be evaluated on *the same terms* as male/female couples and in regard to dominant norms. Those who do not fit into the dominant norms, or do not want to, remain shut out. Those whose financial resources are limited also remain shut out. Issues of region, gender, age, race, language ability, and more still shape the outcomes of these cases. Not just migrants but also citizens find themselves governed in new ways as a result.[48] The demand for equal treatment has certainly had paradoxical results.

Anne Mulhall suggests that this outcome reflects a process whereby the treatment of gay men and lesbians has come "to signify modernity and progress" by the Irish state. This politics of representation has yoked sectors of the lesbian and gay movement into "a mainstreaming, reformist, liberalizing approach that seeks assimilation within existing social and economic structures rather than any whole-scale radical reconstitution of those structures themselves."[49] Recognition of same-sex partnerships— but only when they fit into and conform to the norm of heterosexual marriage—has become one of the mechanisms whereby some lesbian and gay citizens have come to accept mainstream immigration regimes, including officials' inquiries into and policing of sexualities and intimacies and the continual reproduction of new figures of illegal migration as a threat that legitimizes these actions.

Other Struggles: Sex Workers, Domestic Workers

Migrant sex work is another key area where sexualities and intimacies are being policed to remake the legal/illegal distinction, limit migrants' possibilities for transitioning their statuses, and remake the meaning of citizenship. The scholarship on migrant sex work is too vast to review here. As described in chapter 2, however, migrant sex work has become largely understood and policed within a framework of "sex trafficking" that has not prevented migration but rather has routed migrants into situations where they are more vulnerable and exploitable while at the same time ensuring that their paths to legal status are significantly reduced or entirely eliminated.

These discourses and the practices also reshape meanings of citizenship for Irish (and EU) people. Jo Doezema points out that within the dominant trafficking framework, "the 'voluntary' prostitute is a Western sex worker, seen as capable of making independent decisions about whether or not to sell sexual services, while the sex worker from a developing country is deemed unable to make the same choice: she is passive, naïve, and ready prey for traffickers."[50] Rutvica Andrijasevic concludes, "Whereas EU citizens are encouraged to undertake greater labour mobility, anti-trafficking campaigns intervene upon the labour mobility of female non-EU nationals and encourage them to remain at home."[51] Elizabeth Bernstein argues that antitrafficking campaigns serve as a critical means to reassert national identity (and normative models of citizenship) in the face of anxieties caused by Europeanization and globalization.[52]

Domestic work is another area where the connections among sexualities, migrant legal status, and dominant norms of citizenship have been contested and remade. Some ten thousand people, most of them migrants from outside the EU, are currently employed as domestic workers in Ireland. According to the Migrant Rights Centre Ireland, "The isolation and invisibility of domestic workers, many of who live in their employers' homes creates a fertile ground for exploitation. This is a sector that has high incidences of exploitation and forced labour. Common complaints reported to MRCI include, long hours of work, pay below national minimum wage, no day off, no sick pay, no holiday pay, harassment, bullying, retention of identity documents and physical and mental abuse."[53] MRCI has highlighted the struggles that face domestic workers who become pregnant, including their frequent lack of medical coverage, lack of paid leave, and potential or actual job loss:

> One employer responded when told that her employee was
> pregnant that all the neighbors would think that the father was
> the employer's husband. They subsequently attempted to send her

back to her country of origin. Another woman who came to the MRCI 37 weeks pregnant was expected to work right up to the point she went into labour. She was intended [sic] to take a month off (unpaid) and then return to work. She was working without a work permit and was terrified that she would be let go if she made any demands on her employer.[54]

According to Siobhan Mullally, in 2011 the International Labour Organization adopted a Convention and Recommendation on Decent Work for Domestic Workers. The Irish Congress of Trade Unions, in its draft response to the convention, advocated, among other issues, "the right of domestic workers not to be required to undertake a HIV or pregnancy test and not to reveal their HIV or pregnancy status."[55] All of this indicates some of the complex ways that sexualities and legal status may interweave in the lives of migrant domestic workers to create jeopardies, restrictions, and exploitation—while also redefining the norms of the families that employ them and Irishness more generally.

Conclusion

Chapters in this book have tracked how pregnancy and migrant status became interwoven through panics over illegal immigration that had significant consequences for both migrants and citizens. This chapter proposes that sexualities in general provide volatile grounds for struggles over immigration and the remaking of nationalism and citizenship. The struggles described here were generally treated in isolation from one another. But it would be more effective to address them as interlinked, using a critical heteronormativity framework that focuses not stable, transhistorical, or essential identities but rather on critically analyzing dominant norms that produce variously subalternized populations (as captured by Gayle Rubin's concept of a pyramid of sexual normativity). Through such a framework, struggles that may otherwise be dismissed as isolated, local, or the purview of "special interest groups," can instead be usefully analyzed as interlinked within larger social, historical, and political processes, and in ways that invite us to imagine forms of activisms that challenge multiple, ongoing inequalities rather than seeking accommodation within the existing system.[56]

Conclusion

JUDITH BUTLER calls for scholarship and activisms "focused on opposition to state violence and its capacity to produce, exploit, and distribute precarity for the purposes of profit and territorial defense."[1] As she describes and as this book demonstrates, effective opposition requires "thinking sexual politics along with immigration politics in new ways."[2] Thus, this concluding chapter first brings the book's arguments together by reviewing how pregnancy became the basis for claiming that certain migrants were "illegal" and then implementing laws and policies that made them so. Second, this chapter addresses how the production of the figure of the illegal migrant is integrally related to the conceptualization and institutionalization of the norm of the desirable migrant and the good citizen in ways that rearticulate sexualized, gendered, racialized, classed, and geopolitical hierarchies. Third, it suggests that despite the state's framework of "national interest," which legitimized these outcomes, state migration controls have been and remain contested. Yet questions of sexuality have rarely factored into opposition arguments or alternative visions; what would happen if we were to factor sexuality in? The chapter concludes by reviewing areas for further research.

Producing Migrant "Illegality"

Since the late nineteenth century, controlling in-migration has become a crucial element of state building and nationalism and their associated relations of power.[3] With the adoption of the Aliens Act of 1935, the southern Irish state, too, claimed control over in-migration into the national territory. Yet emigration, which the Irish state never directly regulated, remained the defining feature of Irish life throughout most of the twentieth century. Laws and policies concerning in-migration remained rudimentary—until last decade of the century.

State-centered and nationalist perspectives presume that expanding state migration controls are natural and inevitable. Such approaches, however, evacuate histories, erase struggles, and naturalize state logics and practices. By contrast, this book suggests that the significant expansion and dispersion of Irish migration controls in the late twentieth century occurred in response to perceived crises; unfolded in a manner that was always somewhat contingent; enabled what Saskia Sassen characterizes as "renationalization" as well as new exercises of statecraft, all of which rearticulated multiple social hierarchies; and generated struggles whose legacies must be remembered and built upon.[4] The book centralizes sexualities, as these intersected with multiple relations of power, as a lens through which to analyze these developments.

The expansion of Irish migration controls occurred in a context of deepening Europeanization and neoliberalization, as well as a booming economy, which resulted in significantly rising rates of in-migration. Many migrants had been recruited to fill labor niches; others were Irish emigrants who saw opportunities to return; still others were international students or people seeking asylum. Labor migrants were far more numerous than asylum seekers, but government officials conceived labor migrants as temporary and expected them to leave. Asylum seekers were another matter, however. Not only did they arrive in growing numbers but their cases often took years to resolve. Since they were not permitted to engage in paid labor while awaiting the resolution of their cases, their presence entailed welfare costs; and, at least for some, settlement eventually occurred. Thus, control over asylum seekers rather than labor migrants was initially identified as the most pressing migration issue confronting the Irish state at the end of the century.[5] Yet efforts to control asylum seekers created logics and practices that would come to affect all categories of migrants—and citizens too.

The state began ramping up its controls over asylum seekers and introducing processes that resulted in significant rates of denial of asylum claims. In that context, migrants' ability to get legal residency through the birth in Ireland of a child, rather than through the state's recognition of their asylum claims, began to generate an outcry. Mechanisms for gaining legal residency through the birth of a child had been institutionalized after the 1990 *Fajujonu* decision, and migrants who acquired residency accordingly were not in violation of any law. But they became characterized as "abusing" the system in ways that necessitated a crackdown. Claims about "abuse" quickly morphed into assertions that the migrants were, in fact, "illegal." Particularly striking were the ways that pregnancy became the site around which these assertions converged.

An asylum-seeker woman's pregnancy became read as a sign that she was likely "really" an illegal immigrant, and treated as a visible manifestation of inner, inherently undesirable qualities, including that she was a sponger, a lawbreaker, and lacking in good moral character.[6] Moreover, her pregnancy was seen as the means through which these undesirable qualities would become entrenched into Irish society: since her child would be a citizen, she could acquire residency through the child and then bring over chains of similarly undesirable family members to Ireland. While asylum-seeker women were the initial targets of these discourses, pregnant migrants of every legal status quickly became targeted too.

These meanings did not spring from thin air; instead, as Jonathan Inda describes, the construct of migrant illegality gets "made up" in particular ways, which officials, citizens, and migrants both learn about and participate in.[7] The scholarship on the social construction of the illegal migrant has richly analyzed many aspects of that making up process. The fact that pregnant women became constructed as paradigmatic illegal immigrants, however, highlights the importance of sexual regimes in shaping these processes. This is hardly surprising; sexuality has historically been central to state and nation building in a manner that institutionalizes yet naturalizes multiple hierarchies.[8] Contemporary globalization processes have rearticulated and further dispersed these effects. Thus, it is crucial to theorize the ways that sexuality—understood not as personal identity (although it is certainly integral to modern identities) but as a regime of power that produces and polices populations in relation to multiple ends—has shaped designations of who is a legal or illegal migrant.

Sexuality, migration, and economic development have been interwoven with nation and state making processes in shifting configurations throughout Irish history. Thus, the "crisis" over pregnant asylum seekers (and, ultimately, over all pregnant migrants) has to be situated through reference to that longer history. It also has to be analyzed as a catalyst for remaking social and institutional relations at every scale. Chapters 1 and 5 traced some of the discourses that "made up" pregnant migrants as paradigmatic illegal immigrants between 1997 and 2004. Chapter 2 provided alternative understandings of the ways that pregnancy, migration, and legal status variously interconnected in diverse migrants' lives, yet these perspectives remained subordinated by the dominant representations. Figures of pregnant women as illegal migrants, to which dominant meanings and anxieties became attached, included the pregnant, usually African but sometimes Eastern European, asylum seeker; the pregnant citizenship tourist; and Ms. O, Ms. Lobe, Ms. Osayande, and Ms. Chen.

Through the circulation of these figures, pregnancy became the locus where multiple anxieties were assembled and transformed into programs for governing against undesired migrants. At that historical moment, control over illegal migration significantly came to mean exerting control over migrant women's bodies, which were normed as always already reproductive (while frequently demonizing migrant men as sexual predators). Control strategies included inquiring into migrant women's reproductive status upon arrival; generating and circulating data about their pregnancy rates; correlating pregnancy rate data with anxieties about hospital capacity, future social welfare costs, and so on; assembling a legal and administrative apparatus centered on migrant pregnancy and childbearing; and other changes that are described in this book. In the process, new knowledge formations, institutional arrangements, logics of governance, and practices became dispersed throughout the state and its social partners through which, since 1987, governance has been negotiated.[9]

For the Irish state, a critical element of gaining control over so-called illegal migration, as embodied by the pregnant migrant, entailed closing down migrants' paths to acquiring legal status through childbearing. Thus, the 2003 L&O decision ended migrants' ability to gain legal residency through birthing and parenting an Irish child. The 2004 citizenship referendum further routed various migrants into illegal status by denying citizenship to many of their Irish-born children. Not only did this denial render the children more easily deportable but it also prevented migrant parents from seeking residency in other EU countries, which might have been possible if their children were Irish (and therefore EU) citizens. The European Court of Justice's 2011 decision in the Zambrano case, which opened the door to legal status in the EU for non-EU migrant parents with citizen children, illustrated this possibility. Yet the results of the citizenship referendum ensured that the numbers of eligible migrant parents were smaller than might have otherwise been the case.

It is critical to underscore that the *L&O* decision and the citizenship referendum actively reduced migrants' possibilities for gaining legal status and in this sense expanded their likelihood of becoming routed into illegal status. This argument challenges the commonly held assumption that migrants' legal statuses stem from and reflect their personal characteristics or moral worth and shows instead that legal statuses are produced through relations of power and knowledge that have deep roots in histories of colonialism, global capitalism, and the formation of an inequitable global system of nation-states. It also highlights the centrality of nationalist sexual regimes—which are not just sexist and heterosexist but also classist and racist—to these processes.

As described in earlier chapters, claims about migrants' "illegality" were in many instances anticipatory; by characterizing various migrations as illegal, even when migrants were lawfully present, it became possible to change the rules so that the migrants would *become* illegal in the future. While these processes initially cohered around pregnant migrant women, they expanded to encompass other kinds of sexual and intimate ties, as described in chapter 6, and other figures of illegality. Yet, designating growing numbers of migrants as illegal did not address the circumstances that generated their migration nor necessarily reduce actual migration; instead, it primarily made migrants more vulnerable and exploitable.

The Relationality of Legal Statuses: Margins (Re)Define the Centers at Different Scales

The struggles over pregnant migrants make clear that the illegal migrant is never separate from the legal migrant or the citizen; rather, these statuses relationally define one another within a larger framework for governing the whole population.[10] Thus, in Ireland, the figure of the childbearing asylum seeker who was supposedly welfare dependent, conniving, cynical, and using her children to create unearned ties to the Irish nation and its material resources came to stand for the most undesirable and unwanted forms of migration. Once this was in place, a contrasting image of the desirable migrant became elaborated, operationalized, and institutionalized in law and practice. Not surprisingly, the desirable migrant was economically productive and required little or no state resources.[11] Increasingly, many officials felt free to disregard poor and working migrants', asylum seekers', and international students' sexual and intimate ties.[12]

In this context, the sexualities and intimacies of middle class and entrepreneurial migrants who were deemed central to the economy sometimes became bargaining chips to attract and retain them. Thus, Filipino nurses successfully campaigned to have their spouses permitted not just to reside but also to work legally in Ireland, or else, they threatened, they would take their nursing skills elsewhere.[13] Same-sex relationships were also recognized for purposes of migration—but only when the couple could demonstrate that they conformed to middle-class heteronorms of privacy, domesticity, consumption, and shared financial responsibility and that they would not be an economic burden. The restructuring of social welfare in the first decade of the twenty-first century, which resulted in the creation of a separate, inferior system of welfare provision for asylum seekers and then in the adoption of a "habitual residence condition" that made access to welfare conditional on a period of residence in Ireland or the United Kingdom (and that affected not just migrants but also citizens), was another very important element of these processes of defining and institutionalizing relational constructs of undesirable illegal migrant and desirable productive migrant—including in relation to desired sexual and intimate norms and the changing roles that these were expected to fulfill under neoliberal conditions.[14]

The struggles around illegal immigration and resulting changes have impacted on citizens and constructs of citizenship too.[15] Indeed, although illegal migrants are often conceived as marginal to society, the margins inevitably define the center (which generally gets to be unmarked, the invisible norm, and therefore to escape critical scrutiny). One of the ways that the margins define the center is that the categories of undocumented migrant, legal migrant, and citizen exist in a structural relation of inequality to one another. Quite simply, the actual or expected advantages associated with holding citizenship status depend on the continued existence of subordinated migrants who are designated as undocumented, exploitable, and deportable.[16] This is not to ignore that the promises associated with juridical citizenship are never fully realized by citizens who are poor, female, racialized, queer, or otherwise Other. Moreover, Alicia Schmidt Camacho writes, many subaltern citizens have faced diminishing rights and protections under current conditions of globalization.[17] Nonetheless, juridical status, which is often glossed over in U.S. scholarship on citizenship, matters deeply. This is certainly evident from the ways that the Irish state has busily reorganized the logics that determine which migrant holds what status; the material and symbolic significance of the status; and migrants' opportunities for transitioning from one status to another (including, in some cases, to citizenship, although in other cases, not).

The political lesson here might be that rather than arguing for the full realization of the rights and privileges that have been endlessly deferred for so many subaltern citizens, we are better served by fighting for a system where basic rights, protections, and the means to live do not depend on one's legal status in the first place. To be sure, this argument has been pursued through important human rights scholarship and activism. Yet the difficulties of ensuring that human rights frameworks consistently and adequately serve either subaltern citizens or migrants of every status remain very substantial. Indeed, this book has shown how the asylum system, which is supposedly grounded in human rights, nonetheless has become a technology for expanding and diversifying the production of migrants who are designated as illegal. Moreover, human rights frameworks often become a convenient alibi for citizens who do not want to critically interrogate investments in and privileges stemming from our juridical status. Sustained, rigorous attention to the consequences of all juridical statuses is critical for social transformation.

At the same time citizenship is never reducible to juridical status but also involves rights, recognition, and responsibilities. Negotiating these aspects of citizenship enmeshes people in what Aihwa Ong describes as cultural processes of " 'subject-ification' in the Foucauldian sense of self-making and being-made by power relations."[18] These include self-making and being-made as gendered, racialized, sexualized, and class-specific subjects in relation to prevailing institutions and ideologies. Struggles over immigration, however, reorganize dominant norms of citizenship, including in regard to rights, responsibilities, and recognition. Accordingly, the struggles against illegal migrants—who in the 1990s were figured initially as pregnant migrants, and later as other kinds of sexualized and laboring figures—have transformed Irish citizenship norms, and reorganized diverse citizens' relationship to those norms. Those citizens who make up the invisible "center" have had to actively work to refashion themselves while subaltern citizens have experienced changing forms of subalternity.

For instance, the struggles over pregnant migrants have ensured that citizens' heterosexual reproduction became linked with migration controls and a new racial grammar of Irishness that affected citizens in different ways, depending on their racial, gender, sexual, and class positioning. Married heterosexual couples, who supposedly represent the most normative sexual and intimate group, began to find that if they married a non-EU/EEA national, their marriages were subjected to surveillance, scrutiny, uncertainty, and possibly dissolution through deportation of the migrant spouse. At the same time, Anne Mulhall writes, "the racially marked woman as producer of an undesirable future . . . [became] the biopolitical complement to the ethnically desirable, presumptively white, woman who is, on the other hand, legislatively coerced into reproducing the nation's aspirational future."[19] Family rights were redefined; indeed, new questions emerged about who and what actually counts as "family."[20] Efforts to secure recognition of same-sex couples for purposes of immigration were successful, yet this occurred in a manner that marginalized less privileged citizen gay men and lesbians while further drawing others into racializing, neoliberalized nationalism and building symbolic capital for the state. Given that efforts to police against unwanted migrants tend to particularly affect subaltern citizens who are associated with "outsiders," Black Irish women with children became subject to abuse on the street because they were believed to be migrant scammers rather than citizens.[21]

These conditions also ensure that, contrary to state projects and fantasies of "integration," there is no singular path to migrant incorporation and no singular Irish society into which migrants negotiate their incorporation.[22] Instead, as Gray argues, migrants find varied ways to incorporate themselves through processes that are mixed, contradictory, and contingent.[23] The book's discussion of Christabel as well as recent published scholarship suggests that migrants develop transnational, translocal, and creolized identities, identifications, and ways of being that function at once within and beyond the boundaries of the nation-state.[24]

Through struggles over migration, diverse citizens and migrants also renegotiated their relationship to Europeanness. The interconnections between Irishness and Europeanness are multiple, contested, and uneasy, yet political elites remain certain that the national future depends on belonging to Europe, and moreover, as Katy Hayward describes, that Ireland has "important practical and idealised contribution[s]" to offer to the EU.[25] Yet, John Harrington cautions, "escape from nationalist stalemate into the flow of European progress is racially defined from the outset."[26] Robbie McVeigh argues, "The idea of Europe is inherently racist—its legacy of racially coded genocide, colonisation, and enslavement is what defines it.... This tradition of dead generations weighs heavily."[27] Nonetheless, "the EU is currently uniting [through] whiteness. 'Fortress Europe' not 'Sanctuary Europe' remains the defining metaphor for the contemporary European project. This process is institutionally racist."[28] Scholars have analyzed how majority Irish people "became white" in Ireland and the diaspora; recent Europeanization processes have further rearticulated whiteness in ways that reshape who counts as properly Irish and European.[29] Migration policies have been key mechanisms through which these transformations have taken place.

Gender, sexual, and class processes, individually and in their interconnections with each other, are also implicated in the (re)constitution of Europeanness. For example, recent scholarship explores how racialization, sexuality, and gender intersect in public discourses to suggest that Muslims are inherently patriarchal and homophobic, thereby posing a threat to the putative European heritage and culture of gender and sexual equality and tolerance. The claims serve multiple functions, including racializing Muslims or those perceived as Muslim; erasing the reality and possibility of feminist, queer, and antihomophobic Muslim people and movements; transferring the history of Europe's gender, sexual, and religious intolerance onto Muslims while sanitizing Europe and Europeans; using claims about Muslims to "define a new, unified Europe characterized by a tolerant secularism"; and remaking whiteness.[30] Events described in this book certainly suggest that interlinked formations of whiteness, gender, sexuality, Irishness, and Europeanness have also emerged that fulfill these functions.

These shifting relationalities were experienced not only at local, national, or EU scales but also in regard to global geopolitical hierarchies. This becomes clear when we remember that the children and grandchildren born abroad to Irish descended people are still permitted to acquire citizenship, even when they have never set foot in Ireland. The disparity between the treatment of migrants' children in Ireland and the children and grandchildren of the Irish diaspora rearticulates Irishness as blood and genealogy in the most literally racist way. EU and Irish law, which privileges migration for EU citizens while increasingly immobilizing others, further entrenches these results. Effectively, changing state regulations concerning the ways that sexualities interweave with migration and citizenship law have rearticulated global histories and geographies of racism and (neo)colonialism. As Ann Stoler explains, this manner of regulating sexuality, migration, and citizenship has "fix[ed] the conditions under which European privileges could be attained and reproduced" and reveals how "the conduct of private life and the sexual proclivities individuals expressed were tied to corporate profit and the security of the . . . [geopolitically advantaged] state" in a context of neoliberal globalization.[31]

The geopolitical significance of these events is also suggested by the fact that controversies over migrant pregnancies specifically—and migrant sexualities more generally—are by no means unique to Ireland but have occurred in many other regions, and Irish struggles both drew on and contributed to these other struggles. For example, fierce controversies over migrant pregnancies have flared in the United States (where, in recent decades, legislation has been repeatedly introduced to abolish birthright citizenship for children born in the United States to undocumented parents); Hong Kong (which, as of February 2007, requires pregnant migrants to provide a $5,000 bond before entering, and more recently, has begun jailing mainland Chinese women who travel there to give birth); Germany (which recently amended its laws to grant citizenship to children and grandchildren born in Germany to guest workers); and the Dominican Republic (which has been systematically revoking the citizenship of children and grandchildren of Haitian migrants who were born in and have always lived in the Dominican Republic), to name just a few of the many nation-states where migrant pregnancies have generated controversy and change.[32] Struggles over same-sex couple migration, heterosexual marriage migration, migrant sex work, the sexual control of domestic workers, efforts to prevent the spread of sexually transmitted diseases through migration, and many other sexuality-related migration struggles have also taken place around the globe.

Each of these struggles has distinct features, but nation-states also borrow from one another when crafting policy responses, practices, and laws. For example, several Irish Supreme Court justices invoked U.S. immigration law when ruling in the *L&O* case that migrant parents with citizen children could be deported; conversely, advocates and attorneys in Ireland who challenged the citizenship referendum drew "not just examples but inspiration" from U.S. legal traditions.[33] Subsequently, the white supremacist Federation for American Immigration Reform began using Ireland's citizenship referendum as an example that should inspire the U.S. federal government to eliminate birthright citizenship because, they argue, women—portrayed as poor, of color, economically noncontributing, and lacking in good moral and cultural values (sound familiar?)—are deliberately migrating to the United States to give birth, thereby ensuring benefits for the children as well as creating opportunities for themselves to "sponge" off welfare and acquire legal status.[34] Reportedly, New Zealand also used Ireland's example as a justification for changing its citizenship laws.[35] Transnational bodies played important roles in these global interchanges. For example, the International Organization of Migration (IOM) produced a report that warned the Irish government of the consequences of granting residency to migrants who gave birth to a citizen child. The report claimed considerable authority because it drew "lessons from the experiences of other countries" in managing migration.[36]

Other sexuality and migration struggles have similarly transnational dimensions. For instance, Irish advocates of same-sex migration derived arguments, strategies, and legitimacy from the United Kingdom's Stonewall organization. The Williams Institute at the University of California Los Angeles also weighed in with neoliberalizing arguments. A Williams Institute report in support of civil partnership law noted that there are "more than 1,200 Irish-born men and women . . . living with a same-sex partner in the United States. They are predominantly female and highly educated. One in seven is raising children. Civil partnership legislation could provide economic benefit to Ireland, enticing some of these talented same-sex couples to relocate back to Ireland and making the country more competitive in the global creative economy."[37] Similarly, heterosexual marriage migration struggles drew not only on British but also EU examples and initiatives. More research is needed to better understand the articulations and disjunctures among these kinds of sexuality and migration struggles as well as their impacts at local, national, regional, and global levels.

Immigration Controls, National Interest, and Sexualities

Centralizing sexual regimes, this book has analyzed how the boundaries between legal status categories, and migrants' possibilities for transitioning from one to another, were significantly redrawn—in ways that negatively affected many migrants and reshaped the meanings and experiences of citizenship. Emphasizing the active, contested, and never predetermined nature of these changes, chapters in the book drew inspiration from migrants, scholars, and activists who critically analyze migration controls, problematize their associated violence, and envision alternatives. Many individuals and groups have proposed alternative frameworks through which to address migration processes. But the state's framework of "national interest"—in other words, harnessing migration to serve national economic growth according to neoliberal logics—has become and remains hegemonic.

Gerard Boucher suggests that the national interest framework largely forecloses engagement with questions about global inequalities—instead, the global is engaged in strictly neoliberalized economic terms within which state managers accept that growth depends on harnessing Ireland's economy to the global.[38] The national interest framework also refuses to substantively engage with history. Many people have indicated connections between Ireland's sustained history of emigration, which stemmed from Irish experiences of colonization and peripheralization within the global economy, and current migration into Ireland that in many cases is also rooted in global economic inequalities. They argue that this connection creates a historical duty to treat migrants well—but the national interest framework largely overrides these concerns.[39] National interest also allows policymakers to ignore the contradictions, which have been highlighted by scholars and activists, between the state's harsh treatment of unwanted and especially of illegal migrants in Ireland and their advocacy for Irish emigrants abroad, particularly those who are living illegally in the United States.[40] Overall, as Boucher describes, the national interest framework "marginalises internal Irish critiques of managed migration, particularly those that advocate alternative policies based on historical duty, liberal humanism and liberal internationalist perspectives" such as human rights.[41] It also marginalizes competing frameworks that have been proposed by labor, the trade unions, and the antiglobalization movement.

Yet there *are* continuing and ongoing critiques of Irish state approaches to managing migration that attempt to reintroduce questions of global and historical responsibility, and that propose alternative visions that address interlinked inequalities at local, national, and global levels. Each merits further exploration and action. A broad international

scholarship also engages these concerns. For example, scholars vigor-
ously debate the possibilities of open borders—which would rework, if
not entirely erase over time, the citizen/migrant distinction, and the
border control apparatuses and associated inequalities that this distinction produces.[42] Debates also consider how migration and economic development might be connected together in new ways—including suggestions that, unlike current global northern state immigrant selection
criteria, migrants should instead be admitted based on their origins in
the world's poor countries, or countries to which a historical debt is
owed, or countries that need assistance even without a historical debt,
and in ways that are cognizant of gendered, racialized, sexualized, and
neocolonial hierarchies.[43] Stephen Castles, however, points out that
global northern governments are often interested in linking migration
with development because they mistakenly believe this will reduce migration from the global south—not because of commitments to remedy-
ing injustice.[44] Consequently, migration/development initiatives generally continue to significantly serve the interests of privileged sectors
within and across national borders. Moreover, "development" in these
instances remains saturated by neocolonial logic. Other challenges to
migration controls come from human rights scholars and advocates
who use human rights protocols and logics to challenge nation-state
immigration controls that manifestly harm migrants, including the
undocumented.

Other scholars doubt whether migration policies, especially in global
northern states, can or will play an important role in addressing multiple
inequalities and instead propose other strategies through which inequalities could be addressed—which in turn would significantly change migration flows and greatly alter how migration controls are implemented
and their impact. For example, Bill Jordan and Franck Düvell propose
the creation of a "uniform global basic income" that is guaranteed to
everyone—and if this occurred, concerns about migration would look
very different.[45] Aylet Shachar proposes the creation of a "birthright
privilege levy" in which wealthy nation-states are permitted to continue
bestowing national citizenship and associated enhanced life opportunities on selected people, and states pay a levy (that would vary depending on
the state's level of economic development) for each citizen that goes into
a common pot and is used to improve life opportunities in less affluent
nation-states.[46] While her proposal is controversial, it highlights creative

possibilities for, on one hand, preserving nation-based citizenship regimes and state-led migration controls while, on the other hand, attempting to address their role in perpetuating global material inequalities. The proposal certainly resonates with struggles over childbearing that this book addressed. Scholarship that challenges mainstream models of economic development, through which migration controls and citizenship restrictions are overwhelmingly understood and legitimized, offers important possibilities too.

Yet matters of sexuality have rarely figured in these alternatives and challenges, at least not explicitly. Instead sexualities often remain subsumed under rubrics of family, morality, crime, social disorder, welfare, gender, and work.[47] Many migration scholars continue to regard sexualities as separate from and less important than other social and economic realms. This is despite the fact that, as Lisa Duggan explains, "the most successful ruse of neoliberal dominance in both global and domestic affairs is the definition of *economic* policy as primarily a matter of neutral, technical expertise. This expertise is then presented as separate from *politics* and *culture*, and not properly subject to specifically political accountability or cultural critique." Duggan persuasively shows, however, that "despite their overt rhetoric of separation between economic policy on one hand, and political and cultural life on the other, neoliberal politicians and policymakers have never actually separated these domains in practice. . . . The *economy* cannot be transparently abstracted from the *state* or the *family*, from practices of racial apartheid, gender segmentation, or sexual regulation."[48]

Despite scholarship such as Duggan's, sexualities and intimacies are routinely ignored, or else treated as a "lifestyle" issue that is separate from the "real" questions, within many strands of migration scholarship and activism. Sometimes advocates lobby to include select migrants within largely hegemonic sexual norms or else try to tweak the norms a little but without significantly challenging or transforming them. At other times, efforts have entailed attempts to reposition the value of specific *citizens* to the nation-state by asserting those citizens' right to intimate sexual ties with recognized family members who are migrants. As important as these efforts are, they effectively turn migrants' bodies into grounds for struggle among different groups of citizens without necessarily challenging migration control regimes or the hierarchical structural relationships between citizen and migrant. Some migrants, in an effort to construct possibilities for legal admission and residence, strategically deploy sexualities in ways that appear to conform to and affirm dominant logics.[49] I have written elsewhere about the importance of these efforts, but since they operate by mimicking the dominant, their ability to transform the system works through subtlety and over the longer term.[50]

What possibilities might open up if scholars, activists, and advocates were to take up a critical, queer framework that identifies sexualities and intimacies as axes of power, domination, and struggle, including in the construction of the citizen/migrant distinction and the multiple hierarchies that run through those statuses? At a minimum, a queer framework might help us to envision interconnections among struggles that are often seen as separate: struggles over same-sex partner reunification, family reunification in general, marriage migration, migrant sex work, low-wage migrant workers facing sexual harassment and abuse as an ongoing condition of labor, welfare rights, reproductive justice, and more. Moreover, a queer framework might suggest possibilities for productive connections among struggles that are facing migrants and citizens alike. As Cathy Cohen describes, treating struggles as linked does not mean treating them as exactly the same; rather, it means addressing "the systemic relationship among forms of domination" and committing to political practices that are "truly liberating, transformative, and inclusive of all those who stand on the outside of the constructed norm" on whatever basis.[51]

This will not be easy; indeed, queer theory is engaged in extensive debate about how sexualities often serve as bases for complicity with, rather than challenge to, dominant relations of power that are being refashioned through neoliberalism.[52] Yet, since economic and social logics have always worked through particular sexual arrangements, sexualities clearly offer important grounds for challenging the existing order. Indeed, building on this insight, some scholarship seeks to "queer" the heteronormative assumptions that underpin mainstream models of economic development; this work may offer possibilities for challenging migration controls that are rationalized by neoliberal economic logics that supposedly best serve the national interest.[53] Furthermore, as this book has shown, concerns about sexuality provide a powerful means to mobilize people for action on matters of immigration and citizenship. The question is whether there are other ways to mobilize that might produce different outcomes.[54] Queer, feminist, and antiracist scholarship that explores how to mobilize affect for political change has important contributions to offer.

Future Research

The growing scholarship about the social construction of the illegal migrant addresses some of the most pressing inequalities of our time. But sexuality has remained undertheorized—indeed, generally absent—within much of that work. Bringing queer theory into critical conversation with the scholarship on the illegal migrant, this book has explored the centrality of nationalist sexual regimes in shaping whether migrants become designated as illegal or not, and in affecting migrants' possibilities for transitioning among legal statuses. The argument was substantially developed through the analysis of controversies over pregnant migrants, but that focus allowed for the development of a comprehensive framework for understanding how sexual regimes in general are implicated in the designations of migrants as documented or undocumented. Moreover, the book explored how sexual regimes interact with migration controls and citizenship laws in ways that not only affect migrants' legal status possibilities but also remake meanings of citizenship in often contradictory, messy, and inequitable ways.

The book's argument and theoretical approach extends the project of queer migration scholarship, which is dedicated to addressing the ways that sexuality structures and is restructured by *all* migration processes, while at the same time paying close attention to the migration histories and experiences of LGBT people and others who have been deemed "deviant." The book does not frame pregnant migrants as necessarily "queer" subjects but rather insists that a queer framework, grounded in critical analysis of heteronormativity, provides a means for understanding these migrants' struggles—and for situating their struggles in relation to wider logics of sexual rule that affect everyone.[55] In making this argument, the book strives to further build bridges between queer and feminist migration scholarships, which often continue to talk past one another even while extensively drawing on one another's analytic tools and social justice commitments.[56] These kinds of divides are deeply evident in politics and advocacy, too, as issues concerning migrant sexualities, intimacies, affects, and life courses are often treated in isolation from one another rather than within a framework that makes connections among diverse struggles. If this book has one overarching motivation, it is to highlight the importance of treating these diverse issues within a shared framework that is guided by radical critiques of how heteronormativity produces multiple, multiscalar, interlocking, though not necessarily commensurate inequalities.

The book emphasizes that migrants' legal statuses stem from and reflect not their personal characteristics or moral worth but rather the relations of power and knowledge that have deep roots in histories of colonialism, global capitalism, and the formation of an inequitable global system of nation-states. Yet, while illegal status is produced by large structural arrangements of power including those involving global capitalism and nation-states, migrants are not merely helpless victims.[57] Instead I frame pregnancy and childbearing specifically—and sexualities and intimacies more generally—as sites where diverse groups actively struggle over where and how to draw status boundaries between citizens and migrants and among different categories of migrants. In turn these distinctions legitimize unequal rights, protections, and possibilities.[58] Effectively, the book identifies sexuality as a critical site where the interplay between agency, subjectivity, and structural hierarchies of power is contested and remade in struggles over migrants' statuses. This approach enabled me to sidestep binary state logics that posit migrants as either victims or cynical exploiters. It also enabled me to situate migrants and citizens within shared fields of analysis and action in ways that neither ignored the significance of status distinctions between these groups nor fully presumed in advance what those distinctions meant and how they would play out. While I focused on pregnant women, similar struggles have been playing out around a wide range of other sexuality issues, as described in chapter 6. It is my hope that other scholars of migration and citizenship will continue to develop this analysis in conversation with queer theory.

Several specific areas that merit further research have already been identified: for instance, there is a pressing need for histories that thoroughly analyze how migration dynamics (emigration and in-migration together, rather than just one process or the other) have constituted what are considered to be national sexualities, historically and in the present.[59] Such studies promise to greatly enrich and complicate the frameworks through which Irish sexualities, for example, are currently theorized. Contrary to some recent works that celebrate the supposedly declining repression of Irish sexualities, greater attention to in-migration would instead underline the need to address the expanded role of the state as well as the importance of transnational dynamics in producing, regulating, and transforming sexualities in Ireland.

Given that sexuality remains central to nationalism and state building in Ireland and around the world, even in this era of globalization and neoliberalization, we need to know more about how migration control regimes and citizenship regimes co-construct one another through sexuality. We also need to know more about how the creation of new migrant communities transforms nationalist sexualities. Since transformations are never just top-down but also work horizontally and from the ground up, situated ethnographies would shed important light on these questions. For instance, citizens and migrants alike had to learn to view pregnant migrants as likely to be "illegal"; in-depth studies of how this occurred would be invaluable on their own terms and as a way to open up political possibilities.[60] During my time in Ireland, public buses were among the many sites where these kinds of lessons were struggled over in practical ways whenever migrant moms with small children in strollers boarded.[61]

We also need to further explore how these processes rearticulated other social hierarchies, identities, and identifications—and how this necessitates the rethinking of various bodies of scholarship. For instance, the book has drawn on the rich writings on racialization in the Irish experience that have emerged in recent years. The writings theorize Irish experiences in ways that are thoroughly cognizant of U.K. and U.S. racial theories, yet they articulate a distinctly Irish experience and thereby lay the groundwork for effectively addressing racism and racialization in Ireland. This book suggests that theories of racialization in the Irish experience will further benefit from engagement with issues of sexuality (and that sexuality in turn should not be conflated with gender, even though the two are closely linked). Anwen Tormey captures the necessity of exploring these interconnections by describing that responses to pregnant migrants were "illustrative of new ways in which the old story of race continues to be told."[62] She elaborates: "The Irish government's privileging of moral rather than cultural incommensurability is strikingly similar to culturalist rhetorics of exclusion that are often invoked when race is at issue in European public debate on immigration."[63]

Because the processes described in this book were not unique to Ireland but instead were part of wider regional and global transformations, we need to further explore the links, flows, connections, and circuits that shaped interchanges between Ireland and other countries where pregnant migrants—and migrant sexualities and intimacies more generally—became problematized and were used to change laws, remake citizenship, alter migration controls, and redraw social, economic, and cultural boundaries.[64] All analyses would greatly benefit by beginning not from a state-centered perspective that takes for granted and naturalizes state migration controls but instead from a perspective that critically interrogates all state-centered claims about migration and migration controls as well as the work that these claims do.

Historically, capitalism, colonialism, and nation-states have deployed sexual and intimate norms as tools to differentiate among, distribute, and govern populations. Nayan Shah characterizes these as processes of estrangement: " 'Estrangement' is an active process of forcible dislocation, removing people from 'an accustomed place or set of associations,' souring the grounds of 'shared membership' by sowing feelings of hostility, distrust, and 'unsympathetic and indifferent' regard."[65] The events analyzed in this book could certainly be conceived as processes of estranging people from one another by remaking not just hierarchies of legal status, gender, sexuality, race, class, and geopolitics but also rearticulating what those hierarchies will materially and symbolically mean and who will accordingly be valued or let die. Yet, through the lens of a queer of color critique of heteronormativity that goes beyond a gay/straight binary, the book captures the ways that people from all walks of life struggled against forms of estrangement, devaluation, and selectively sanctioned death that were being introduced and legitimized through migration controls.[66] Elizabeth Povinelli suggests that questions of power, inequality, and transformation are implicitly present even when doing something as ordinary as kissing our lovers goodbye for the day. Kissing lovers and others, and everyday acts of sociality, variously implicate us all in the struggles described in this book—and challenge us to imagine theories, politics, and ways of living that do not reinscribe but instead interrupt migration controls and citizenship processes that systematically "cripple and rot certain worlds while over-investing others with wealth and hope."[67]

Acknowledgments

Even when there is only one author name on the cover, every book is a collaborative project. This book would not have been possible without generous support, practical assistance, and inspiration from many people. Warmest thanks to the migrants who shared aspects of their daily lives and perspectives with me. A huge thanks to the staff and volunteers at Derek Stewart and Company, the Vincentian Refugee Centre, and Residents against Racism, particularly Derek Stewart, Hilkka Becker, Sr. Breege Keenan, and Rosanna Flynn, each of whom was extraordinarily generous in answering questions and creating opportunities for me to learn how the system works.

Throughout the research in Ireland, Ronit Lentin unfailingly provided practical tips, contacts, and connections; reading recommendations; and a critical perspective. The book could never have been completed without her support and inspiration or the new ground that she has broken through her intellectual work and publications. Breda Gray generously arranged a visiting scholar opportunity at the Institute for the Study of Knowledge of Society at the University of Limerick, for which I am very grateful. Breda's encouragement, insightful feedback, and outstanding published works have greatly benefitted the book. Mary Lovett warmly and unfailingly offered contacts, access, insightful perspectives, and support; thanks a million, sis. Heather in Lucan, from whom I rented a room one summer, also offered invaluable perspectives, historical information, access to legal materials, and wonderful humor. Bob Pritchard and Breege Fahy shared their knowledge, offered friendship, and fed me deliciously.

I am very grateful to the migrants who shared their stories with me but whose names must remain anonymous. I am also very grateful for information received from the following people, some of whom now have different institutional affiliations: Nerilee Ceathu at the Immigrant Council of Ireland, Dug Cubie at the Irish Refugee Council, Dr. Michael

Forde SC, Noreen Giffney at University College Dublin, Fr. Bobby Gilmore at the Migrant Rights Centre Ireland, Rabia Golden at the Islamic Cultural Centre, Patricia Kennedy at University College Dublin, Mark Lacey at GLUE, John McDermott at the Refugee Information Service, Fr. Brian Moore at the Vincentian Refugee Centre, Sharon Murphy, Katherine O'Donnell at University College Dublin, Peter O'Mahoney at the Irish Refugee Council, Cathleen O'Neill at SAOL, Andy Storey at University College Dublin, David Walshe, Gillian Wylie at Trinity College Dublin, and Abel Ugba at the University of East London.

Once I began transforming the research into a book, Arlene Keizer offered continual encouragement as well as helpful feedback on several chapters. Karma Chávez provided unfailing encouragement and insightful feedback on chapter 5. Jane Juffer's generous suggestions greatly improved chapter 5. Jyoti Puri provided a very helpful reading of chapter 3. Adam Geary closely read and provided valuable comments on the Introduction. In the final stretch, chapter exchanges with Liz Kennedy kept me going, and her suggestions and questions improved the manuscript. Rob Buffington's extraordinary support included reading and commenting on an entire draft of the manuscript. Vicki Patraka also supported this work in numerous ways. Maja Halilovic-Pastuovic and Shannon Randall provided skilled research assistance, for which I am very grateful.

Members of the Sexualities, Subjectivities, and Political Cultures Research Cluster at the University of Arizona's Institute for LGBT Studies, particularly Laura Briggs, Cat Euler, Adam Geary, Laura Gutiérrez, Liz Kennedy, Miranda Joseph, Sallie Marston, Spike Peterson, Hai Ren, and Sandra Soto, provided feedback and helpful suggestions.

Scholarly audiences also provided helpful feedback and insightful questions about various chapters from the book. Warmest thanks to audiences at the Migrant Women Transforming Ireland Conference at Trinity College, Dublin, Ireland (2003); the Mellon Faculty Seminar on Race, Sexuality, and the Transnational, Macalester College, Minnesota (2004); the Workshop on the Cultural Logics and Political Economy of Transnational Families at the University of Washington (2004); the Reproductive Disruptions Conference at the University of Michigan (2005); the Feminist Dialogues in Social Justice: Forging Articulations across U.S.-Based Anti-Racist and Transnational Feminisms Conference at the University of Washington (2005); the Lineae Terrarum International Borders Conference at the University of Texas, El Paso (2006); the Global Society and Justice Workshop at the James E. Rogers College of Law, University of Arizona (2006); the History Department Brown Bag Series at the University of Arizona (2006); the Global Sexualities Research Collaborative at the University of Minnesota (2007); the Global Race/Ethnicity/Migration Seminar at the University of Minnesota (2008); the Department of Latin American and Latino Studies at DePaul University (April 2008); the University of Limerick (2008); the Lesbian, Bisexual, and Gay Studies program at Cornell University (2009); the symposium on Immigration, Race, Ethnicity, and the Law, organized by the Women, Gender, and Sexuality Studies Program at Harvard University (2009); the public lecture organized by the interdisciplinary reading group The Deconstruction and Reconstitution of the Intimate within the Context of Mobilities and Migration at the National University of Singapore (2009); Williams College, Massachusetts (2009); the Committee on Social Theory Lecture Series at the University of Kentucky (2010); the Theory Now Conference at Cornell University (2010); the Dislocating Queer: Race, Region, and Sexual Diasporas Graduate Student Conference at the University of Illinois at Urbana-Champaign (2011); the Citizenship and Its Others Symposium at the Centre on Migration Policy and Society, Oxford (2012); the Symposium on Bodies in Motion, States of Unrest: Sexuality, Citizenship, and the Freedom of Movement as a Human Right at the University of Connecticut (2012); and the Conference on Queer Places, Practices, and Lives at Ohio State University (2012).

Research funding was generously provided by the Wenner Gren Foundation for anthropological research; a social and behavioral sciences summer research grant development stipend from the University of Arizona; and the Scholar's Assistance Program Award from Bowling Green State University. The project also greatly benefitted from a scholar-in-residence fellowship at the Institute for the Study of Culture and Society at Bowling Green State University and a visiting scholar opportunity at the Institute for the Study of Knowledge of Society at the University of Limerick.

Warmest thanks to Richard Morrison, the editorial director at the University of Minnesota Press, and Roderick Ferguson, one of the editors of the Difference Incorporated series, for their generous readings, thoughtful suggestions, practical assistance, and unfailing encouragement. I am very grateful to the manuscript's external reviewers, Monisha

Das Gupta and Gillian Wylie, for their careful reading and very helpful suggestions that have improved the book. Thanks to Erin Warholm-Wohlenhaus for her effective editorial assistance.

Throughout the entire process, Hai Ren provided unfailing support including excellent feedback on grant applications; hands-on training in participant ethnography; thoughtful suggestions on chapter drafts; outstanding graphic assistance; an inspiring example of intellectual work; and love, practical assistance, and creative humor.

The book is dedicated to migrants in Ireland, especially those who feel that they cannot go on, yet do anyway—and to Hai.

Notes

A Note on Terminology

1. Martin Ruhs and Bridget Anderson, "Semi-compliance and Illegality in Migrant Labour Markets: An Analysis of Migrant Employers and the State in the U.K.," *Population, Place and Space* 16 (2010): 195–211.

2. Luin Goldring, Carolina Berinstein, and Judith K. Bernhard, "Institutionalizing Precarious Migratory Status in Canada," *Citizenship Studies* 13, no. 3 (June 2009): 255.

3. Bridget Anderson and Martin Ruhs, "Guest Editorial: Researching Illegality and Labour Migration," *Population, Space and Place* 16 (2010): 175.

4. Ibid., 176.

5. Underscoring the contradictions and inconsistencies associated with terms such as "migrant" and "immigrant," Breda Gray explains that "EU policy defines the migration of EU citizens within Europe as 'mobility' and of third country nationals as 'immigration,' so that the presence of EU nationals is legitimised and the presence of third country nationals is identified as requiring regulation and surveillance." See Breda Gray "Migrant Integration Policy: A Nationalist Fantasy of Management and Control?" *Translocations* 1, no. 1 (Autumn 2006): 134.

Introduction

1. The term "Celtic Tiger" deliberately registers a comparison with the four Asian Tiger economies of the time. The Irish government's strategy was an extension and reworking of an earlier economic strategy, launched in 1958, which embraced global investment as the path for Irish economic development.

2. Donal Hickey, "State Alert as Pregnant Asylum Seekers Aim for Ireland," *Irish Examiner*, December 4, 2001.

3. For example, Kate Goldade, "Babies and Belonging: Reproduction, Citizenship, and Undocumented Nicaraguan Labor Migrant Women in Costa Rica," *Medical Anthropology* 30, no. 5 (2011): 545–68; Carolyn F. Sargent and Stéphanie Larchanché-Kim, "Liminal Lives: Immigration Status, Gender, and

the Construction of Identity among Malian Migrants in Paris," *American Be-havioral Scientist* 50, no. 1 (2006): 9–26; Carolyn F. Sargent, "Lamenting the 'Winter' of French Fertility: Politics, Power, and Reproduction among Malian Migrants in Paris," *Curare* 29, no. 1 (2006): 71–80; Heide Castañeda, "Paternity for Sale: Anxieties over 'Demographic Theft' and Undocumented Migrant Re-production in Germany," *Medical Anthropology Quarterly* 22, no. 4 (December 2008): 340–59; Sharon La Franiere, "Mainland Chinese Flock to Hong Kong to Give Birth," *New York Times*, February 22, 2012; Sarah Willen, "Birthing 'Invis-ible' Children: State Power, NGO Activism, and Reproductive Health among 'Illegal Migrant' Workers in Tel Aviv, Israel," *Journal of Middle East Women's Studies* 1, no. 2 (2005): 55–88; J. M. Mancini and Graham Finlay, "Citizenship Matters: Lessons from the Irish Citizenship Referendum," *American Quarterly* 60, no. 3 (2008): 578 and 595–96n18; and Leo Chavez, "Latina Sexuality, Re-production and Fertility as Threats to the Nation" and "Latina Fertility and Reproduction Reconsidered," in his *The Latino Threat: Constructing Immi-grants, Citizens, and the Nation* (Stanford, Calif.: Stanford University Press, 2008), 70–110.

4. Siobhan Somerville, "Queer," in *Keywords in American Cultural Studies*, ed. Bruce Burgett and Glenn Hendler (New York: New York University Press, 2007), 189. Michael Warner is popularly credited with coining the concept of heteronormativity. Michael Warner, ed., "Introduction," in *Fear of a Queer Plan-et: Queer Politics and Social Theory* (Minneapolis: University of Minnesota Press, 1993), vii–xxxi.

5. Heteronormativity is not the same as heterosexuality (although the two are closely related), since various heterosexualities—for example, among com-munities of color, in working-class communities, and across racial lines—are frequently stigmatized and policed. See Somerville, "Queer."

6. M. Jacqui Alexander, "Erotic Autonomy as a Politics of Decolonization: An Anatomy of Feminist and State Practices in the Bahamas Tourist Econo-my," in *Feminist Genealogies, Colonial Legacies, Democratic Futures*, ed. M. Jac-qui Alexander and Chandra Talpade Mohanty, 63–100 (New York: Routledge, 1997); and Warner, "Introduction."

7. Somerville, "Queer," 190. Importantly, Somerville clarifies that this does not mean "destroying or abandoning identity categories altogether" (ibid.). In-stead, focusing on the socially constructed nature of identities, especially as a result of regimes of power, violence, normalization, and oppression, Somerville suggests that queer theory invites us to seek interconnections and possibilities for coalition-building among social justice struggles that are often conceived as distinct (ibid.).

8. Michel Foucault, *Discipline and Punish: The Birth of the Prison*, trans. Alan Sheridan (New York: Vintage, 1979), 146, 149, 180, 181, 190.

9. Gayle Rubin, "Thinking Sex: Notes for a Radical Theory of the Politics of Sexuality," in *The Lesbian and Gay Studies Reader*, ed. Henry Abelove, Michèle Aina Barale, and David M. Halperin (New York: Routledge, 1993), 11.

10. Ibid., 11–12.

11. Somerville elaborates: "Heteronormativity derives much of its power from the ways in which it (often silently) shores up as well as depends on naturalized categories of racial difference." Somerville, "Queer," 190.

12. Cathy Cohen, "Punks, Bulldaggers and Welfare Queens: The Radical Potential of Queer Politics?" in *Black Queer Studies: A Critical Anthology*, ed. E. Patrick Johnson and Mae G. Henderson (Durham, N.C.: Duke University Press, 2005), 38.

13. Ibid., 43.

14. See also María do Mar Castro Varela, Nikita Dhawan, and Antke Engel, eds., *Hegemony and Heteronormativity: Revisiting the Political in Queer Politics* (Surrey, U.K.: Ashgate, 2011).

15. For example, see Ann Laura Stoler, *Carnal Knowledge and Imperial Power: Race and the Intimate in Colonial Rule* (Berkeley: University of California Press, 2002); and Elizabeth Povinelli, *The Empire of Love: Toward a Theory of Intimacy, Genealogy, and Carnality* (Durham, N.C.: Duke University Press, 2006).

16. Cindy Patton, "Stealth Bombers of Desire: The Globalization of 'Alterity' in Emerging Democracies," in *Queer Globalizations: Citizenship and the Afterlife of Colonialism*, ed. Arnaldo Cruz Malavé and Martin F. Manalansan IV (New York: New York University Press, 2002), 195.

17. Alice Miller, "Gay Enough: Some Tensions in Seeking the Grant of Asylum and Protecting Global Sexual Diversity," in *Passing Lines: Sexuality and Immigration*, ed. Brad Epps, Keja Valens, and Bill Johnson Gonzalez, 137–87 (Cambridge, Mass.: Harvard University Press, 2005).

18. For example, M. Jacqui Alexander, *Pedagogies of Crossing: Meditations on Feminism, Sexual Politics, Memory, and the Sacred* (Durham, N.C.: Duke University Press, 2006); Lionel Cantú Jr., *The Sexuality of Migration: Border Crossings and Mexican Immigrant Men*, ed. Nancy A. Naples and Salvador Vidal-Ortiz (New York: New York University Press, 2009); Carlos Ulises Decena, *Tacit Subjects: Belonging and Same-Sex Desire among Dominican Immigrant Men* (Durham, N.C.: Duke University Press, 2011); "Queer/Migration," special issue, *GLQ* 14, nos. 2–3 (2008); "Homoerotic, Lesbian, and Gay Ethnic and Immigrant Histories," special issue, *Journal of American Ethnic History* 29, no. 4 (summer 2010); Eithne Luibhéid, *Entry Denied: Controlling Sexuality at the Border* (Minneapolis: University of Minnesota Press, 2002); Eithne Luibhéid and Lionel Cantú Jr., eds., *Queer Migrations: Sexuality, U.S. Citizenship, and Border Crossings* (Minneapolis: University of Minnesota Press, 2005); Lawrence La Fountain-Stokes, *Queer Ricans: Cultures and Sexualities in the Diaspora*

(Minneapolis: University of Minnesota Press, 2009); Martin F. Manalansan IV, *Global Divas: Filipino Gay Men in the Diaspora* (Durham, N.C.: Duke University Press, 2003); and Erica Rand, *The Ellis Island Snow Globe* (Durham, N.C.: Duke University Press, 2005).

19. Manalansan, *Global Divas.*

20. See Eithne Luibhéid, "Heteronormativity and Immigration Scholarship: A Call for Change," *GLQ* 10, no. 2 (2004): 227–35.

21. Valsamis Mitsilegas, Jörg Monar, and Wyn Rees, *The European Union and Internal Security* (Basingstoke, U.K.: Palgrave Macmillan, 2003), 42–43, 48.

22. Foregrounding the fact that law, politics, and society construct illegal status is not intended to erase migrants' agency and subjectivity, including as they maneuver and strategize possibilities for themselves in relation to this status.

23. The growing scholarly interest in irregular or undocumented migration is reflected by the proliferation of journal special issues on the topic, including *International Migration* 45, no. 3 (2007); *Social Science Information* 47, no. 4 (2008); *Ethics and International Affairs* 22, no. 2 (2008); *Population, Space, and Place* 16 (2010); *European Journal of Migration and Law* 12, no. 2 (2010); *Ethnic and Racial Studies* 34, no. 8 (August 2011); and *International Migration* 49, no. 5 (2011). Alice Bloch and Milena Chimienti, "Irregular Migration in a Globalizing World," *Ethnic and Racial Studies* 34, no. 8 (August 2011): 1271–85, provides an overview of key areas of research.

24. Saskia Sassen, "Why Migration?" *NACLA Report on the Americas* 26, no. 1 (July 1992): 14–19; see also Stephen Castles and Mark J. Miller, *The Age of Migration: International Population Movements in the Modern World,* 4th ed. (Basingstoke, U.K.: Palgrave Macmillan, 2009).

25. Douglas Massey, Joaquin Arango, Graeme Hugo, Ali Kouaouci, Adela Pellegrino, and J. Edward Taylor, *Worlds in Motion: Understanding International Migration at the End of the Millennium* (Oxford: Clarendon Press, 1998), 45–46.

26. Illegal status significantly exacerbates migrants' vulnerability.

27. Catherine Dauvergne, *Making People Illegal: What Globalization Means for Migration and Law* (Cambridge: Cambridge University Press, 2008), 124, 123.

28. Goldring, Berinstein, and Bernhard, "Institutionalizing Precarious Migratory Status," 245.

29. Ironically, as scholars have documented, neoliberalizing changes that drive global migration at present have also given rise to new restrictions on admission, which results in expanded illegalization. For example, see Douglas S. Massey, Jorge Durand, and Nolan J. Malone, *Beyond Smoke and Mirrors: Mexican Immigration in an Era of Economic Integration* (New York: Russell Sage Foundation, 2002).

30. Bloch and Chimienti, "Irregular Migration in a Globalizing World," 1273.

31. Castles and Miller, *Age of Migration*, 34.

32. Matthew Coleman, "Immigration Geopolitics beyond the Mexico-U.S. Border," *Antipode* 38 (2007): 64, 70.

33. Migrants are also vulnerable to individuals and vigilantes who take it upon themselves to police everyday life based on their perceptions about who is and is not a citizen.

34. Migrant Rights Centre Ireland, *Life in the Shadows. An Exploration of Irregular Migration in Ireland* (Dublin: MRCI, December 2007), 38.

35. Crosscare, *Invisible Pathways: A Critique of the Irish Immigration System and How It Can Contribute to People Becoming Undocumented* (Dublin: Crosscare, 2009), 7.

36. Note that only certain forms of legal presence are intended to lead to the possibility of citizenship. Those on temporary tourist visas, for example, are legally present but rarely on track for eventual citizenship. Also note that in Ireland migrants have no automatic right to naturalize; rather, naturalization occurs at the discretion of the Minster for Justice when migrants demonstrate they have met all the necessary requirements.

37. Mae Ngai, *Impossible Subjects: Illegal Aliens and the Making of Modern America* (Princeton, N.J.: Princeton University Press, 2004), 6.

38. Franck Düvell, "Irregular Migration: A Global, Historical and Economic Perspective," in *Illegal Immigration in Europe Beyond Control?*, ed. Franck Düvell (Basingstoke, U.K.: Palgrave McMillan, 2006), 26. See also Godfried Engberse and Joanne Van Der Leun, "The Social Construction of Illegality and Criminality," *European Journal on Criminal Policy and Research* 9, no. 1 (2001): 51–70.

39. This process was further expanded as Europeanization was institutionalized under the Maastricht, Amsterdam, Nice, and Lisbon Treaties.

40. Hélène Pellerin, "Migration and Border Controls in the EU: Economic and Security Factors," in *Soft or Hard Borders? Managing the Divide in an Enlarged Europe*, ed. Joan DeBardeleben (Aldershot, U.K.: Ashgate, 2005), 108.

41. As Bloch and Chimienti describe, "the expansion of the EU means that people from traditional migrant-sending countries from the south and east of Europe are now able to move freely within the EU zone and, if previously irregular, have been able to regularize their situation," while at the same time "the majority of irregular migrants today now come from non-European countries." See Bloch and Chimienti, "Irregular Migration in a Globalizing World," 1275.

42. Franck Düvell, "Reframing the Irregular Migration Dilemma," in *Illegal Immigration in Europe Beyond Control?*, ed. Franck Düvell (Basingstoke, U.K.: Palgrave McMillan, 2006), 239. See also Anna Triandafyllidou, "Introduction,"

in *Irregular Migration in Europe: Myths and Realities,* ed. Anna Triandafyllidou, 9–13 (Farnham, U.K.: Ashgate, 2010).

43. Düvell, "Irregular Migration," 25.

44. Virginie Guiraudon, and Christian Joppke, "Controlling a New Migration World," in *Controlling a New Migration World,* ed. Virginie Guiraudon and Christian Joppke, 12–14 (London: Routledge, 2001).

45. Düvell, "Irregular Migration," 28.

46. For an overview of EU policies on irregular migration, see Anna Triandafyllidou and Maria Iles, "EU Irregular Migration Policies" in *Irregular Migration in the EU: Myths and Realities,* ed. Anna Triandafyllidou, 24–40 (Farnham, U.K.: Ashgate, 2010).

47. Bloch and Chimienti, "Irregular Migration in a Globalizing World," 1273.

48. Nicholas De Genova, "Migrant 'Illegality' and Deportability in Everyday Life," *Annual Review of Anthropology* 31 (2002): 419–47; Joseph Nevins, *Operation Gatekeeper: The Rise of the 'Illegal Alien' and the Making of the U.S.-Mexico Boundary* (New York: Routledge, 2002); and Ngai, *Impossible Subjects.*

49. I began developing this argument in Luibhéid, "Sexuality, Migration, and the Shifting Line between Legal and Illegal Status," *GLQ* 14, nos. 2–3 (April 2008): 289–316.

50. Peadar Kirby, Luke Gibbons, and Michael Cronin, "Introduction: The Reinvention of Ireland: A Critical Perspective," in *Reinventing Ireland: Culture, Society and the Global Economy,* ed. Peadar Kirby, Luke Gibbons, and Michael Cronin (London: Pluto Press, 2002), 13.

51. Martin Ruhs, "Ireland: From Rapid Immigration to Recession," Migration Information Source, September 2009, www.migrationinformation.org /Feature/display.cfm?ID=740.

52. Antje Roeder, "Polish Migration to Ireland: A Literature Review," 3, accessed April 17, 2012, www.tcd.ie/sociology/assets/docs/Polish%20migration %20to%20Ireland%20-%20A%20literature%20review.pdf.

53. Nicola Yeates, "Ireland's Contributions to the Global Health Care Crisis," in *Globalization, Migration and Social Transformation. Ireland in Europe and the World,* ed. Bryan Fanning and Ronaldo Munck, 35–50 (Surrey, U.K.: Ashgate, 2011); see especially 41–45.

54. Enterprise Ireland, *International Students in Higher Education in Ireland 2009/2010* (Dublin: Enterprise Ireland, May 2010).

55. Statistics from the Office of the Refugee Applications Commissioner show that those from Nigeria consistently ranked as the number one applicant group for asylum in Ireland, with Romanians generally ranking second, until 2007, when they became ineligible. Between 2007–10 the other consistently large applicant groups came from Pakistan, China, and the Democratic Republic of Congo. See www.orac.ie/pages/Stats/statistics.htm, accessed April 21, 2012.

56. Ruhs, "Ireland."

57. The EU/EEA is itself a tiered and hierarchical structure whose disparities are partly reflected by the fact that official Irish statistics continue to differentiate between the original EU fifteen and the subsequent EU twelve members.

58. Central Statistics Office, *Census 2006: Non-Nationals Living in Ireland* (Dublin: Central Statistics Office, 2008), 8.

59. Ibid., 5.

60. Asylum seekers are migrants who are seeking protection from persecution. They arrive without permission and in unpredictable numbers. But they cannot just be turned away as "illegals" because by requesting asylum they invoke international human rights standards that nation-states cannot afford to openly ignore. Instead, nation-states must evaluate on a case-by-case basis whether asylum seekers' experiences match up to the international definition for refugees.

61. Peter O'Mahoney, "Supporting Asylum Seekers," in *Sanctuary in Ireland,* ed. Ursula Fraser and Colin Harvey (Dublin: Institute for Public Administration, 2003), 129. Information about the numbers of migrants granted permission to remain based on having an Irish child has been difficult to ascertain. Liam Coakley and Claire Healy offer what seems to be a reliable summary: "From 1996 until early January 2003, a total of 10,584 people were granted residency, with few problems, on the basis of their Irish children" (23). This number included not just asylum seekers but also other categories of migrant, including workers and students. Nearly 11,500 applications for residency based on a child were pending in February 2003 when the government announced that it would no longer accept such applications and froze the processing of the pending applications (ibid., 23). Under the IBC/05 scheme announced in January 2005, "close to 17,000 people were granted permission to remain in Ireland by the Minister for Justice" based on their parentage of an Irish child (ibid., 21). See Coakley and Healy, *Looking Forward, Looking Back. Experiences of Irish Citizen Children Families* (Dublin: Integrating Ireland, 2007).

62. Heaven Crawley suggests that the "issue of asylum dominates political and public debates in many countries of the world and both directly and indirectly drives the direction and content of policies relating to all other international migration flows." See Crawley, "Forced Migration and the Politics of Asylum: The Missing Pieces of the International Migration Puzzle?" *International Migration* 44, no. 1 (2006), 23. Moreover, Crawley suggests the need to understand "economic migrant" and "asylum seeker" as relational terms, and to grasp how negative constructions of asylum seekers shape the constructions of economic migrants.

63. I mean "managing" in a Foucauldian sense, which entails developing a rationale for and defining objectives to be accomplished or avoided through migration control.

64. See Liisa Malkki, "Refugees and Exile: From 'Refugee Studies' to the National Order of Things," *Annual Review of Anthropology* 24 (1995): 495–523; and Nevzat Soguk, *States and Strangers: Refugees and the Displacements of Statecraft* (Minneapolis: University of Minnesota Press, 1999).

65. Malkki, "Refugees and Exile," 496.

66. Ashkaan Rahimi, "The Evolution of EU Asylum Policy," Center for European Integration Studies, Bonn, Germany, Discussion Paper C 142 (2005), 5.

67. For example, the implementation of a visa system combined with carrier sanctions seemed "designed . . . to prevent asylum seekers from getting to the territory of Member States lawfully so they can apply for asylum." Elspeth Guild, "The Legal Framework: Who Is Entitled to Move?" in *Controlling Frontiers: Free Movement Into and Within Europe,* ed. Didier Bigo and Elspeth Guild (Aldershot, U.K.: Ashgate, 2005), 35.

68. See Alice Bloch and Liza Schuster, "At the Extremes of Exclusion: Deportation, Detention, and Dispersal," *Ethnic and Racial Studies* 28, no. 3 (May 2005): 492; more generally, see Liza Schuster, "Asylum and the Lessons of History," *Race and Class* 44, no. 2 (2002): 40–56.

69. Franck Düvell, "Introduction: The Pathways In and Out of Irregular Migration in the EU: A Comparative Analysis," *European Journal of Migration and Law* 13, no. 3 (2011), 245–46.

70. As Düvell explains, "During the 1990s, the concept of 'illegal' or 'irregular' immigration has been frequently confused with refugees and asylum seekers. . . . The reasons behind such confusions are multiple. Refugees do not usually have a visa when they appear at the point of entry, and because they have no visa they cannot enter legally and therefore often find access through illegal means. Moreover, because states have more or less closed their front doors, this has left only the asylum path open to would-be migrants. . . . Also, undocumented immigrants, when they have been apprehended, have often applied for asylum in order to prevent immediate deportation. Finally, post–Cold War refugees and asylum seekers have generally been perceived as a burden and are not much desired in Europe, which has prompted a general scapegoating and stereotyping" (Düvell, "Irregular Migration," 28–29).

71. Siobhan Mullally, "Too Fast to be Safe? Regular/Irregular Asylum Determination Procedures," in *Sanctuary in Ireland: Perspectives on Asylum Law and Policy,* ed. Ursula Fraser and Colin Harvey (Dublin: Institute of Public Administration 2003), 146.

72. Ronit Lentin and Robbie McVeigh, *After Optimism? Ireland, Racism and Globalisation* (Dublin: Metro Eireann Publications, 2006), 45.

73. For example, Irish Refugee Council, *Asylum in Ireland: A Report on the Fairness and Sustainability of Asylum Determinations in the First Instance* (Dublin: Irish Refugee Council, 2000).

74. For example, Siobhán Kilfeather, "Sexual Discourse in English before the Act of Union: Prescription and Dissent, 1685–1801," in *The Field Day Anthology of Irish Writing*, vol. 4, *Irish Women's Writing and Traditions*, ed. Angela Bourke, Mairín Ní Dhonneadha, Siobhán Kilfeather, Maria Luddy, Margaret MacCurtain, Geraldine Meaney, Mary O'Dowd, and Clair Wills, 761–65 (Cork: Cork University Press in association with Field Day, 2002).

75. Clair Wills, "Women, Domesticity and the Family: Recent Feminist Work in Irish Cultural Studies," *Cultural Studies* 15, no. 1 (2001): 41.

76. Geraldine Meaney, "Sex and Nation: Women in Irish Culture and Politics," in *Irish Women's Studies Reader*, ed. Ailbhe Smyth (Dublin: Attic Press, 1993), 233. Put differently, since the founding of the postcolonial Irish state in the 1920s, "the overwhelming push to define Ireland as 'not-English' led to a search for distinguishing marks of identity," of which women's reproductive sexuality became key. Siobhán Mullally, "Debating Reproductive Rights in Ireland," *Human Rights Quarterly* 27, no. 1 (2005): 82.

77. Bunreacht na hÉireann, Constitution of Ireland (Dublin: Stationery Office, 1937), Article 41.1.1.

78. A short overview of Irish citizenship law can be found in Bernard Ryan, "The Celtic Cubs: The Controversy over Birthright Citizenship in Ireland," *European Journal of Migration and Law* 6 (2004): 173–93.

79. Shalini Sinha, "The Right to Irishness: Implications of Ethnicity, Nation and State towards a Truly Multi-Cultural Ireland," in *The Expanding Nation: Towards a Multi-Ethnic Ireland*, ed. Ronit Lentin (Dublin: Trinity College Dublin, 1998), 24; see also Ronit Lentin, "Racialising (Our) Dark Rosaleen: Feminism, Citizenship, Racism, Anti-Semitism," in *Women's Studies Review* 6 (1999): 1–17.

80. For example, see Laury Oaks, "Irishness, Eurocitizens and Reproductive Rights," in *Reproducing Reproduction*, ed. Sarah Franklin and Helena Ragoné, 132–55 (Philadelphia: University of Pennsylvania Press, 1997). Regrettably, the analysis of Irish heterosexuality has often focused less on heteronormativity as an oppressive system than on the ways that *Irish* heteronormativity has varied from its metropolitan counterparts (and on evaluating the extent to which it is converging with imagined norms of "liberated" heterosexuality in metropolitan cores).

81. Eithne Luibhéid, "Childbearing against the State? Asylum Seeker Women in the Irish Republic," *Women's Studies International Forum* 27, no. 4 (2004): 335–50; and Anwen Tormey, "'Everyone with Eyes Can See the Problem': Moral Citizens and the Space of Irish Nationhood," *International Migration* 45, no. 3 (2007): 69–98.

82. Drazen Nozinic, "One Refugee Experience in Ireland," in *Racism and Anti-Racism in Ireland*, ed. Ronit Lentin and Robbie McVeigh (Belfast: Beyond the Pale, 2002), 82.

83. Eithne Luibhéid, "Rescuing National Sovereignty through Asylum Seekers' Sexualities," talk delivered at Macalester College, St. Paul, Minnesota, May 22, 2004.

84. Claims of illegality therefore work to justify changes that will, in the future, ensure that more migrants *become* illegal. Thus, they are anticipatory.

85. The grounds for refusal were that they had previously sought and been refused asylum in the United Kingdom. Under Dublin Convention rules, asylum seekers were not permitted to seek asylum in another EU country after being refused in an initial EU jurisdiction.

86. *L. and O. v. Minister for Justice, Equality and Law Reform* [2003] IESC 1 (January 23, 2003).

87. Alexander, "Erotic Autonomy," 65.

88. Ngai, *Impossible Subjects*, 6.

89. For a discussion of how individuals may take up certain legal immigration statuses for their own ends, see, for example, Bridget Anderson, "What's in a Name? Immigration Control and Subjectivities: The Case of Au Pair and Domestic Worker Visa Holders in the UK," *Subjectivity* 29, no. 1 (2009): 407–24.

90. Yen Le Espiritu explains, "Differential inclusion [is] a process whereby a group of people is deemed integral to the nation's economy, culture, identity, and power—but integral only or precisely because of their designated subordinate standing." Yen Le Espiritu, *Home Bound: Filipino American Lives across Cultures, Communities, and Countries* (Berkeley: University of California Press, 2003), 47. Through one group's subordination, other groups achieve dominant status that benefits them materially and symbolically yet is normalized.

91. One of the important differences between asylum seekers and refugees is that the latter, under the law, have already had their claims recognized and are therefore entitled to certain rights and protections. Asylum seekers, by contrast, are seeking recognition that they constitute "refugees" under circumstances where the burden of proof is stacked against them. Many important works overlook this critical distinction.

92. These practices mirrored trends evident throughout the European Union.

93. Moreover, contrary to state claims, controls do not prevent migration but instead convert humans into a bureaucratic category called "migrants" whose lesser rights and entitlements are sanctioned by law while contributing to inequitable forms of nation-making, statecraft, citizenship making, capital accumulation, and human differentiation. Nandita Sharma, *Home Economics: Nationalism and the Making of "Migrant Workers" in Canada* (Toronto: University of Toronto Press, 2006), 139–67.

94. Geraldine Pratt, *Families Apart: Migrant Mothers and the Conflicts of Labor and Love* (Minneapolis: University of Minnesota Press, 2012), 5–7.

95. Leanne Weber and Sharon Pickering, *Globalization and Borders: Death at the Global Frontier* (Basingstoke, U.K.: Palgrave Macmillan 2011), 6, 198.

96. A manuscript reviewer inquired why my ethnography seemed to be "on the side of the migrants" and suggested that there was much to learn from engaging in ethnography of state institutions that address migration and migrants. I completely agree that ethnographies of these institutions represent an important future research direction. For example, see Alison Mountz, *Seeing Asylum: Human Smuggling and Bureaucracy at the Border* (Minneapolis: University of Minnesota Press, 2010). However, when working with migrants, I was never not dealing with the state; on the contrary, most of my time was spent helping migrants to understand and negotiate the state systems that were in place, becoming formed, or being transformed.

97. Stuart Hall, "Cultural Identity and Diaspora," in *Identity: Community, Culture, Difference,* ed. Jonathan Rutherford (London: Lawrence and Wishart, 1990), 229.

98. Ibid., 225.

99. For statistics in Irish return migration from 1996 to 2007, see Philip J. O'Connell and Corona Joyce, "International Migration in Ireland 2009," ESRI Working Paper 339 (March 2010), 12, accessed August 26, 2011, www.esri.ie /UserFiles/publications/WP339.pdf.

100. Walter P. Jacob, "Diversity Visas: Muddled Thinking and Pork Barrel Politics," *Georgetown Immigration Law Journal* 6, no. 2 (1992): 297–344.

101. For example, Ronit Lentin, "Illegal in Ireland, Irish Illegals: Diaspora Nation as Racial State," *Irish Political Studies* 22, no. 4 (December 2007): 433–53.

102. Breda Gray, "Remembering a 'Multicultural' Future through a History of Emigration: Towards a Feminist Politics of Solidarity across Difference," *Women's Studies International Forum* 27, no. 4 (2004): 418.

103. Ibid., 422.

104. Ibid., 423.

1. Shifting Boundaries through Discourses of Childbearing

1. See Anne McClintock, *Imperial Leather: Race, Gender and Sexuality in the Colonial Context* (New York: Routledge, 1994); and Floya Anthias and Nira Yuval-Davis, *Racialized Boundaries: Race, Nation, Gender, Colour, and Class and the Anti-Racist Struggle* (New York: Routledge, 1993).

2. Scholarship and popular representations about Baartman's life are extensive. Recent works include Deborah Willis, ed., *Black Venus 2010: They Called Her "Hottentot"* (Philadelphia: Temple University Press, 2010); and

Natasha Gordon-Chipembere, ed., *Representation and Black Women: The Legacy of Sarah Baartman* (Basingstoke, U.K.: Palgrave Macmillan, 2011).

3. Robyn Wiegman, *American Anatomies: Theorizing Race and Gender* (Durham, N.C.: Duke University Press, 1995), 58.

4. Bill Rolston and Michael Shannon, *Encounters: How Racism Came to Ireland* (Belfast: Beyond the Pale Publications, 2002), 4. According to these authors, Baartmann was exhibited in Limerick in 1812 where she was "visited by very few" (70).

5. L. P. Curtis, *Apes and Angels: The Irishman in Victorian Caricature* (Washington, D.C.: Smithsonian Institution Press, 1971), 19–20.

6. Ibid.

7. As many scholars have noted, the Celtic/Saxon dichotomy positioned Celts as a "feminized race." However, even within "feminized races," gender distinctions remained salient. My argument concerns the extent to which theories and studies of bodies gendered as female shaped the articulation of "Celtic" racial identity.

8. Curtis, *Apes and Angels*, 16.

9. Bronwyn Walter, *Outsiders Inside: Whiteness, Place, and Irish Women* (London: Routledge, 2001), 91.

10. Ann Stoler suggests that all "national" sexualities are formed through transnational routes; in the Irish case, I argue, migration is one of the key mechanisms for the transnational formation of what is frequently named "Irish" sexuality. See Stoler, *Carnal Knowledge and Imperial Power*.

11. F. S. L. Lyons, *Ireland since the Famine* (London: Weidenfeld and Nicolson, 1971), 36.

12. Tom Inlis, *Lessons in Irish Sexuality* (Dublin: University College Dublin Press, 1998), 33. For more extended discussion, see Inglis, *Moral Monopoly: The Rise and Fall of the Catholic Church in Modern Ireland* (London: Gill and Macmillan, 1987).

13. Inglis, *Lessons in Irish Sexuality*, 34.

14. Joseph J. Lee, *Ireland, 1912–1985: Politics and Society* (Cambridge: Cambridge University Press, 1995), 71.

15. Jim MacLaughlin, "Emigration and the Construction of Nationalist Hegemony in Ireland: The Historical Background to 'New Wave' Irish Emigration," in *Location and Dislocation in Contemporary Irish Society: Emigration and Irish Identities*, ed. Jim MacLaughlin (Cork: Cork University Press, 1997), 13.

16. Wills, "Women, Domesticity, and the Family," 46.

17. Ibid.

18. All of these processes entailed not simply handing over control of sexuality to the Catholic Church; rather, as James M. Smith describes, after independence, the state worked in tandem with the Catholic Church to "close off inter-

nal challenges and contradictions even as they represented society as pure and untainted by external corruption" (3). Thus, the state was "an active agent and willing partner" (47) in the church's regulation of sexuality. See James M. Smith, *Ireland's Magdalene Laundries and the Nation's Architecture of Containment* (Notre Dame, Ind.: University of Notre Dame Press, 2007).

19. The term "settled" refers to non-Traveller people who are privileged as a result of their settled, nonnomadic status. Travellers are a distinct group that has experienced institutionalized racism, discrimination, and exclusion in Ireland. Their origins are disputed. Some claim that they are "descendants of peasants forced into landlessness and mobility by the evictions and famines suffered by the Irish" during British rule while others trace their origins to a much earlier period in Irish history (Helleiner, 30). In either case, accounts of their origins "have focused not on 'where' they're from," since they're presumed to be an indigenous Irish minority, but on "'when' and 'why' they emerged as a distinct group within Ireland" (ibid.). Some scholars suggest that anti-Traveller racism is integrally connected to their nomadic way of living, which is seen as antithetical and threatening to the sedentarist requirements of capitalisms and nationalisms grounded in liberal models of property ownership (e.g., McVeigh, 41–44). Significantly, even while neoliberal globalization processes foster particular forms of mobility as a mode of self-cultivation and a route to economic advancement, the mobility associated with Travellers (and unauthorized migrants and certain other mobile populations) remains a basis for institutionalized discrimination. Historically, Travellers have occupied distinct niches in the Irish economy, although these have been radically affected by recent globalization, and speak distinct languages (Shelta and Cant) as well as English. The policies of the Irish state have "wavered between [forced] assimilation, . . . expulsion (the elimination of bodies from the territory), and lastly a recognition of cultural difference" (Garner, 145). Yet recognition of cultural difference has done little to alter the state's ultimately assimilationist stance (Fanning, 152), nor to substantively address institutionalized discrimination against Travellers in every domain of social life. Moreover, although the Irish state recognizes them as a social group, it refuses to recognize them as an ethnic group. John O'Connell summarizes, "Travellers fare poorly on every indicator used to measure disadvantage: unemployment, poverty, social exclusion, health status, infant mortality, life expectancy, illiteracy, education and training levels, access to decision making and political representation, gender equality, access to credit, accommodation and living conditions" (49). For further information, see Bryan Fanning, *Racism and Social Change in the Republic of Ireland* (Manchester, U.K.: Manchester University Press, 2002); Steve Garner, *Racism in the Irish Experience* (London: Pluto Press, 2004); Jane Helleiner, *Irish Travellers: Racism and the Politics of Culture* (Toronto: University of Toronto Press, 2000);

Jim MacLaughlin, *Travellers and Ireland: Whose Country? Whose History?* (Cork: Cork University Press, 1995); Robbie McVeigh, "The Specificity of Irish Racism," *Race and Class* 33, no. 4 (1992): 31–45; John O'Connell, "Travellers in Ireland: An Examination of Discrimination and Racism," in *Racism and Anti-Racism in Ireland,* ed. Ronit Lentin and Robbie McVeigh (Belfast: Beyond the Pale Publications, 2002), 49–62; and materials at the Pavee Point Travellers' Centre in Dublin (http://paveepoint.ie/). "White" is a term that is generally applied to people with "light"-colored skin and "European" features. Yet whiteness is by no means reducible to these phenotypical characteristics; in the Irish Republic, Travellers generally share these characteristics but remain subjected to racism and are not seen as representative of the nation. See Sinéad Ní Shúinéar, "Othering the Irish (Travellers)," in Lentin and McVeigh, *Racism and Anti-Racism in Ireland,* 177–92.

20. Such analysis acknowledges the fact that even "majority" white Irish women have been racialized—but this does not mean that they cannot, in turn, act in racist ways toward others or seek to secure a more advantageous position within racial hierarchies that structure society. See Robbie McVeigh and Ronit Lentin, "Situated Racisms: A Theoretical Introduction," in Lentin and McVeigh, *Racism and Anti-Racism in Ireland,* 17–30.

21. Ibid.

22. According to Steve Garner, "the existence of an Irish 'race' is still a core belief in contemporary Ireland." Garner, *Racism in the Irish Experience,* 152. On historical notions of Irishness as racial, see not only scholarship on the Celtic/Saxon dichotomy but also works such as Fanning, *Racism and Social Change in the Republic of Ireland;* Garner, *Racism in the Irish Experience;* Lentin and McVeigh, *Racism and Anti-Racism in Ireland;* Catherine Nash, *Of Irish Descent: Origin Stories, Genealogy, and the Politics of Belonging* (Syracuse, N.Y.: Syracuse University Press, 2008); and Peter O'Neill and David Lloyd, eds., *The Black and Green Atlantic: Cross-Currents of the African and Irish Diasporas* (Basingstoke, U.K.: Palgrave and Macmillan, 2009).

23. The homogeneity of the South at the time of independence remains debated. On one hand, Lee suggests that the process through which the island was partitioned resulted in an overwhelmingly homogenous South, peopled mainly by "white," settled Catholics. Moreover, in his view, the partition process exported racial and religious conflict to the North. Lee, *Ireland 1912–1985,* 77. Other scholars, however, stress that while the South at the time of independence was significantly homogenous, there were nonetheless small populations of Travellers, Jews, Protestants, and other nonmajority people within the territory. Moreover, as Rolston and Shannon (2002) and Lentin and McVeigh (2002) argue, Irish people had a long history of interactions with diverse peoples—through invasions of Ireland, Irish participation in British colonial

processes, and emigration. Lentin and McVeigh thus write, "Ireland was never the monoculture it told itself it was." Lentin and McVeigh, *Racism and Anti-Racism in Ireland,* 21. See also Rolston and Shannon, *Encounters.*

24. Moreover, this perpetuates the idea that that "race" is a substance that is significantly transmitted through childbearing (and enhanced or further realized through particular child-rearing practices).

25. Helleiner, *Irish Travellers,* 65.

26. Ibid. Moreover, Traveller men were constructed as threatening the domestic ideal that relegated mainstream Irish women to "the home" (ibid., 67–68).

27. As we know, racialization dynamics are not stable; rather, groups' positions within racial hierarchies and the grounds for their racialization regularly shift. The arrival of pregnant asylum seekers would provide a moment when racialization dynamics associated with childbearing would shift again.

28. Pauric Travers, " 'There Was Nothing for Me There': Irish Female Emigration 1922–71," in *Irish Women and Irish Migration,* ed. Patrick O'Sullivan (London: Leicester University Press, 1995), 155.

29. Ibid., 154.

30. According to Travers, this failure "illustrates the way in which key elements of the rural economy outweighed government policy or the desire to end emigration" (ibid., 156).

31. Ibid., 154. See also John O'Brien, ed., *The Vanishing Irish: The Enigma of the Modern World* (New York: McGraw Hill, 1953).

32. Finola Kennedy, *Cottage to Creche: Family Change in Ireland* (Dublin: Institute of Public Administration, 2001), 29.

33. Fanning, *Racism and Social Change,* 89.

34. Ibid., 90, 91.

35. Ibid., 91. A handful of Jews fleeing the Nazis and European anti-Semitism were admitted to Ireland before World War II. "However, requests that Ireland take larger numbers of Jewish refugees during and after the war were refused, mainly on the pretext that they would be an undue burden on a weak Irish economy." O'Mahony, "Supporting Asylum Seekers," 128. Anti-Semitism, however, was also a significant factor shaping their refusal; Charles Bewley, a key Berlin-based Irish diplomat, "pursued a de facto policy of minimizing the number of Jewish refugees allowed into Ireland, basing his argument on their putative cultural inability to assimilate and the threat posed by Jewish values for Catholic Ireland." Garner, *Racism in the Irish Experience,* 143. Consequently, "Ireland admitted approximately sixty adults between 1939 and 1945, followed by 147 Jewish war orphans in 1947, all of whom were relocated abroad within twelve months." O'Mahony, "Supporting Asylum Seekers," 128. After admitting small numbers of Hungarians, Ireland accepted small numbers of additional refugee cohorts: 120 Chileans in 1973; 212 (eventually 582) Vietnamese refugees in 1979;

25 Iranian Baha'is in 1985; approximately 1,000 Bosnians in 1991; and others. According to UNHCR, "Ireland [now] operates an annual resettlement quota of 200 people on referral from UNHCR or identified through selection missions to existing UNHCR refugee operations." See www.unhcr.ie/resettlement .html, accessed June 16, 2011. When asylum seekers began to arrive in significant numbers in the late 1990s, however, state services were quickly overwhelmed. Moreover, asylum seekers were not the same as refugees. Most importantly, they have not already been granted refugee status before arrival; rather, they are seeking recognition as refugees.

36. Quoted in Walter, *Outsiders Inside*, 204.

37. Lindsey Earner-Byrne, "'Moral Repatriation': The Response to Irish Unmarried Mothers in Britain, 1920s–1960s," in *To and from Ireland: Planned Migration Schemes c. 1600–2000*, ed. Patrick J. Duffy (Dublin: Geography Publications, 2004), 155–73; and Louise Ryan, "Sexualising Emigration: Discourses of Irish Female Emigration in the 1930s," *Women's Studies International Forum* 25, no. 1 (2002): 51–65.

38. For example, Eoin Collins, "Editor's Introduction," in *Lesbian and Gay Visions of Ireland: Towards the Twenty-First Century*, ed. Íde B. O'Carroll and Eoin Collins (London: Cassell, 1995), 7–10; Eithne Luibhéid, "The Pink Tide: Narrating Ireland's Lesbian and Gay Migrations," *Journal of Commonwealth and Postcolonial Studies* 7, no. 1 (2000): 149–68.

39. Íde B. O'Carroll, "Breaking the Silence from a Distance: Irish Women Speak on Sexual Abuse," in *Irish Women and Irish Migration*, ed. Patrick O'Sullivan, 192–200 (Leicester: Leicester University Press, 1995).

40. For example, Margaret McCarthy, *My Eyes Only Look Out: Experiences of Irish People of Mixed Race Parentage* (Dingle, Co. Kerry: Brandon, 2001), 164–83. See also the scholarship on intermarriage among Irish and Caribbean migrants in Britain, and on Black British children with white Irish emigrant mothers, including Jacqueline Nassy Brown's wonderful *Dropping Anchor, Setting Sail: Geographies of Race in Black Liverpool* (Princeton, N.J.: Princeton University Press, 2005).

41. A thorough history of the connections among emigration, sexuality, economy, and nation and state building remains to be written.

42. In recent decades Irish sexual norms have been transformed not only by migration but also as a result of the declining Catholic Church monopoly over morality; the state's changed strategies for integration into global capitalism; entry into the European Union; urbanization; social movements; mass media; and expanding commodification. See, for example, Tony Fahey and Richard Layte, "Family and Sexuality," in *Best of Times? The Social Impact of the Celtic Tiger*, ed. Tony Fahey, Helen Russell, and Christopher T. Whelan, 155–74 (Dublin:

Institute for Public Administration, 2007); Inglis, *Lessons in Irish Sexuality;* Hilary Tovey and Perry Share, *A Sociology of Ireland,* 2nd ed. (Dublin, Gill and Macmillan, 2003), esp. chapter 9.

43. June 2001 fieldnotes.

44. As Ursula Fraser succinctly summarizes, "The practical results of the *Fajujonu* case were that non-national parents and siblings of Irish born children [were] effectively 'undeportable' from Ireland." Ursula Fraser, "Two-Tier Citizenship—The Lobe and Osayande Case," in *Women's Movement: Migrant Women Transforming Ireland,* ed. Ronit Lentin and Eithne Luibhéid, 26–34, at 27; accessed May 8, 2011, www.tcd.ie/sociology/ethnicracialstudies/assets /documents/migrantwomenpapers.pdf.

45. Note that Ireland did not (and currently does not) allow same-sex couples to get married (although civil partnerships are recognized). These two women married in a large public but informal ceremony that was not recognized by the state. As of January 2011 Ireland offers civil partnership to same-sex couples.

46. Each narrative involved specific configurations of gender and legal status (and legal status, in turn, was often taken as a proxy for "race" or nationality); all of the narratives were heteronormalizing.

47. Quoted in Garner, *Racism and the Irish Experience,* 180; also Paul Cullen, *Refugees and Asylum Seekers in Ireland* (Cork: Cork University Press, 2000), 39.

48. Nozinic, "One Refugee Experience in Ireland," 82.

49. August 2002 fieldnotes.

50. Katrina Goldstone, "Christianity, Conversion, and the Tricky Business of Names: Images of Jews and Blacks in the Nationalist Irish Catholic Discourse," in Lentin and McVeigh, *Racism and Anti-Racism in Ireland,* 167–176, quotation from p. 169.

51. Hickey, "State Alert as Pregnant Asylum Seekers Aim for Ireland."

52. For critique of colonialist constructions of "third-world women" as total victims who supposedly need rescue from patriarchal cultures, see Chandra Talpade Mohanty, "Under Western Eyes: Feminist Scholarship and Colonial Discourse," in *Third World Women and the Politics of Feminism,* ed. Chandra Talpade Mohanty, Ann Russo, and Lourdes Torres (Bloomington: Indiana University Press, 1991), 50–80. For discussion of how these constructions operate through particularly reifying sexuality as the site of alleged victimhood, see Inderpal Grewal, *Transnational America: Feminisms, Diasporas, Neoliberalisms* (Durham, N.C.: Duke University Press, 2003), esp. chapter 3.

53. "State 'Must Accept Asylum Seekers,'" *Irish Times,* November 25, 1999. See also Office of the Houses of the Oireachtas website, www.irlgov.ie/debates -99/24nov99/sect3.htm.

54. Personal interview, July 16, 2001.

55. Fieldnotes, June 20, 2002.

56. Jonathan Inda, *Targeting Immigrants* (Malden, Mass.: Blackwell Publishing, 2006), 5.

57. In other words, heterosexist, patriarchal, racist, and class-specific assumptions underpin the minister's comments about women's sexualities.

58. The articles are "Surge in Births Leads to Department Move" and "Expulsion Threat to Immigrants with Irish Children," both written by Paul Cullen and published in the *Irish Times* on December 1, 2001.

59. Yet, although the minister's concerns thoroughly implicated gender and sexuality dynamics, gender and sexuality were rarely explicitly acknowledged. Instead, as suggested by the section heading—which is drawn from a ministerial statement—the minister sometimes appeared to go to great lengths to avoid acknowledging the gender and sexual dynamics that were involved. The mismatch in his statement between "people" and who can actually become pregnant is very obvious. The statement was reported by Hickey, "State Alert as Pregnant Asylum Seekers Aim for Ireland."

60. Both at the level of constructing "knowledge" about asylum seekers and developing changed procedures for managing them, these two cases would become much bigger than the individuals involved.

61. Foucault, *Discipline and Punish,* 191.

62. Opening remarks by Lauren Berlant at the salon "The Scenarios of War, the Event of the Case: A 'Critical Inquiry'" at the Cultural Studies Association Conference, New York, May 23, 2008; also Lauren Berlant, "On the Case," *Critical Inquiry* 33 (Summer 2007), 663–72; Lauren Berlant, "Introduction: What Does It Matter Who One Is?" *Critical Inquiry* 34 (Autumn 2007): 1–4.

63. Off the record, some interviewees speculated that the families' national origins were not a coincidence; Nigerians were consistently the largest nationality group seeking asylum, and Nigerians and the Roma were particular targets of racist fearmongering and racialization.

64. The Dublin Convention requires that migrants must seek asylum in the first "safe country" in which they arrive, and if they apply for asylum in an EU state and are refused, then they cannot move on to and reapply in another European country.

65. Emma Quinn (2005) gives a slightly different account: that the families were refused asylum on Dublin Convention grounds and a deportation order was issued. "The applicant then issued judicial review proceedings against the deportation order. The Minister gave an undertaking not to deport the applicant pending the determination of the proceedings, during which time a child was born in Ireland" (26). See Emma Quinn, *Migration and Asylum in Ireland: Summary of Legislation, Case Law, and Policy Measures and Directory of Organ-*

isations, Researchers, and Research 2005 (Dublin: ESRI and European Migration Network, 2005).

66. Such mobilization of statistics affirms Inda's argument that numerical technologies have been key to "making up" undocumented immigrants as a category of problematic subjects against whom the state must take action. See Inda, *Targeting Immigrants*, 64–65, 74–93.

67. Nikolas Rose, *Powers of Freedom: Reframing Political Thought* (Cambridge, U.K.: Cambridge University Press, 1999), 204–5.

68. Arguably, one way to create the perception that there *is* a problem is by mobilizing statistics.

69. This shows the process of selecting individual cases through reference to an aggregate and then using these individual cases as instruments to transform the aggregate. As Berlant argues, "The case can incite an opening, an altered way of feeling things out," and furthermore, cases are "actuarial," raising "questions of precedent and futurity." Berlant, "On the Case," 666.

70. At that time, the backlog always exceeded the number of cases that were filed for the individual year.

71. Also rendered invisible is the fact that wealthy men had for years sent their wives to Ireland to birth children, and no one raised concerns about that.

72. See Thomas Robert Malthus, *An Essay on the Principle of Population* (1798; repr., New York: Oxford University Press, 1999).

73. See writings about the so-called immigration multiplier, which is defined as the total number of migrants who will arrive as a result of the admission of a single immigrant; these statistically based alarmist stories merit critical analysis.

74. "Holles Street Can't Keep Up with Baby Boom," *Irish Times,* August 4, 2001.

75. Pat Guerin, "Racism and the Media in Ireland: Setting the Anti-Immigrant Agenda," in Lentin and McVeigh, *Racism and Anti-Racism in Ireland,* 93.

76. For example, for the 50 percent figure ("up to half of female asylum-seekers are pregnant at the time of making their applications"), see Nuala Haughey, "State Contesting the Right of Non-EU Parents to Stay," *Irish Times,* January 9, 2002; for the 80 percent figure ("officials say some 80 percent of women of child-bearing age who have sought asylum in the past year were visibly pregnant when they lodged their applications"), see Nuala Haughey, "New Clinic Set Up for Pregnant Asylum Seekers," *Irish Times,* December 17, 2002.

77. For example, Nuala Haughey, "Immigrant Baby Boom Puts Pressure on the Coombe," *Irish Times,* August 14, 2000; "Holles Street Can't Keep Up"; and Nuala Haughey, "Unique Attitude to Irish Citizens," *Irish Times,* February 21, 2002; plus subsequent chapters of this book.

78. Muiris Houston, "Difficulties for Pregnant Refugees," *Irish Times,* April 18, 2001. The study by Patricia Kennedy and Jo Murphy-Lawless, *The Maternity Care Needs of Refugee and Asylum Seeking Women* (Swords, Co. Dublin: Northern Area Health Board, 2002), represents a unique effort to connect statistical information with qualitative information gained from refugees and asylum seekers themselves.

79. For thorough analysis of the limits of government statistical claims, see Dervla King, *Immigration and Citizenship in Ireland* (Dublin: Children's Rights Alliance, 2004).

80. In this section, my use of the term "making up" comes from Jonathan Inda, who describes that governments render "the illegal" immigrant "thinkable, calculable, and manageable" through particular technologies, especially those associated with statistics and enumeration (*Targeting Immigrants,* 7, 16, 24–25, 60).

81. Cullen, "Expulsion Threat to Immigrants with Irish Children."

82. Dervla King describes that these numerically limited but spectacularized events became mixed up with more general claims about women who arrived late or unbooked at maternity hospitals, all of whom were presumed to be "abusing" the system. But, as King discusses, not all late-term arrivals were coming from outside the state; such women had a range of legal statuses, not just that of asylum seeker; and there were often important reasons for their late arrival. Moreover, airlines place restrictions on women who travel very late in their pregnancies. See King, *Immigration and Citizenship in Ireland,* 15–16, 18–20.

83. Guerin, "Racism and the Media in Ireland," 94.

84. Fanning, *Racism and Social Change,* 101.

85. Fionnán Sheahan, "Banishing Myth of Asylum 'Spongers,' " *Irish Examiner,* February 7, 2002.

86. Marie O'Halloran, "No Change Planned in Automatic Citizenship for Refugees' Children," *Irish Times,* December 6, 2001.

87. This logic pits asylum seekers against Irish people rather than raising questions about the larger neoliberal economic logic through which national development—along with growing gaps between the haves and the have nots—was being produced.

88. Hickey, "State Alert as Pregnant Asylum Seekers Aim for Ireland."

89. Ralph Riegel and Geraldine Niland, "Racial Time Bomb Set to Explode as Crisis Deepens," *Irish Independent,* January 27, 2002.

90. Kathy Donaghy, " 'Racial Hatred' Leaflets Probed by Gardai," *Irish Independent,* January 21, 2002.

91. Quoted in Alison Healy, "Immigrants 'A Poll Issue,' " *Irish Times,* February 11, 2002.

92. Guerin, "Racism and the Media in Ireland," 94.

93. Hickey, "State Alert as Pregnant Asylum Seekers Aim for Ireland."

94. Accounts by asylum-seeker women would surely frame the matter differently, but their thoughts and voices are not included. Indeed, the minister's construction seems to replicate the (hetero)sexist construction that was so roundly critiqued by an earlier generation of feminist advocates—the idea that asylum-seeker women were merely appendages of husbands, without independent claims of their own, and without any existence apart from the men who define them.

95. Nuala Haughey, "Birth Rights: The Ruling," *Irish Times,* June 7, 2003.

2. Counternarratives of Migration Law and Childbearing

1. Dauvergne, *Making People Illegal,* 15.

2. There are limitations on the data that I obtained from asylum seekers. As described in the introduction, a strict condition of my participant observation at the drop-in center was the requirement that I should never ask anyone why they came to Ireland, or for details about how they made their journeys. All staff and volunteers at the center were bound by this requirement, which was imposed for ethical reasons that I accepted. I applied this approach to dealing with migrants outside of the center, too, but once they got to know me, some told me anyway about how and why they came.

3. Nicholas De Genova captures some of what may have been at stake in migrants' efforts: "The social space of 'illegality' is an erasure of legal personhood—a space of forced invisibility, exclusion, subjugation, and repression that [materializes] . . . in the form of real effects ranging from hunger to unemployment (or more typically, severe exploitation) to violence to death." De Genova, "Migrant 'Illegality' and Deportability," 427.

4. The chapter thus contributes to scholarship that historicizes illegal status as being produced in multiple, changing ways; as not having a singular meaning; and as something that migrants may strategize to avoid through any available means. Yet it extends that scholarship by centering queer theory's insistence on the importance of sexuality in its intersections with other social hierarchies as an axis of power, domination, and contestation.

5. As Minister O'Donoghue had indicated, Ireland was unique among EU countries in offering not only birthright citizenship but also the possibility for non-EU parents to acquire residency through their citizen child.

6. Irish Refugee Council, "Factsheet on the Dublin Convention," April 2002. Copy in author's possession.

7. Ibid.

8. These statistics concern recognition rates in the first instance (i.e., they don't include cases that were initially denied but then granted on appeal).

9. Brian Barrington, *The Single Protection Procedure: A Chance for Change* (Dublin: Irish Refugee Council, 2009), 13.

10. Irish Refugee Council, "Factsheet on the Dublin Convention," 2.

11. Ursula Fraser, "Complementary Protection and Temporary Protection" in *Sanctuary in Ireland: Perspectives on Asylum Law and Policy,* ed. Ursula Fraser and Colin Harvey (Dublin: Institute for Public Administration, 2003), 204.

12. Ibid., 212.

13. As UNHRC Ireland explains, "Anyone who fears indiscriminate violence in their home country must wait until they have been refused asylum and issued with a notification of intent to deport before they can make an application for protection from indiscriminate violence." See UNHCR Ireland statement on the need for introduction of single procedure, February 11, 2011, accessed May 12, 2011, www.unhcr.ie/feb_statement_2011.html.

14. Fraser, "Complementary Protection and Temporary Protection," 213–14.

15. In 2004 the EU Qualifications Directive set out a legal framework for providing subsidiary protection for those who may not meet the refugee definition but who nonetheless faced the risk of serious harm if returned to their countries of origin. In 2006 these provisions were incorporated into Irish law. For a discussion of the strengths and weaknesses of this legislation, see Integrating Ireland and the Irish Refugee Council Information Note, "Subsidiary Protection under the Qualifications Directive," September 2006. Copy in author's possession.

16. For an overview, see John Stanley, Corona Joyce, and Emma Quinn, *The Practices in Ireland Concerning the Granting of Non-EU Harmonised Protection Statuses* (Dublin: ESRI, 2010).

17. Emma Quinn, *The Organisation of Asylum and Migration Policies in Ireland* (Dublin: ESRI and European Migration Network, February 2009), 24n30.

18. Corona Joyce, *Annual Policy Report on Migration and Asylum 2008: Ireland* (Dublin: ESRI and European Migration Network, 2009), 25.

19. Corona Joyce, *Annual Policy Report on Migration and Asylum 2009: Ireland* (Dublin: ESRI and European Migration Network, 2010), 14. Moreover, while the introduction of provisions for subsidiary protection are positive, Integrating Ireland and the Irish Refugee Council raise concerns including the fact that citizens of EU Member States are not eligible for consideration, and that the system differentiates between the rights afforded those with refugee status versus those granted subsidiary protection. See Integrating Ireland and the Irish Refugee Council Information Note, "Subsidiary Protection under the Qualifications Directive."

20. Barrington, *Single Protection Procedure,* 12.

21. Technically, the minister did not seek to overturn *Fajujonu* but rather to differentiate *L&O* from *Fajujonu* and then get a decision in *L&O* that allowed

his office to stop granting residency to migrant parents of citizen children, which is what happened.

22. Nuala Haughey, "I Give Up. I Couldn't Win Because What Am I? I Am Just an Immigrant," *Irish Times,* January 25, 2003.

23. Ibid.

24. Bridget Anderson and Rutvica Andrijasevic, "Sex, Slaves, and Citizens: The Politics of Anti-trafficking," *Soundings* 40 (Winter 2008): 136; emphasis in the original.

25. Don Flynn, "Human Trafficking and Forced Labour: What Perspectives to Challenge Exploitation?" Platform for Cooperation on Undocumented Migrants (PICUM), April 2007, accessed May 26, 2010, http://picum.org/picum .org/uploads/publication/HumanTraffickingandForcedLabour.pdf.

26. Ibid.

27. Ibid.; emphasis in the original.

28. The Irish state's Anti-Trafficking Unit's official site, Blue Blindfold, under the Department of Justice, offers a definition of trafficking at www.blueblindfold .gov.ie/website/bbf/bbfweb.nsf/page/humantrafficking-overview-en, accessed May 19, 2010. The site also attempts to define the distinction between trafficking and smuggling but the resulting definition is confusing.

29. Anderson and Andrijasevic, "Sex, Slaves, and Citizens," 141.

30. Ibid. See also Mike Kaye, "The Migration/Trafficking Nexus: Combating Trafficking through the Protection of Migrants' Human Rights," Anti-Slavery International, 2003, www.antislavery.org/includes/documents/cm_docs/2009 /t/the_migration_trafficking_nexus_2003.pdf.

31. Anderson and Andrijasevic, "Sex, Slaves, and Citizens," 138.

32. Kamala Kempadoo, "Introduction: From Moral Panic to Global Justice; Changing Perspectives on Trafficking," in *Trafficking and Prostitution Reconsidered,* ed. Kamala Kempadoo (Boulder, Colo.: Paradigm Publishers, 2005), xiii.

33. Ibid., xiv.

34. The Child Trafficking and Pornography Act 1998 made it an offense to organize or knowingly facilitate the entry into, transit through, accommodation in, or exit from the State of a child for purposes of sexual exploitation. See Immigrant Council of Ireland (ICI) in collaboration with the Women's Health Project (HSE) and Ruhama, *Globalisation, Sex Trafficking and Prostitution: The Experiences of Migrant Women in Ireland* (Dublin, Immigrant Council of Ireland, 2009), 121.

35. Eilís Ward and Gillian Wylie, *The Nature and Extent of Trafficking of Women into Ireland for the Purposes of Sexual Exploitation 2000–2006: A Report from Findings,* SSRC Research Papers and Reports No. 39 (Social Science Research Centre, NUI Galway, 2007), 5. The authors also make clear how they define trafficking "into" Ireland, and how they define "Ireland."

36. Other antitrafficking operations include Operation Hotel (November 2005), Operation Snow (focused on children) and Operation Abbey.

37. Gillian Wylie, "Doing the Impossible? Collecting Data on the Extent of Trafficking," in *Trafficking and Women's Rights*, ed. Christien Van den Anker and Jeroen Doomernick (Basingstoke, U.K.: Palgrave Macmillan, 2006), 75.

38. Pauline Conroy, *Trafficking in Unaccompanied Minors in Ireland* (Dublin: International Organization for Migration, 2003).

39. Ward and Wylie, *Nature and Extent of Trafficking*, 6.

40. Ibid., 9–10.

41. Ibid., 10.

42. Ibid.

43. According to the Immigrant Council of Ireland (ICI), "The 'adult entertainment' business has grown significantly over the past two decades with the opening of sex shops, lap-dancing clubs and massage parlours, all of which are legal in Ireland" (ICI, *Sex Trafficking and Prostitution*, 81). "Since the 1990s, the core of the prostitution industry in Ireland has moved indoors. The widespread use of the internet and mobile phones has made the buying of sex paradoxically more accessible but less overt. Women are available in rented private apartments or houses and do both in-calls and callouts to hotel rooms or residences of buyers" (ibid., 83). "The flow of foreign women into Ireland for the purpose of prostitution started in the early 2000s" (ibid., 84). See also Ward and Wylie, *Nature and Extent of Trafficking*, 6.

44. MRCI, *No Way Forward, No Going Back: Identifying the Problem of Trafficking for Forced Labour in Ireland* (Dublin: MRCI in association with Dublin City University, 2006).

45. See MCRI, *Forced Labour: The Case for Criminalisation* (Dublin: MCRI, 2010), 2.

46. Notably, therefore, the law separates sexual exploitation from labor exploitation, which has a range of important implications for those in the sex industry.

47. ICI, *Globalisation, Sex Trafficking and Prostitution*, 121.

48. Initially there was a forty-five-day period, which was then expanded to sixty days.

49. ICI, *Globalisation, Sex Trafficking and Prostitution*, 2.

50. Ibid., 22.

51. Joyce, *Annual Policy Report, 2008*, 40: those identified as trafficked may receive temporary residence from the minister for justice, equality and law reform for up to six months if the person has severed all ties with the trafficker and is assisting the gardai with an investigation or prosecution.

52. ICI, *Sex Trafficking and Prostitution*, 123.

53. Roger Rouse, "Making Sense of Settlement: Class Transformation, Cultural Struggle, and Transnationalism among Mexican Migrants in the United States," in *Towards a Transnational Perspective on Migration: Race, Class, Ethnicity, and Nationalism Reconsidered*, ed. Nina Glick-Schiller, Linda Basch, and Cristina Blanc-Szanton (New York: New York Academy of Sciences, 1992), 25–26.

54. Nina Glick-Schiller, Linda Basch, and Cristina Blanc-Szanton, "Towards a Definition of Transnationalism," in Glick-Schiller, Basch, and Blanc-Szanton, *Towards a Transnational Perspective on Migration*, 1.

55. Deborah Fahy Bryceson, and Ulla Vuorela, "Transnational Families in the Twenty-First Century," in *The Transnational Family: New European Frontiers and Global Networks*, ed. Deborah Fahy Bryceson and Ulla Vuorela (Oxford: Berg Publishers, 2002), 12.

56. Brenda S. A. Yeoh, Shirlena Huang, and Theodora Lam, "Transnationalizing the 'Asian' Family: Imaginaries, Intimacies, and Strategic Intents," *Global Networks* 5, no. 4 (2005), 308. These authors describe "the 'transnational family' as a formation [that] derives its lived reality not only from material bonds of collective welfare among physically dispersed members but also a shared imaginary of 'belonging' which transcends particular periods and places to encompass past trajectories and future continuities" (308).

57. Leah Schmalzbauer, "Searching for Wages and Mothering from Afar: The Case of Honduran Transnational Families," *Journal of Marriage and Family* 66, no. 5 (2004), 1329.

58. Yeoh et al., "Transnationalizing the 'Asian' Family," 312. The scholarship on transnational families is now vast.

59. For example, see the scholarship on the "global chain of care," which explores how women from the global south leave behind their families to work and care for more affluent families in the global north, in a global division of reproductive labor. According to Martin Manalansan, however, many scholars have debated these ideas in ways that reinscribe heteronormative models of gender, sexuality, affect, and family that need to be challenged. See Martin F. Manalansan IV, "Queering the Chain of Care Paradigm," *Scholar and Feminist Online* 6, no. 3 (Summer 2008), special issue, *Borders on Belonging: Gender and Immigration*, accessed May 18, 2010, http://sfonline.barnard.edu/immigration/manalansan_01.htm. In regard to Irish writings about the global chain of care, see for example Nicola Yeates, *Globalizing Care Economies and Migrant Workers: Explorations in Global Care Chains* (Palgrave Macmillan, 2009).

60. Kieran Allen, "Neo-liberalism and Immigration," in *Immigration and Social Change in the Republic of Ireland*, ed. Bryan Fanning (Manchester, U.K.: University of Manchester Press, 2007), 90. Even worse, permits were held by

the employer, not the worker, and bound the worker to a specific employer. In 2000 a work visa system was developed for more skilled employees that granted them somewhat more rights. But in both cases "their relation to wider Irish society was defined as temporary and it was assumed that they would leave once the boom ended" (ibid., 86). Accordingly, family reunification was not guaranteed to workers (although Filipino nurses managed to get an exception), and their place in Irish social institutions was not considered or addressed in policy. Policies on worker rights and restrictions have continued to change; for updated information, see the Citizen's Information website at www.citizensinformation.ie/en/employment/migrant_workers/.

61. This discussion is informed by the work of Aihwa Ong, who, in *Flexible Citizenship: The Cultural Logics of Transnationality* (Durham, N.C.: Duke University Press, 1999), argues that under contemporary conditions of transnationalization and globalization, people often strategize ways to acquire legal status in other nation-states in order to protect against uncertainties or create new opportunities.

62. Women like this informant are similar in some respects to so-called astronaut parents. The scholarship about astronaut families generally focuses on the middle and upper middle classes from Asia, who strategically relocate their children to global northern countries to study and acquire residency rights. Sometimes mothers accompany the children while fathers remain in Asia, earning salaries. As Ong describes, the purpose of strategically deploying various family members across borders in these ways is to maximize opportunities. There were obvious class similarities between these astronaut mothers and the women described by my informant. But there were differences, too, including the contrasting manner in which they entered destination countries as well as the fact that astronaut mothers generally could not depend on the state for support of themselves and their children. For example, see Lan-Hung Nora Chiang, "'Astronaut Families': Transnational Lives of Middle-Class Taiwanese Married Women in Canada," *Journal of Social and Cultural Geography* 9, no. 5 (August 2008): 505–18; and Min Zhou, "'Parachute Kids' in Southern California: The Educational Experience of Chinese Children in Transnational Families," *Educational Policy* 12, no. 2 (1998): 682–704.

63. Elisabetta Zontini, "Resisting Fortress Europe: The Everyday Politics of Female Transnational Migrants," *Focaal: European Journal of Anthropology* 51 (2008): 19.

64. Ibid., 16.

65. Dianna J. Shandy and David V. Power, "The Birth of the African-Irish Diaspora: Pregnancy and Post-Natal Experiences of African Immigrant Women in Ireland," *International Migration* 46, no. 5 (2008): 129.

66. Ibid.

67. Ireland also has a long history of participation in transnational flows of medical personnel, which has taken on new dimensions as a result of Europeanization.

68. Dervla King writes, "Pregnant women may be fleeing their country of origin because of concerns about the safety of their unborn child. . . . It is not uncommon for rape to be used as a weapon in wars and internal conflicts. . . . According to a British study of social care staff who worked closely with asylum seekers and refugees, 31% of them had encountered women who were pregnant as a result of rape" (King, *Immigration and Citizenship in Ireland,* 17). Women in flight or in refugee camps are also routinely at risk of sexual harassment and assault, which may result in pregnancy.

69. Ireland's 1996 Refugee Act recognizes persecution on account of the five grounds described by the Geneva Convention *and* on account of gender, sexual orientation, or trade union membership.

70. Quoted in "Amina's Sentence: Pregnant Nigerian Seeks Asylum in Cyprus," posted by Women's Rights Watch Nigeria, accessed April 27, 2004. Copy in author's possession. See also "Pregnant Nigerian Seeks Sharia Asylum" *Religion News Blog,* August 23, 2002, accessed June 10, 2010, www.religionnewsblog .com/archives/00000515.html. Note that although Fatimo needed protection, this would not be available to her under the Geneva Convention.

71. The percentage of asylum claims that Ireland recognizes as legitimate has been low; in January 2011, a new report from Eurostat showed that "Ireland's acceptance rate of refugees at first instance [i.e., before an appeal], at 1.3 per cent, is significantly lower than those of most EU states, including Britain (24 per cent), Sweden (36 per cent) and France (13 per cent)," and consequently, "Ireland has overtaken Greece as the EU state with the lowest acceptance rate of claims for refugee status." Jamie Smyth, "Irish Acceptance of Asylum Claims Lowest in the EU," *Irish Times,* January 21, 2011.

72. In other words, this route to residency was also fraught with risks, and people had to decide whether these risks outweighed the possibility of deportation. Women and men faced very different pressures as they negotiated these risks, including because the consequences of pregnancy are *definitely* gendered.

73. For example, in April 2011 two Iranian asylum seekers in the United Kingdom went on a hunger strike and sewed their lips shut after their applications were denied. "Iranian Asylum Seekers Sew Lips Together in Hunger Strike," *BBC,* April 27, 2011, accessed June 20, 2011, www.bbc.co.uk/news/uk -england-london-13216143.

74. Hannah Arendt, "The Decline of the Nation State and the End of the Rights of Man," in *The Origins of Totalitarianism* (New York: Meridian Books, 1958), 286–87. Arendt's argument is intended to illuminate the nightmarish position of the asylum seeker under the law. Students in my spring 2011 seminar,

Transnational Feminism, rightly argued that any belief that the criminal justice system is just, fair, reasonable, or transparent is not supported.

75. Then the second girl began to laugh because my suggestion reminded her of a story that she had heard. She related that in her country, people sometimes try to get money by standing in the road and letting a car hit them. Then, when the driver offers to take them to hospital, they say "no, instead give me some money and I will leave you alone." There were two men who were friends, and one came back to the village and found his friend had opened a shop. He was very impressed and asked his friend where he got the money. The friend said he waited in the road and when he saw a car approaching he stepped out and the driver hit him. When the driver offered to take him to hospital, he said no and took money instead, which enabled him to open the shop. It was just a little car that hit him, he said. His friend thought, if this man got enough money to open a shop from being hit by a small car, then I will let something bigger hit me so I can make enough money to open a supermarket. So he stood by the road, and when he saw a big trailer coming, he stepped into the road and the trailer hit him. He was lying in the road, and the friend who came with him negotiated with the driver for money. Then the friend shook the man in the road. But although the man seemed to be grinning, he was dead. The girl concluded, "In my country, you see many bodies like that, they look like they are grinning in death."

76. Notably, many countries now routinely incarcerate people under very poor conditions solely because they sought asylum. That is different from the situation that I am discussing here.

77. A teacher in the prison system who worked with incarcerated nonnationals confirmed that she knew at least one person who committed a crime so that he would not be deported to his country of origin.

78. See chapter 4 for further discussion.

79. Patricia Kennedy and Jo Murphy-Lawless, "The Maternity Care Needs of Refugee and Asylum Seeking Women in Ireland," *Feminist Review* 73 (2003): 50.

80. Patricia Kennedy and Jo Murphy-Lawless, *The Maternity Care Needs of Refugee and Asylum-Seeking Women: A Research Study Conducted for the Women's Health Unit, Northern Area Health Board, Eastern Regional Health Authority* (Swords, Co. Dublin: Northern Area Health Board, 2002), 51.

81. Thus, the interviewer's questions not only evoked trauma but also demanded knowledge that the girl could not possibly have. This is not to suggest that the interviewer was insensitive but to highlight the fact that asylum seekers are *required* to recall and relate traumatic events in order for their applications to be considered.

82. For state rates of recognition of asylum claims, see the *Annual Reports* issued by the Office of the Refugee Applications Commissioner (www.orac.ie /pages/Stats/statistics.htm). Corona Joyce provides information on recogni-

tion rates from 2004 to 2010 in Corona Joyce, *Annual Policy Report 2010: Ireland* (Dublin: ESRI and EMN, 2011), 65.

83. Noting the more stringent measures, the *Irish Times* described, "Already, many asylum-seekers who have children here are being required to show they form a stable family unit. Asylum-seeker fathers have been asked to undergo DNA tests to prove their paternity." Paul Cullen, "Surge in Births Leads to Department Move," *Irish Times,* December 1, 2001.

84. FÁS was the Irish National Training and Employment Authority. Note that after May 2004, when the Habitual Residence Condition was introduced, the receipt of regular welfare became far more difficult.

85. Furthermore, citizenship was granted at the minister's discretion rather than automatically, even for those who fulfilled all the criteria.

86. Fieldnotes, May 27, 2003: "Today, a man came into the Centre. He has an Irish born child, but he's not living with the mother anymore, so the department of Justice refused to renew his residency. 'That's happening more, now,' said the director."

87. For example, see Crosscare Migrant Project, *Invisible Pathways.*

88. There is a growing literature on "mixed status" families (i.e., families whose members have different legal statuses, which differentially affects their life chances). U.S. literature includes Jeffrey Fix and Wendy Zimmerman, "All under One Roof: Mixed Status Families in an Era of Reform," *International Migration Review* 35, no. 2 (2001): 397–419; Karina Fortuny, Randy Capps, Margaret Sims, and Ajay Chaudry, *Children of Immigrants: National and State Characteristics* (Washington, D.C.: Urban Institute, 2009); Lynn Fujiwara, *Mothers without Citizenship: Asian Immigrant Families and the Consequences of Welfare Reform* (Minneapolis: University of Minnesota Press, 2008); and Hirokazu Yoshikawa, *Immigrants Raising Citizens: Undocumented Parents and Their Young Children* (New York: Russell Sage Foundation, 2011).

89. Lorna Siggins, "Stark Choice: Residency or Refugee?" *Irish Times,* January 25, 2003. Officials have consistently denied that they ever advised anyone to opt for residency based on a child. They also claimed that when someone decided to follow that route, the consequences were explained to them, including in written form. I saw a copy of the letter that was given to migrants who decided to drop their asylum claims in favor of seeking residency through a child. The letter effectively said, "Your case is closed; we are returning your documents; future inquiries should be directed to the following; and remember to use your 69/ number when making inquiries." To me, that did not constitute an adequate explanation of consequences.

90. Migrants may have responded in these ways in part because I was white, Irish-born and -raised, and represented the mainstream in their eyes. But their responses may also reflect their internalization, adoption, and reworking of

mainstream neo-liberal heteronormative and "enterprise culture" norms, including as a way to respond to experiences of discrimination. As Beth Baker-
Cristales describes, dominant xenophobia "shape(s) the ways in which [mi-
grants] . . . formulate and reformulate their evolving political identities, their
ideas about civic participation and citizenship, governance and rights, and undoubtedly the kinds of struggles to which they are willing to commit or even
acknowledge as legitimate." Beth Baker-Cristales, "Mediated Resistance: The
Construction of Neoliberal Citizenship in the Immigrant Rights Movement,"
Latino Studies 7, no. 1 (2009): 77. Taking the analysis a step further, Natalie
Peutz describes how migrants often "desire 'the law' of the very state that imprisoned, detained, and excluded them." Natalie Peutz, "Out-laws: Deportees,
Desire, and 'the Law,'" *International Migration* 45, no. 3 (2007): 183. Certainly,
many migrants with whom I interacted were presumed by mainstream society
to have violated the law, and had, in turn, been violated by the law. Those who
received legal residency continued to be violated not only by the law but also by
multiple structural barriers that blocked their access to employment and made
their everyday lives very difficult. These experiences constitute forms of "abuse"
that certainly need to be highlighted—and I regard interviewee comments that
are discussed in this chapter as part of the process of reframing what counts as
abuse that needs to be addressed.

3. Baby Gives Birth to Parents

1. Jost Halfmann, "Welfare State and Territory," in *Immigration and Welfare:
Challenging the Borders of the Welfare State,* ed. Michael Bommes and Andrew
Geddes (New York: Routledge, 2000), 45.

2. Ibid., 41.

3. Michelle Millar, "Social Inclusion and the Welfare State: Who Cares?" in
Contesting the State: Lessons from the Irish Case, ed. Maura Adshead, Peadar
Kirby, and Michelle Millar (Manchester, U.K.: Manchester University Press,
2008), 103.

4. Bryan Fanning, "Locating Irish Social Policy," in *Theorising Irish Social
Policy,* ed. Bryan Fanning, Patricia Kennedy, Gabriel Kiely, and Suzanne Quin
(Dublin: University College Dublin Press, 2004), 8.

5. Bryan Fanning, "The New Welfare Economy," in *Care and Social Change
in the Irish Welfare Economy,* ed. Bryan Fanning and Michael Rush (Dublin:
University College Dublin Press, 2006), 14.

6. Ibid., 18.

7. Millar, "Social Inclusion and the Welfare State," 107. At the same time, the
government spent little on social welfare relative to other EU countries.

8. Aihwa Ong, *Buddha Is Hiding: Refugees, Citizenship, the New America* (Berkeley: University of California Press, 2003), 78–79.

9. Aihwa Ong, "Cultural Citizenship as Subject-Making: Immigrants Negotiate Racial and Cultural Boundaries in the United States," in *Race, Identity, and Citizenship: A Reader*, ed. Rodolfo D. Torres, Louis F. Mirón, and Jonathan Xavier Inda (Malden, Mass.: Blackwell Publishers, 1997), 263.

10. Ibid., 264.

11. In recent years, not only have migrants become subjectified through their engagement with the welfare system (among other institutions), but transformations in welfare have also produced sharper divisions between migrants and citizens. As Fanning describes, differential welfare access was steadily introduced and codified in a manner that reflected and continually reproduced stratifications between migrants and citizens, on one hand, and within various categories of migrants, on the other hand. Fanning, "New Welfare Economy." These transformations occurred not only in Ireland but also much more widely.

12. Nasc, *Hidden Cork: The Perspectives of Asylum Seekers on Direct Provision and the Asylum Legal System* (Cork: Nasc, 2007), 4.

13. Pauline Faughnan, Niamh Humphries, and Sadhbh Whelan, *Patching Up the System: The Community Welfare Service and Asylum Seekers* (Dublin: University College Dublin, Social Science Research Centre, 2002), 17.

14. Nasc, *Hidden Cork*, 4.

15. According to the Free Legal Advice Centre (FLAC), the Directorate of Asylum Support Services, or DASS, "was established at the end of 1999 under the aegis of the Minister for Justice, Equality and Law Reform to coordinate the schemes of dispersal and Direct Provision for asylum seekers." On April 2, 2001, the Reception and Integration Agency (RIA) was established "following the merger of the Directorate of Asylum Support Services or DASS and the Refugee Agency." FLAC, *Direct Discrimination? An Analysis of the Scheme of Direct Provision in Ireland* (Dublin: FLAC, 2003), 9n5.

16. Comhlámh, *Refugee Lives* (Dublin: Comhlámh, 2001), 22–23; and FLAC, *One Size Doesn't Fit All: A Legal Analysis of the Direct Provision and Dispersal System in Ireland, 10 Years On* (Dublin: FLAC, 2009), 19.

17. Steve Loyal describes that some private companies continue turning a hefty profit by providing for asylum seekers. See Loyal, "The Business of Direct Provision: Outside the Integration Debate," *Dark Matter in the Ruins of Imperial Culture*, June 17, 2008; accessed April 19, 2009, www.darkmatter101.org/site/2008/06/17/the-business-of-direct-provision-outside-the-integration-debate/; and FLAC, "The Direct Provision Industry," in *One Size Doesn't Fit All*, 26–30. For a state analysis, see Reception and Integration Agency (RIA), *Value for Money and Policy Review: Asylum Seeker Accommodation Programme, Final*

Report, May 2010, accessed June 17, 2011, www.ria.gov.ie/en/RIA/FINAL%20
VFM%20Report%20on%20Asylum%20Seeker%20Accomm%20July272010.pdf
/Files/FINAL%20VFM%20Report%20on%20Asylum%20Seeker%20Accomm
%20July272010.pdf. For discussion of the report, see Jamie Smyth, "State Spon-
sored Poverty a Cash Cow for Big Business," *Irish Times,* September 1, 2010.

    18. Loyal, "Business of Direct Provision."

    19. In recent years asylum seekers are provided with an informational book-
let, *House Rules and Procedures,* but this provides only general information.

    20. *Refugee Lives* explains how this odd and meager sum was derived: "The
Department decided that the needs of asylum seekers were analogous to those
of people in long-term institutional care, who received [that same sum] for
'hospital comforts'" (Comhlámh, *Refugee Lives,* 16–17).

    21. As FLAC summarizes, "The decision to introduce the scheme was based
on a policy of deterrence rather than on any attempt to address the needs of
asylum seekers as a class or as individuals" (*Direct Discrimination?,* 39). Joe
Moran further explains the government's logic: "Depriving them of full welfare
entitlements will discourage asylum seekers who, it is argued by governments,
are not genuine in the first place, from trying to enter European states and live off
their generous welfare provisions." Moran, "Refugees and Social Policy," in *Contemporary Irish Social Policy,* ed. Suzanne Quin, Patricia Kennedy, Anne Mat-
thews, and Gabriel Kiely (Dublin: University College Dublin Press, 2005), 269.

    22. Nuala Haughey, "Government Aims to Tackle Asylum Seeker Crisis,"
Irish Times, December 13, 1999.

    23. FLAC, *Direct Discrimination?,* 36.

    24. Faughnan, Humphries, and Whelan, *Patching Up the System,* 87.

    25. Ibid., 10.

    26. Ibid., 11.

    27. Ibid., 19.

    28. These desired outcomes are significantly different than the aims of regu-
lar welfare systems under neoliberal capitalism, which strive to produce entrepreneurial subjects of choice.

    29. Nasc, *Hidden Cork,* 27–28.

    30. For information about the complaint procedure, see FLAC, *One Size
Doesn't Fit All,* 34–40. As the report notes, "Despite the reassurances given in
the house rules booklet to the contrary, many residents believe that any attempt to bring grievances to the attention of those in charge may result in a
negative decision on their asylum application or some other form of punitive
measure" (ibid., 40).

    31. AkiDwA, *"Am Only Saying It Now": Experiences of Women Seeking Asylum
in Ireland* (Dublin: AkiDwA, March 2010), 16.

    32. Ibid.

33. FLAC, *One Size Doesn't Fit All*, 45–46.

34. Currently asylum seekers remain eligible for "exceptional needs" payments, which may be "granted to 'help meet exceptional, once-off expenditures which a person could not be reasonably expected to meet out of their weekly income.'... In practice, direct provision residents receive two payments per year to cover clothing expenses: €150 per annum for a child and €300 per annum for an adult" (FLAC, *One Size Doesn't Fit All*, 47). They are also eligible for "urgent needs" payments for "purchase of an item which is of vital necessity to applicant.... The rate will depend on the type of assistance needed" (ibid., 47). Finally, those asylum seekers with school-age children are eligible for a back-to-school clothing and footwear allowance (ibid., 48).

35. Bryan Fanning, Angela Veale, and Dawn O'Connor, *Beyond the Pale: Asylum-Seeking Children and Social Exclusion in Ireland* (Dublin: Irish Refugee Council, 2001), 5.

36. "Food poverty may be defined in a number of ways, from a nutritional, social exclusion and/or food security perspective." Health Service Executive, *National Intercultural Health Strategy, 2007–2012* (Dublin: Health Service Executive, 2008), 42.

37. Irish Refugee Council, *Fact Sheet on Asylum Seekers and Accommodation Centres: Social Policy Information Note No. 1*, June 2002. Copy in author's possession.

38. Meave Foreman, "HIV and 'Direct Provision'—Learning from the Experiences of Asylum Seekers in Ireland," *Translocations: Migration and Social Change* 4, no. 1 (Winter 2008): 68.

39. See Health Services Executive, *National Intercultural Health Strategy, 2007–2012*.

40. Foreman, "HIV and Direct Provision," 68.

41. "Dr. Philip Crowley, the Deputy Chief Medical Officer of the Department of Health and Children, summarised the main issues pertaining to the mental health of asylum seekers: 'Their mental health is adversely affected by social isolation, pre- and post-arrival trauma, culture shock, language barriers, fear of deportation coupled with lack of understanding about services, poverty, and poor housing" (FLAC, *One Size Doesn't Fit All*, 108).

42. See FLAC, *Direct Discrimination?*, 35; and Irish Refugee Council, *Fact Sheet on Asylum Seekers and Accommodation Centres: Social Policy Information Note No. 1*.

43. Comhlámh, *Refugee Lives*, 39.

44. Dermot Ryan, Ciarán Benson, and Barbara Dooley, "Forced Migration and Psychological Stress," in *Immigration and Social Change in the Republic of Ireland*, ed. Bryan Fanning (Manchester, U.K.: Manchester University Press, 2007), 121–22.

45. AkiDwA, *"Am Only Saying It Now,"* 16.

46. Ibid., 14.

47. "Much of an asylum seeker's child's welfare is effectively beyond the parent's control, dictated by the ways in which the centre is run"; ibid., 15.

48. For example, Moran, "Refugees and Social Policy," 271; FLAC, *Direct Discrimination?*; Claire Breen, "The Policy of Direct Provision in Ireland: A Violation of Asylum Seekers' Right to an Adequate Standard of Housing," *International Journal of Refugee Law* 20, no. 4 (2008), 611–36; Lentin and McVeigh, *After Optimism?*; and Louise Beirne and Vinodh Jaichand, *Breaking Down Barriers: Tackling Racism in Ireland at the Level of the State and Its Institutions* (Galway: Irish Centre for Human Rights, National University of Ireland, Galway, 2006), accessed June 19, 2011, www.nuigalway.ie/human_rights/documents /breaking_down_barriers_ir_report1.pdf, 70.

49. Moran, "Refugees and Social Policy," 271.

50. Dauvergne, *Making People Illegal*, 151.

51. Frances McGinnity, Philip J. O'Connell, Emma Quinn, and James Williams, *Migrants' Experiences of Racism and Discrimination in Ireland* (Dublin: ESRI, 2006), 63.

52. Bryan Fanning, "Racism, Rules and Rights," in *Immigration and Social Change in the Republic of Ireland*, ed. Bryan Fanning (Manchester, U.K.: Manchester University Press, 2007), 16.

53. In recent years the state has dismantled significant elements of the equality infrastructure. In 2008 the Equality Authority's budget was cut by 43 percent, and the Human Rights Commission's budget was cut by 24 percent. The National Consultative Committee on Racism and Interculturalism closed in December 2008. Combat Poverty was subsumed under the Department of Social Protection. The National Action Plan against Racism was concluded and funding for other equality initiatives was stalled.

54. Upon arrival all migrants encounter new histories and structures of racial classification and inequality within which they must negotiate their place. This is because "race is a global social fact, a sociocultural category that structures social hierarchies of power and prestige, determines access to resources, and organizes individual and collective identities and action. Yet, racial classification systems vary in different places." José Itzigsohn, Silvia Giorguli, and Obed Vazquez, "Immigrant Incorporation and Racial Identity: Racial Self-Identification among Dominican Immigrants," *Ethnic and Racial Studies* 28, no. 1 (January 2005): 51. At the same time, their arrival often contributes to transformations in racial identities, hierarchies, and social relations. It is important to explore how the direct provision system fits into these processes.

55. Stacy Vandenhurst, "Identity in Refuge: The Distinct Experiences of Asylum Seekers in Ireland," *Notre Dame Journal of Undergraduate Research* (2007), accessed June 19, 2011, www.nd.edu/~ujournal/assets/files/06-07 /identity.pdf, 14.

56. Ibid., 15. See also Nasc, *Hidden Cork,* 23–24.

57. Vandenhurst, "Identity in Refuge," 15.

58. For example, as early as 2001 the Irish Refugee Council recommended that "comprehensive anti-racism and intercultural awareness training should be provided for all staff working with asylum seekers, in particular for the staff involved in overseeing complaints." Irish Refugee Council, *Direct Provision and Dispersal, 18 Months On* (IRC: Dublin, 2001), 3. Similarly, "It is also recommended that staff of direct provision centres be given training in dealing with asylum seekers such as communications training, listening skills, anti-racist training and multicultural training." Waterford Area Partnership, Men's Development Network and RAPID, *The Needs of Asylum Seeker Men Living in Viking House Direct Provision Centre, Waterford* (Waterford: Waterford Area Partnership, 2007), 7.

59. Katharine M. Donato, Donna Gabaccia, Jennifer Holdaway, Martin Manalansan IV, and Patricia R. Pessar, "A Glass Half Full? Gender in Migration Studies," *International Migration Review* 40, no. 1 (Spring 2006): 4, 13.

60. This scholarship therefore challenges the imperialist logics and self-congratulatory postures evident in the belief that migration to the global north must inevitably "liberate" or improve women's lot.

61. Despite the law's recognition of gender as a basis or mechanism of persecution, migrants who rely on these provisions face significant struggles to ensure that their experiences are appropriately understood and evaluated by state decision makers.

62. Waterford Area Partnership, *Needs of Asylum Seeker Men,* 2.

63. Ibid.

64. Ibid., 12–13.

65. AkiDwA, *"Am Only Saying It Now,"* 10.

66. Ibid.

67. As Espiritu indicates, minority and immigrant communities often strive to assert their worth and challenge racist characterizations by foregrounding the morality and gender propriety of women within the community. Yet this antiracism strategy reinforces patriarchy and heterosexism, and marginalizes many women, queer people, and other nonconformists. See Yen Le Espiritu, " 'We Don't Sleep Around like White Girls Do': Family, Culture, and Gender in Filipina American Lives," in *Gender and U.S. Immigration: Contemporary Trends,* ed. Pierette Hondagneu-Sotelo (Berkeley: University of California Press, 2003), 263–84.

68. AkiDwA, *"Am Only Saying It Now,"* 5.

69. Domestic Violence Advocacy Service (DVAS), "Domestic Violence in Direct Provision (Sligo, Leitrim, and West Cavan)," March 2010. Copy in author's possession.

70. The authors provide a definition of domestic violence: It "is never about one or two incidents of abuse. It is a systemic pattern of behaviour that is designed to gain control" over another. Men experience domestic violence, but women experience it at a much greater rate.

71. DVAS, "Domestic Violence in Direct Provision."

72. Ibid.

73. Ibid.

74. AkiDwA recommends the establishment of "separate women only supportive accommodation . . . within the direct provision system, ensuring women can have the choice of women only centres. This is especially important for women who have suffered gender based violence in their countries of origin or who have been trafficked into Ireland" (*"Am Only Saying It Now,"* 28). It might also be helpful for single women and women facing domestic violence.

75. DVAS, "Domestic Violence in Direct Provision."

76. AkiDwA, *"Am Only Saying It Now,"* 20.

77. DVAS, "Domestic Violence in Direct Provision."

78. Ibid.

79. Ibid.

80. Espiritu, "We Don't Sleep Around like White Girls Do," 264.

81. Ibid. Otherwise, the experiences, needs, and contradictions facing migrant women who are also marginalized on the basis of race, culture, class, sexuality, religion, or other factors will remain silenced, ignored, or "resist telling." Kimberlé Crenshaw, "Mapping the Margins: Intersectionality, Identity Politics, and Violence against Women of Color," *Stanford Law Review* 43 (1993): 1242.

82. We also need to interrogate the definitions of "family" through which centers organize their provision of supports as well as the ways gender and sexual norms are spatialized and enacted. Research on direct provision suggests that the centers' definitions of family, the spatialization of gender and sexual norms, the services provided, and the day-to-day cultures that permeate centers construct and enforce particular kinds of sexual norms that merit critical scrutiny. Yet I have been unable to locate studies that explicitly address how direct provision constructs and enforces particular sexual regimes.

83. Quentin Fottrell, "Lifting the Veil of Suspicion That Clouds Asylum Cases," *Irish Times,* March 11, 2008.

84. Ireland's *Gay Community News* should not be confused with *Gay Community News* that was published in Boston, Massachusetts. I am referring to the former.

85. According to their website, "Outhouse is a community and resource centre for LGBT people, their families, and their friends. It is based in Dublin." Accessed December 17, 2012, at www.outhouse.ie/aboutoverview.html.

86. Jeanette Rehnstrom, "Queer and Here: Gay Immigrants to Ireland Tell Their Stories: Olive Namuddu from Uganda," *Gay Community News*, no. 229 (January 2009), 37.

87. LGBTI stands for lesbian, gay, bisexual, transgender, and intersex.

88. Sabine Jansen and Thomas Spijkerboer, *Fleeing Homophobia: Asylum Claims Related to Sexual Orientation and Gender Identity in Europe* (Amsterdam: COC Nederland and Vrije Universiteit Amsterdam, 2011), 77–78.

89. Eoin Burke Kennedy, "LGBT Migrants Fear Disclosing Sexuality," *Irish Times*, January 31, 2012.

90. FLAC's *One Size Doesn't Fit All* is exceptional in stating that sexual orientation may make people particularly vulnerable, and that provisions for asylum seekers need to take this into account (137, 141).

91. Ryan, Benson, and Dooley, "Forced Migration and Psychological Stress," 126–27.

92. Ibid.

93. Ibid.

94. For example, "Irish Police End Afghans' Protest," *BBC World*, May 20, 2006, http://news.bbc.co.uk/2/hi/europe/5000202.stm; CNN, "Afghans' Irish Hunger Strike Ends," May 21, 2006, http://articles.cnn.com/2006-05-21/world /ireland.afghans_1_hunger-strike-afghan-asylum-seekers-police-custody?_ s=PM:WORLD; and "Afghans Wage Hunger Strike in Ireland," CBS, May 20, 2006, www.cbsnews.com/stories/2006/05/20/world/main1638186.shtml, all accessed June 20, 2011.

95. Ronit Lentin, "Asylum Seekers Are Not 'Things,'" *Free Radical*, August 8, 2010, accessed June 20, 2011, www.ronitlentin.net/2010/08/08/asylum-seekers -are-not-things/#more-274.

96. Irish Refugee Council, *Without Rights or Recognition* (Dublin: Irish Refugee Council, December 2010), 2.

97. Roland Bank, "Europeanising the Reception of Asylum Seekers: The Opposite of Welfare State Polices," in Bommes and Geddes, *Immigration and Welfare*, 149.

98. FLAC, *Direct Discrimination?*, 10.

99. After the Supreme Court's *L&O* decision in January 2003, the birth of a child no longer offered a route to legal residency for migrant parents.

100. Liam Thornton, "'Upon the Limits of Rights Regimes': Reception Conditions of Asylum Seekers in the Republic of Ireland," *Refuge* 24, no. 2 (2007): 89.

101. FLAC, *Direct Discrimination?*, 10.

102. Faughnan, Humphries, and Whelan, *Patching Up the System*, 24.

103. Ibid., 25–27; and Fanning, Veale, and O'Connor, *Beyond the Pale*, 7.

104. Faughnan, Humphries, and Whelan, *Patching Up the System*, 25–27.

105. Ibid.

106. In Ireland, a "lone" parent refers to a parent who is parenting alone—but is not necessarily single or unmarried. For instance, migrants' spouses were often in countries of origin; therefore, migrants were effectively raising children as "lone parents" in Ireland, even when they were married.

107. Fanning, Veale, and O'Connor, *Beyond the Pale*, 7.

108. For example, a Nigerian mother of an Irish child described moving out of direct provision and gaining residence as "'freedom' and a chance to settle down." Insa Lichtsinn and Angela Veale, "Between 'Here' and 'There': Nigerian Lone Mothers in Ireland," in *Immigration and Social Change in the Irish Republic*, ed. Bryan Fanning (Manchester, U.K.: Manchester University Press, 2007), 109.

109. Moreover, she found that many Irish people seemed unworldly, including in terms of their lack of familiarity with racial and ethnic diversity, which is a hallmark of life in Nigeria.

110. According to Foucault, "Technologies of the self . . . permit individuals to effect by their own means or with the help of others a certain number of operations on their own bodies and souls, thoughts, conduct, and way of being, so as to transform themselves in order to attain a certain state of happiness, purity, wisdom, perfection, or immortality." Quoted in Luther Martin, Huck Gutman, and Patrick Hutton, eds., *Technologies of the Self: A Seminar with Michel Foucault* (Amherst: University of Massachusetts Press, 1988), 18.

111. Significantly, the Irish asylum system channels asylum seekers into volunteer work, which they undertake while waiting for decisions on their asylum claims. Critical analysis of the ways asylum seekers are mobilized as volunteer labor—until their claims are decided—merits further critical analysis. See Su Yin Yap, Angela Byrne, and Sarah Davidson, "From Refugee to Good Citizen: A Discourse Analysis of Volunteering," *Journal of Refugee Studies* 24, no. 1 (2010): 157–70.

112. For example, see *White Paper on a Framework for Supporting Voluntary Activity and for Developing the Relationship Between the State and the Community and Voluntary Sector*, n.d., accessed June 21, 2011, http://socialpolicy.ucc.ie /Supporting_Voluntary_Activity%20_A_White_Paper_415709.pdf.

113. In this respect Christabel demonstrated and enacted understanding of citizenship as entailing not just rights and entitlements but also responsibilities.

114. Note that this was before Ireland began to use the euro as currency.

115. My narrative acknowledges that migrants negotiate subjectivities and possibilities within the constraints available to them—including dominant neoliberal logics. This should not surprise us; subjectivity does not exist in a

relationship of exteriority to power. For further discussion, see Baker-Cristales, "Mediated Resistance."

116. The Training and Employment Authority. In July 2011 the minister for education and skills announced that FÁS would be replaced by a new agency, SOLAS, under the new Department of Social Protection.

117. For rich discussion of the ways that the IBC/05 scheme, which provided residency to nearly seventeen thousand migrant parents of Irish children, subjectified migrants by making continued residency conditional on securing employment and other requirements, see Siobhán Ní Chatháin, "Transnational Migrants' Negotiations of Formal and Informal Citizenship," *Irish Journal of Sociology* 19, no. 2 (2011): 27–42.

118. For example, Rose, *Powers of Freedom*; and Anna Marie Smith, *Welfare Reform and Sexual Regulation* (Cambridge: Cambridge University Press, 2007).

119. See Inda, *Targeting Immigrants*, 24.

120. Giorgio Agamben, *Homo Sacer: Sovereign Power and Bare Life*, trans. Daniel Heller-Roazen (Stanford, Calif.: Stanford University Press, 1998).

121. For a useful review of feminist scholarship that builds on but extends Agamben's framework, see Alison Mountz, "Where Asylum Seekers Wait: Feminist Counter-Topographies of Sites between States," *Gender, Place and Culture* 18, no. 3 (June 2011): 381–99.

122. Heterosexual reproduction as "life" was literalized to an extraordinary degree by these Irish policies.

123. According to FLAC, the minister for justice framed asylum seekers' preference for private rented accommodation over Direct Provision as a matter of asylum seekers "reject[ing] a legitimate offer of accommodation, thereby rendering themselves homeless"; therefore, he argued, they "should not be awarded the full rate of Supplementary Welfare Allowance or have their accommodation needs met in either emergency accommodation or the private rented sector except in very exceptional cases' " (*Direct Discrimination?*, 9).

124. Nuala Haughey, "State Housing for New Asylum Seekers," *Irish Times*, June 12, 2003.

125. Thornton, "Upon the Limits of Rights Regimes," 90. Note, however, that in 2008 Social Welfare Appeals officers held that four women who were in the asylum/leave to remain process *did* meet the HRC and therefore qualified for child benefit. The decision was appealed, and DFSA issued new *Guidelines for Deciding Officers* that state, "An asylum seeker cannot satisfy either the habitual residence condition or the normal residence condition for any DFSA payments." Nonetheless, FLAC continues to challenge the argument that asylum seekers as a class cannot meet the HRC. See FLAC, "Policy Document: Briefing Note on the Habitual Residence Condition," September 2009, accessed June 17, 2011, www.flac.ie/publications/briefing-note-on-the-habitual-residence-condition/.

126. Fanning and colleagues offer a definition of social exclusion: "The *Partnership 2000 Agreement* (1996) defined social exclusion in terms of 'cumulative marginalisation: from production (employment), from consumption (income poverty), from social networks (community, family and neighbours), from decision making and from an adequate quality of life.'" See Fanning, Veale, and O'Connor, *Beyond the Pale*, 13.

127. Nasc, *Hidden Cork*, 12.

128. Ibid., 2: "Much has been said about the quality of the Irish asylum system by Government and Government representatives. It is not the experience of Nasc, nor is it evident in the research, that the Irish system meets the best standards in terms of transparency, consistency and justice."

129. RIA, *Value for Money and Policy Review*, 64.

130. Ibid., 65.

131. Nasc, *Hidden Cork*, 35.

4. The "Right to Life of the Unborn" and Migration Controls

1. Article 40.3.3 states: "The State acknowledges the right to life of the unborn and, with due regard to the equal right to life of the mother, guarantees in its laws to respect, and, as far as practicable, by its laws to defend and vindicate that right." See *Bunreacht na hÉireann, Constitution of Ireland* (Dublin: Government Publications, 1937).

2. This is a legal term that results in reduced scope for appealing a negative judgment.

3. Carol Coulter, "AG to Argue that Unborn Child Is Not a Person," *Irish Times,* January 9, 2002.

4. These included the arguments that her unborn child was legally a person and therefore a deportation order should also have been issued against the unborn child (which it was not); and that Ms. O's asylum claim had not been reviewed according to "fair procedures." Mary Carolan, "Court Appeal against Deportation Fails," *Irish Times,* February 15, 2002.

5. Mary Carolan, "Status of the Unborn at the Centre of a Plea against Deportation," *Irish Times,* February 6, 2002.

6. Crystal Hug, *The Politics of Sexual Morality in Ireland* (New York: St. Martin's, 1999), 143.

7. Mullally, "Debating Reproductive Rights in Ireland," 82. As Anthias and Yuval-Davis describe, women's sexuality is central to gendered nationalist projects because women reproduce the next generation not only biologically but also culturally; furthermore, women's sexualities provide a means to demarcate group boundaries. See Floya Anthias and Nira Yuval-Davis, "Introduc-

tion," in *Woman, Nation, State,* ed. Nira Yuval-Davis and Floya Anthias, 1–15 (New York: Saint Martin's, 1989). M. Jacqui Alexander extends their argument, showing that these processes require nation-states to engage in forcefully heterosexualizing their citizenry, thereby stigmatizing and dispossessing lesbians, gay men, sex workers, and non-heteronormative people in ways that rearticulate racial, class, gendered, and neocolonial hierarchies. See Alexander, *Pedagogies of Crossing.*

8. Article 41.2.1 of the Constitution says, "The State recognises that by her life within the home, woman gives to the State a support without which the common good cannot be achieved." Consequently, according to Article 41.2.2, "The State shall . . . endeavour to ensure that mothers shall not be obliged by economic necessity to engage in labour to the neglect of their duties in the home."

9. Ruth Fletcher characterizes that construction as pronatalist, treating population as a valuable resource for the postcolonial nation (367, 369, 383). See Ruth Fletcher, "Reproducing Irishness: Race, Gender, and Abortion Law," *Canadian Journal of Women and the Law* 17, no. 2 (2005): 365–404.

10. Mullally describes that "adherence to the Roman Catholic teachings on issues involving the family, sexuality, and reproductive health served to distinguish 'Irish laws and Irish ways' from the 'polluting' forces of English law." Mullally "Debating Reproductive Rights in Ireland," 84. The 1929 Censorship of Publications Act prohibited selling, publishing, distributing, or importing any publications related to contraception or abortion; the Criminal Law (Amendment) Act 1935 prohibited the sale, importation, or distribution (but not the use) of contraceptives.

11. For example, see Ronit Lentin, " 'Irishness,' the 1937 Constitution, and Citizenship: A Gender and Ethnicity View," *Irish Journal of Sociology* 8 (1998): 5–24. Ruth Fletcher suggests that "post-colonial nationalism . . . reclaimed a racialized Irishness to some extent and celebrated the superiority of the Catholic Celts and their reproducing women" ("Reproducing Irishness," 377).

12. Oaks, "Irishness, Eurocitizens, and Reproductive Rights," 133.

13. The decision is *McGee v. Attorney General* [1974 I.R. 284].

14. Mullally, "Debating Reproductive Rights in Ireland," 89.

15. Fletcher, "Reproducing Irishness," 383.

16. Ibid., 384; and Mullally, "Debating Reproductive Rights in Ireland," 90.

17. Fletcher, "Reproducing Irishness," 384.

18. See Tom Hesketh, *The Second Partitioning of Ireland: The Abortion Referendum of 1983* (Dublin: Brandsma Books, 1990).

19. For recent valuable discussions about Article 40.3.3, see Jennifer Schweppe, ed., *The Unborn Child, Article 40.3.3 and Abortion in Ireland: Twenty-Five Years of Protection?* (Cork: Liffey Press, 2008).

20. M. A. G. O'Tuathaigh, "The Historical Pattern of Irish Emigration: Some Labour Aspects," in *The Emigrant Experience*, ed. Galway Labour History Group (Galway: Galway Labour History Group, 1991), 9.

21. MacLaughlin, "Emigration and the Construction of Nationalist Hegemony in Ireland," 6, 13; see also Lee, *Ireland 1912–1985*, 374.

22. Alternatively, they endured confinement within what James M. Smith describes as Ireland's "architecture of containment," including Magdalene Laundries. See Smith, *Ireland's Magdalene Laundries and the Nation's Architecture of Containment*.

23. Luibhéid, "Pink Tide"; and O'Carroll, "Breaking the Silence from a Distance."

24. Earner-Byrne, "'Moral Repatriation,'" 155; see also Ryan, "Sexualising Emigration."

25. Earner-Byrne, "'Moral Repatriation,'" 156. Only in the 1930s, under considerable pressure, did the state actively respond by sanctioning a repatriation program for pregnant unmarried Irish women in Britain. Earner-Byrne relates that "repatriation as a tool of reversal or change was utterly unsuccessful because it responded only to the symptoms not the causes of this prenatal emigration" (172). Causes that Earner-Byrnes names include being rejected socially; being discriminated against; the likelihood of being detained in an institution; being held liable for the cost of one's child's maintenance in an institution; being subjected to religious manipulation; and being viewed as a financial and moral burden (170).

26. Ibid., 155.

27. Moreover, practices of seeking abortion in Britain generated and institutionalized transnational networks of solidarity between women in Ireland and Britain. See Ann Rossiter, *Ireland's Hidden Diaspora: The "Abortion Trail" and the Making of a London-Irish Underground, 1980–2000* (London: IASC Publishing, 2009).

28. Hug, *Politics of Sexual Morality in Ireland*, 160–1.

29. Sherie de Burgh, *The Irish Journey: Women's Stories of Abortion* (Dublin: Irish Family Planning Association, 2000), 5.

30. Ibid., 35, 37.

31. See Irish Family Planning Association, "Statistics," accessed May 25, 2010, www.ifpa.ie/Hot-Topics/Abortion/Statistics.

32. "Ireland was pure and abortion free. Irish abortion was exported," according to Tony O'Brien. See O'Brien, "Abortion in Ireland: Abortion Law in the Republic of Ireland," in *Abortion Law and Politics Today*, ed. Ellie Lee (New York: St. Martin's, 1998), 112.

33. In addition to seeking abortions in Britain, "Irish women have also had abortions in other European countries; in the United States, in Canada, Aus-

tralia, New Zealand.'" Medb Ruane, *The Irish Journey: Women's Stories of Abortion* (Dublin: IFPA, 2000), 10. But Britain remains the primary destination.

34. Jo Murphy-Lawless, "Fertility, Bodies and Politics: The Irish Case," *Reproductive Health Matters* 2 (November 1993): 57.

35. Lisa Smyth, *Abortion and Nation: The Politics of Reproduction in Contemporary Ireland* (Aldershot, U.K.: Ashgate, 2005), 112–13. Internment is a process of confining or imprisoning people without trial, often on political grounds. It has a long history in Ireland (north and south). Most recently, it was introduced into Northern Ireland on August 9, 1971, and used primarily against those suspected of belonging to Irish Republican groups. The interrogation techniques that were often employed resulted in a judgment by the European Court of Human Rights that Britain had engaged in inhuman and degrading treatment. While it was in effect, internment resulted in tremendous alienation and anger among Northern Ireland's Catholic minority.

36. According to Smyth, "characterizations of X and her family as respectable, middle class and law abiding were particularly important in generating the reaction." Smyth, *Abortion and Nation*, 1. See also Fletcher, "Reproducing Irishness."

37. Mullally, "Debating Reproductive Rights in Ireland," 92. "Many Irish people faced the contempt of fellow Europeans for what was judged to be a barbaric ruling." Murphy-Lawless, "Fertility, Bodies and Politics," 57.

38. Mullally, "Debating Reproductive Rights in Ireland," 92. "Fearing an adverse impact on market forces and the image of the Irish abroad, the government actually volunteered to pay the costs of the Supreme Court appeal, so anxious were they to have the issue resolved." Murphy-Lawless, "Fertility, Bodies and Politics," 57.

39. "The Supreme Court lifted the injunction, reversing the High Court's ruling on the substantive question of abortion. Pointing out the state's duty to have 'due regard' for the life of the mother [according to Article 40.3.3], the Supreme Court concluded that abortion was lawful in Ireland when there was a 'real and substantial risk' to the life, as distinct to the health, of the mother." Mullally, "Debating Reproductive Rights in Ireland," 92.

40. Murphy-Lawless, "Fertility, Bodies and Politics," 57; see also Katie Conrad, *Locked in the Family Cell* (Madison: University of Wisconsin Press, 2004), 102.

41. Madeleine Reid, "Abortion Law in Ireland after the Maastricht Referendum," in *The Abortion Papers, Ireland*, ed. Ailbhe Smyth (Dublin: Attic Press, 1992), 26.

42. Ibid.

43. As Justice Findlay summarizes, "It was submitted on behalf of the defendants . . . that even if orders restraining the first defendant [X] from leaving the

jurisdiction for purposes of having an abortion carried out, were permissible under Irish constitutional law, they were prohibited by European community law as being in breach of the Treaty of Rome, which provides a freedom for persons to travel from one Member state to another for the purpose of availing of a service in that other Member state, the performance of an operation of abortion being, within the meaning of European law, such a service." See *The Attorney General v. X,* 1 I.R. [1992] at 59.

44. Mullally, "Debating Reproductive Rights in Ireland," 93.

45. Oaks, "Irishness, Eurocitizens, and Reproductive Rights," 140.

46. Ruane, *The Irish Journey: Women's Stories of Abortion,* 23.

47. EU citizenship "derived from holding the citizenship of a member state and thereby complementing, not replacing, national citizenship." Andrew Geddes, *Immigration and European Integration,* 2nd ed. (Manchester, U.K.: Manchester University Press, 2008), 104. Contrary to claims about supranational citizenship, this structure reinforced rather than eroded the importance of holding citizenship in a member nation.

48. See ibid.; and Bill Jordan and Franck Düvell, *Irregular Migration* (Cheltenham, U.K.: Edward Elgar, 2004), 41–43.

49. Murphy-Lawless, "Fertility, Bodies and Politics," 57. According to Oaks, pro-life activists working through pro-life conservative senator Des Hanafin ensured that the protocol would be included in the treaty. Oaks, "Irishness, Eurocitizens, and Reproductive Rights," 136.

50. For example, see Oaks, "Irishness, Eurocitizens, and Reproductive Rights."

51. Ibid., 149. Importantly, Oaks continues, "As changes have transformed the meaning of Irishness, so too 'European' identities are being explicitly reformulated within and across the European Union." Ibid.

52. Murphy-Lawless, "Fertility, Bodies, and Politics," 57; see also Smyth, *Abortion and Nation;* and Conrad, *Locked in the Family Cell,* 106–7.

53. Ailbhe Smyth, "'And Nobody Was Any the Wiser': Irish Abortion Rights and the European Union," in *Sexual Politics and the European Union: The New Feminist Challenge,* ed. R. Amy Elman (Providence, R.I.: Berghahn Books, 1996), 111.

54. However, vulnerable women's right and capacity to travel abroad for abortions are still not unequivocal. In 2007 Ms. D, a seventeen-year-old who was in the care of the Health Services Executive, learned that her fetus had anencephaly and would most likely die soon after birth. Ms. D had to resort to the courts in order to secure the right to travel abroad for an abortion. Her situation illustrates that minors, those in care of the state, prisoners, and those with limited income remain without assurance as to their right or capacity to travel for abortions.

55. According to Jane Helleiner, "Anti-Traveller racism was very much part of the ethos and practice of the post-colonial state." Helleiner, *Irish Travellers,* 74.

56. Garner, *Racism in the Irish Experience,* 144.

57. O'Connell, "Travellers in Ireland," 49.

58. Helleiner, *Irish Travellers,* 162–63. Settled people also tend perceive Traveller marriage as particularly oppressive to Traveller women (ibid., 181). Yet, the extent to which institutionalized racism and (hetero)sexism in the mainstream severely limits Traveller women's horizons of possibility is rarely acknowledged.

59. Ibid., 166.

60. Ní Shúineár, "Othering the Irish (Travellers)," 189.

61. Ibid., 188, 189.

62. Helleiner, *Irish Travellers,* 71.

63. Fletcher, "Reproducing Irishness," 389.

64. Ibid., 388.

65. Ibid.

66. Ibid.

67. Ibid., 390.

68. Ibid.

69. Daniel J. Kanstroom, *Deportation Nation: Outsiders in American History* (Harvard, Mass.: Harvard University Press, 2007).

70. Matthew J. Gibney, "Asylum and the Expansion of Deportation in the United Kingdom," *Government and Opposition* 43, no. 2 (2008): 147.

71. Quoted in Kanstroom, *Deportation Nation,* 18

72. Gibney, "Asylum and the Expansion of Deportation in the United Kingdom," 147.

73. There are several types of "forced return" to which migrants may be subjected: deportation, removal, or Dublin II transfers. For discussion of the differences, see Emma Quinn, *Programmes and Strategies in Ireland for Fostering Assisted Return to and Reintegration into Third Countries* (Dublin: ESRI, 2010). As this report notes, various forms of assisted voluntary return also exist.

74. Decisions to grant leave to remain are entirely at the minister's discretion.

75. Emma Quinn and Gerard Hughes, *Illegally Resident Third Country Nationals in Ireland: State Approaches toward Their Situation* (Dublin: ESRI, 2005), 23.

76. Ibid., 36.

77. Liz Fekete, "The Deportation Machine: Europe, Asylum, and Human Rights," *Race and Class* 47, no. 1 (2005): 71.

78. Ibid., 72–73.

79. Ibid., 74.

80. Quinn and Hughes, *Illegally Resident Third Country Nationals,* 36.

81. For helpful analysis of deportation in the EU and globally, see Nicolas De Genova and Natalie Peutz, eds., *The Deportation Regime: Sovereignty, Space, and Freedom of Movement* (Durham, N.C.: Duke University Press, 2010).

82. For example, see Quinn, *Migration and Asylum in Ireland*; and Quinn, *Organisation of Migration and Asylum Policies in Ireland.*

83. Lentin and McVeigh, *After Optimism?*, 49.

84. Quinn, *Migration and Asylum in Ireland*, 5.

85. For example, see Charlie Taylor, "New Immigration Bill Published," *Irish Times*, July 2, 2010; the Immigrant Council of Ireland (ICI), "The Immigration, Residence and Protection Bill, 2010—A Critical Overview," September 2010, www.immigrantcouncil.ie/images/stories/ICI_critical_overview_-_IRP_Bill _2010_final_0910.pdf; and the Irish Refugee Council, "The Right to Protection: Submission to the Joint Oireachtas Committee on Justice, Equality, Defence, and Women's Rights on the Protection Aspects of the Immigration, Residence and Protection Bill, 2008," accessed December 17, 2012, www .irishrefugeecouncil.ie/wp-content/uploads/2011/08/IRC-Submission-on-the -IRP-Bill-2008.pdf.

86. According to Lentin and McVeigh (*After Optimism?*, 49), the state justifies such deportations as an important means for ensuring the integrity of the asylum system—in other words, the fact the state can deport those with unsuccessful claims ensures that the state can at the same time provide protection to "genuine" asylum seekers. But this argument does not really stand up to scrutiny, especially when we consider Ireland's low rates for refugee recognition and the practical and administrative difficulties facing those needing protection. Instead the situation suggests that the chimera of the "genuine asylum seeker" allows the state to relentlessly expand its deportation regimes even while claiming to uphold human rights. This argument extends Jacqueline Bhabha's suggestion that the asylum system helps to keep restrictive immigration defensible. Bhabha, "Internationalist Gatekeepers? The Tension between Asylum Advocacy and Human Rights," *Harvard Human Rights Journal* 15 (2002): 155–82.

87. Quinn, *Programmes and Strategies in Ireland*, 7.

88. *Baby O. v. Minister for Justice, Equality and Law Reform* [2002] IESC 44 (6th June, 2002), online at Supreme Court of Ireland Decisions, www.bailii.org /ie/cases/IESC/2002/44.html.

89. Fletcher, "Reproducing Irishness," 391.

90. This complex case therefore required analysis not only of gender and sexual hierarchies but also intersecting racial and immigration hierarchies.

91. Coulter, "AG to Argue That Unborn Person Is Not a Child."

92. *Baby O. v. Minister for Justice, Equality and Law Reform*, 8.

93. Ibid.

94. Carol Coulter, "State Fails to Argue Foetus Is Not a Person," *Irish Times*, January 10, 2002.

95. As Ruth Fletcher explains, "This position stands in marked contrast to [the state's] explicit representation of the 'unborn' as a distinct legal entity in the context of abortion information law" (391). Moreover, the position contra-

dicts the decision in the *X* case, "where the 'unborn's' rights were deemed capable of limiting women's rights"—including in the realm of travel across international borders. See Fletcher, "Reproducing Irishness," 392.

96. Coulter, "State Fails to Argue Foetus Is Not a Person."

97. "High Court Challenge by Nigerian Woman Is Dismissed," *Irish Times,* January 19, 2002.

98. *Baby O. v. Minister for Justice, Equality and Law Reform,* 8.

99. A pessimistic reading suggests that "the court is concerned with the 'unborn's' rights only insofar as they limit women's right to abortion." Fletcher, "Reproducing Irishness," 393–94.

100. Mullally, "Debating Reproductive Rights in Ireland," 101.

101. Fletcher, "Reproducing Irishness," 393.

102. Ibid.

103. Ibid., 395.

104. Ibid., 394.

105. Smyth, *Abortion and Nation,* 127.

106. Fletcher, "Reproducing Irishness," 394.

107. The importance of thinking about state regimes for governing immigration in tandem with emigration is suggested by the fact that even as immigration continues to occur, so also does emigration. For the most recent immigration *and* emigration figures for Ireland, see Joyce, *Annual Policy Report on Migration and Asylum 2009,* 49.

108. In August 2005 three women who were forced to travel from Ireland to England to secure abortions filed a grievance against the Irish state in the European Court of Human Rights. Their case, known as *A, B and C v. Ireland,* raises important questions about the connections between travel across borders, abortion access, and women's rights.

109. In 2008 the Irish Family Planning Association received a grant of €75,000 to establish the Majira project, with input from AkiDwA. "The aim of the project is to improve the quality of reproductive and sexual health for refugees and asylum seekers by providing sustainable medical care, psychological care, training and information. . . . On 8th July, 2009, 29 women seeking asylum in Ireland graduated from a 10-week empowerment course focusing on sexual and reproductive health and rights." "Abortion and Society," Abortion in Ireland website, accessed June 3, 2012, www.abortioninireland.org/republic -of-ireland/abortion-and-society.

110. "Ireland 2001," Women on Waves website, accessed June 27, 2008, www .womenonwaves.org/set-309-nl.html. Others included "women who had been raped, schoolgirls who would not find a feasible excuse to go to England for a couple of days, [and] mothers who could not pay childcare during their journey to England."

111. Carol Coulter, "Asylum Seekers Permitted to Go Abroad for Abortions 'for Years,'" *Irish Times*, October 15, 2001.

112. Ibid.

113. Human Rights Watch, *A State of Isolation: Access to Abortion for Women in Ireland* (New York: Human Rights Watch, 2010), 33–34.

114. Two women were granted temporary exit and reentry visas to enable them to travel to Britain for an abortion in 2000; eight women received such documents in 2001; thirty-three women received such documents in 2003; through July 31, 2004, ten women received the documents. See Joe Humphries, "Issue of Travel Visas for Abortions Defended," *Irish Times*, July 12, 2004; and Joe Humphries, "60 Asylum Seekers Left the State to Seek Abortions in the U.K.," *Irish Times*, September 17, 2004. The most recent information suggests that "according to figures from the Department of Justice, the number of asylum seekers recorded as travelling abroad for abortions has dropped from . . . 22 in 2005 to just one in 2008, and none at all this year [2009]." Danielle Barron, "The Practice of Illegal Abortion (in Ireland)," *Irish Medical News*, November 16, 2009, www.choiceireland.org/content/imn-practice-illegal-abortion-ireland.

115. Fletcher, "Reproducing Irishness," 398.

116. Ibid., 399.

117. Costs include "direct costs such as travel and accommodation [and] indirect costs, including childcare, loss of income and the costs of a traveling companion." Human Rights Watch, *A State of Isolation*, 31. Those needing visas or translation services must pay these costs. In addition, women must pay for the cost of the abortion procedure itself, which varies depending on the clinic where it is done and the stage of the pregnancy. "Irish service providers estimated the total costs to be between €800 and €1,000." Ibid.

118. Fletcher, "Reproducing Irishness," 399.

119. All this has to be accomplished by women who lack the financial and support networks that are available to citizens, long-term residents, and other migrants.

120. Human Rights Watch, *A State of Isolation*, 33.

121. Ibid. Even with the correct travel documents, some women who "tried to come back through Northern Ireland, have been stopped by immigration officials in Belfast and detained in Macebearer prison." Kitty Holland, "Asylum Seekers Granted Visas for U.K. Abortions," *Irish Times*, August 30, 2003.

122. Kitty Holland, "Woman Not Allowed to Travel for Abortion," *Irish Times*, February 22, 2005.

123. Ibid. The article also describes a single mother from Nigeria who made an appointment for an abortion in England but was similarly refused travel documents and therefore had to cancel. A fortnight after cancelling, she had

"lost" the baby, which raised questions about whether she had resorted to a back-street abortion in Dublin.

124. Fletcher, "Reproducing Irishness," 397.

125. Thus, in 2006 the *Irish Independent* reported the experiences of a Lithuanian migrant worker who worked two jobs but remained under severe financial pressure since she needed to send money home to her parents while also assisting an unemployed brother in Ireland. When she learned that she was pregnant, her male partner pressured her to abort the baby and eventually left her. She paid a Russian-speaking man for an abortifacient that induced bleeding. The woman gave birth to a boy at thirty-six weeks, alone in a field. "The baby was not breathing and was blue, and . . . she held him in her arms for a long time." An inquest determined that "the baby had died 'of undetermined causes, following a self-induced miscarriage,'" and the director of public prosecutions declined to press charges. Breandán Morley, "Mother Gave Birth in Field after Abortion," *Irish Independent*, November 30, 2006. The woman's experiences evoke those of Anne Lovett, a fifteen-year-old girl who, in 1984, died alone in a field in County Longford while giving birth to a child. Her death shocked the nation and opened up a sustained public discussion.

126. The Migrant Rights Centre Ireland (MCRI), *Private Homes a Public Concern: The Experiences of Twenty Migrant Women Employed in the Private Home in Ireland* (Dublin: MCRI, December 2004), 29.

127. Jimmy Walshe, "O'Meara Appalled by Back-Street Abortions," *Irish Times*, July 9, 2004.

128. Georgina O'Halloran and Shane Phelan, "Mum Who Used Pill for Home Abortion Likely to Avoid Charges," *Irish Independent*, May 23, 2008; see also Georgina O'Halloran, "Woman Fled Ireland for Philippines after Inducing Abortion," *Irish Independent*, May 23, 2008.

129. See Center for Reproductive Rights, fact sheet, "*A, B and C v. Ireland*," accessed December 21, 2012, http://reproductiverights.org/sites/crr.civicactions.net/files/documents/crr_ABC_Factsheet.pdf.

5. Reproductive Futurism and the Temporality of Migration Control

1. Michael McDowell, "Proposed Citizenship Referendum: Article by Minister for Justice, Equality, and Law Reform Mr. Michael McDowell, T.D.," *Sunday Independent*, March 14, 2004, accessed November 24, 2008, www.inis.gov.ie/en/inis/article.pdf/Files/article.pdf.

2. Lee Edelman, *Queer Theory and the Death Drive* (Durham, N.C.: Duke University Press, 2004). For further analysis of how heteronormative politics and visions of the national future authorize violence against immigrants, queers, communities of color, and poor or working-class people, see Lauren

Berlant, *The Queen of America Goes to Washington City* (Durham, N.C.: Duke University Press, 1997). For critical analysis of the claim that gay men, lesbians, and queer people threaten not only the national future but also "Western civilization," see Janet Jakobsen, "Can Homosexuals End Western Civilization as We Know It? Family Values in a Global Economy," in *Queer Globalizations: Citizenship and the Afterlife of Colonialism*, ed. Arnaldo Cruz-Malavé and Martin F. Manalansan IV (New York: New York University Press, 2002), 49–70.

3. Moreover, this inequity is generally naturalized rather than historicized and critically questioned.

4. Diaspora was temporally imagined as stretching from an impoverished national past that generated mass emigration to an imagined prosperous future where emigration would no longer be necessary.

5. The original Article 2 of the 1937 constitution laid claim to the entire island of Ireland, rather than just the twenty-six southern counties, and included an assertion that Northern Ireland was within the "national territory." Article 3, which was also amended as part of the peace process, made similar claims on Northern Ireland.

6. For example, see Lentin and McVeigh, *After Optimism?*, 51–55, for a summary of the history of Irish citizenship; see also Siobhan Mullally, "Citizenship and Family Life in Ireland: Adding the Question 'Who Belongs,'" *Legal Studies* 25, no. 4 (2005): 578–600; and Bernard Ryan, "The Celtic Cubs: The Controversy over Birthright Citizenship in Ireland," *European Journal of Migration and Law* 6 (2004): 173–93.

7. The referendum did not alter Article 2; rather, voters were asked whether to insert a new section into Article 9, saying, "Notwithstanding any other provision of this Constitution, a person born in the island of Ireland, which includes its islands and seas, who does not have at the time of his or her birth at least one parent who is an Irish citizen or entitled to be an Irish citizen is not entitled to Irish citizenship or nationality, unless otherwise provided for by law." That change then allowed the Oireachtas (parliament) to pass a law that restricted who was entitled to birthright citizenship.

8. Ryan, "Celtic Cubs," 178.

9. Breda Gray, *Women and the Irish Diaspora* (London: Routledge, 2004), 32, 33.

10. Breda Gray, "Diaspora—New or Old Logics of Affiliation? A Case Study of the Irish Diaspora," plenary address at the conference "Neither Here nor There: Writing the Irish Diaspora," University of Limerick, October 30, 2008.

11. Nash, *Of Irish Descent*, 27, 39.

12. Katy Hayward and Kevin Howard, "Cherry-Picking the Diaspora," in *Immigration and Social Change in the Republic of Ireland*, ed. Bryan Fanning (Manchester, U.K.: Manchester University Press, 2007), 57–58. These authors

argue that the focus on recruiting Irish-born and Irish-descended labor reflects a model of "connection" based on descent combined with culture. The authors further describe that when Irish emigrants proved insufficient in numbers to meet the state's labor needs, recruitment strategies broadened in a manner that reflected an "implicit hierarchy in the type of immigrants sought" (51): from skilled Irish emigrants, to members of the Irish diaspora, to "qualified non-nationals from Britain, EU Member states, East European states (including Russia), and then English speaking states (including India)" (51)—but not, for instance, Anglophone Africa, except for the case of white South Africans.

13. Gray, "Diaspora—New or Old Logics of Affiliation." Gray proposes that in the new millennium, the model has changed from that of the Irish family to that of the Irish family firm. Also see Breda Gray, "Curious Hybridities: Transnational Negotiations of Migrancy through Generation," *Irish Studies Review* 14, no. 2 (2006): 207–23.

14. Nash, *Of Irish Descent*, 55. For a valuable discussion of the ways that Irishness became normed as white through the intersection of national and global histories, see McVeigh and Lentin, "Situated Racisms, 1–48. See also McVeigh and Lentin, *After Optimism*.

15. *L. and O. v. Minister for Justice, Equality and Law Reform* [2003] IESC 1 (January 23, 2003).

16. Ibid., per Chief Justice Ronan Keane, at para. 103.

17. Ibid., per Justice John Murray, at para. 189.

18. Moreover, the minister ordered that when migrant parents left, they were to bring their Irish citizen children with them or else face charges. Thus, the ruling resulted in forced exiling of minor Irish citizens who were by definition ethnic minorities (since their parents were migrants).

19. This strategy was problematic in many ways, including because it was deeply heteronormative, erased women, and created a focus on citizen children that minimized consideration of migrants' lives or robust critique of migration policy from a migrant rather than citizen perspective. But it was also a strategic decision. See Pratt, *Families Apart*, for discussion of the risks and possible gains of these kinds of representational strategies.

20. Thus, the imagery created binarized, essentializing representations of "race," Irishness, and legal status that were very problematic—but that did reflect how many people understood the issues.

21. Michael O'Farrell, "Immigrants Protest at Dail against Deportations," *Irish Examiner*, July 4, 2003. See also Nuala Haughey, "Parents Protest at Threatened Deportations," *Irish Times*, July 4, 2003.

22. "Michael McDowell, hear us say . . ." would alternate with "Bertie Ahern, hear us say . . . ," "Fianna Fail, hear us say . . . ," and "Immigration police, hear us say. . . ."

23. Personal conversation with Ronit Lentin, July 2003.

24. Department of Justice, Equality and Law Reform, "Notice to Non-National Parents of Irish Born Children," *Irish Times*, July 18, 2003, 8. Nuala Haughey clarifies the significance of item 4: if they leave voluntarily, they will receive assistance with costs, and "they would be free in the future to apply to come back to Ireland, perhaps as migrant workers." Nuala Haughey, "Position of Immigrant Parents Clarified," *Irish Times*, July 18, 2003.

25. Copy in the author's possession.

26. Carl O'Brien, "Refugees Face Being Deported after New Deadline," *Irish Times*, August 12, 2003.

27. Nuala Haughey, "Immigrant Parents Face Deportation," *Irish Times*, July 28, 2003.

28. Coakley and Healy, *Looking Forward, Looking Back*, 24.

29. This is the lead-in to an article by Ursula Fraser, "Immigration Act Places Duty on Asylum Seekers to Prove Persecution," *Metro Eireann* 4, no. 8 (August 2003): 8.

30. This is not to suggest that the government or opponents of the referendum explicitly used the language of reproductive futurism but rather that we can usefully read their materials through that lens.

31. Department of Justice, Equality and Law Reform, *Information Note on Proposal for Constitutional Amendment and Legislation Concerning the Issue of Irish Citizenship for Children of Non-National Parents* (Dublin: DJLER, 2004), heading that introduces paragraph 9, accessed January 10, 2010, www.inis.gov.ie/en/INIS/information%20note.pdf/files/information%20note.pdf (hereafter *Information Note*).

32. Statistics about asylum-seeker women's rates of pregnancy are included not only in the main text of the Information Note but also in section 3.1 of appendix 1, "Pregnant Asylum Applicants," with more than a page of tables of the pregnancy rates of women who sought asylum, month by month, for March to December 2002 and January to December 2003. No explanation is offered about how the statistics were generated.

33. *Information Note*, para. 11.

34. Ibid., para. 14.

35. Ibid., para. 17. Even Peter Schuck and Roger Smith, the original framers of the thesis that pregnant women engage in unauthorized migration so as to secure the benefits of birthright citizenship in a wealthy nation-state for their child, admitted that their evidence was primarily anecdotal. Schuck and Smith, *Citizenship without Consent: Illegal Aliens and the American Polity* (New Haven, Conn.: Yale University Press, 1985). Moreover, such a framing ignores the wider transnational relations that structure migration—and ignores the role of the state in generating significant levels of migration, including through labor recruitment.

36. This framing, of course, created a particular bounded notion of the categories "Ireland" and "Irish people."

37. *Information Note*, para. 17.

38. Ibid., para. 13. Similarly, according to McDowell, "our maternity services come under pressure" (which repeats a long-standing discourse that suggests problems accessing health care as attributable to immigrants rather than to difficulties within the state and the system). See McDowell, "Proposed Citizenship Referendum."

39. McDowell, "Proposed Citizenship Referendum."

40. Ibid.

41. According to the information note, the government considered two options: "to legislate based on the current constitutional provisions; or, alternatively, to promote a constitutional referendum to allow for a significant legislative change" (para. 18). The legislative option was "not considered viable" (para. 19), so the government pursued a referendum.

42. Many naturalize this link. For critical discussion, see Jacqueline Stevens, *Reproducing the State* (Princeton, N.J.: Princeton University Press, 1999).

43. This argument reworks, from a queer migration theory angle, Arendt's important insight that when people were unable to claim nationality and citizenship, they were unable to claim and access "human rights"—which makes clear that many (though not all) "rights" must be translated and leveraged through discourses of nation and national citizenship. The Irish situation demands that we route Arendt's insights through a critique of reproductive futurism and heteronormative logics. See Arendt, "Decline of the Nation-State."

44. For example, Julie-Anne Barnes, "Doctors Reject 'Scapegoat' Role for Decision by McDowell," *Irish Times,* March 11, 2004; "Masters Pleaded with Him, says McDowell," *Irish Times,* March 12, 2004; and Liam Reid, "Masters Deny Seeking Change of Status on Non-Nationals," *Irish Times,* March 13, 2004.

45. King, *Immigration and Citizenship in Ireland.*

46. Ibid., 6.

47. Ibid., v.

48. "Masters Urged Tighter Controls on Immigration," *Irish Times,* April 22, 2004.

49. *Information Note,* para. 12.

50. Significantly, nowhere are these women described as entering in violation of immigration laws. In that sense, they are not "illegal immigrants" as that term is commonly understood, even though the minister positions them that way.

51. National Consultative Committee on Racism and Interculturalism, "The Citizenship Referendum: Issues, Observations, and Concerns," Advocacy Paper

Series, Paper No. 3, June 2004, accessed December 17, 2012, www.nccri.ie/pdf/AdvocacyPaper3.pdf, p. 3. For a critique of the claims that migrants seek the "entitlements" associated with citizenship while shucking off associated responsibilities, see Helga Leitner and Patricia Ehrkamp, "Transnationalism and Migrants' Imagining of Citizenship," *Environment and Planning A* 38 (2006): 1615–32.

52. "Masters Urged Tighter Controls on Immigration," *Irish Times*, April 22, 2004. Dervla King discusses various legitimate reasons why women present at late stages for maternity care (which the citizenship referendum would not address). See King, *Immigration and Citizenship*, iv.

53. According to Dr. Declan Keane, master of the National Maternity Hospital, "More recently we have noticed a change whereby African women and eastern European patients who are living in Paris, Holland, and indeed Britain, and are getting their full antenatal care there, are coming to this country at the last moment, at 35, 36 weeks. Now, they cannot be coming for medical reasons because these countries offer extremely good maternity and obstetrical care, so I do believe that they are coming for one reason and one reason only, and that is for citizenship reasons." Quoted in Eithne Donnellan, "Rotunda Master Anxious over Late Arrivals," *Irish Times*, April 23, 2004.

54. Mark Brennock, "'Citizenship Tourists' a Tiny Group, Statistics Indicate," *Irish Times*, April 22, 2004.

55. Marie O'Halloran, "Gormley Insists 442 People 'Does Not Represent a Crisis,'" *Irish Times*, April 23, 2004.

56. Marie O'Halloran, "Citizenship System 'Being Abused,'" *Irish Times*, March 31, 2004.

57. Mary Raftery, "Opinion: Delivering Fact from Fiction," *Irish Times*, April 1, 2004.

58. Opinion of Advocate General Tizzano delivered on May 18, 2004, Case C-200/02, *Man Lavette Chen and Kunqian Catherine Zhu v. Secretary of State for the Home Department*, accessed November 20, 2008, www.irishtimes.com/newspaper/special/2004/chen_case/index.htm; hereafter *Opinion*.

59. The *Opinion* describes him as Mr. Chen, but since married Chinese couples often do not share the same last names, and the children are named as "Zhu," it seems possible he is Mr. Zhu.

60. *Opinion*, para. 11.

61. Britain does not automatically grant citizenship to anyone born there.

62. See note 7 above, explaining that under the revised Article 2 of the constitution, anyone born anywhere on the island of Ireland was entitled to birthright citizenship.

63. Carol Coulter and Mark Brennock, "U.K. Case May Have a Bearing on Citizenship Referendum," *Irish Times*, April 3, 2004.

64. "EU Ruling Reiterates Need for Referendum—McDowell," *Irish Times*, May 18, 2004.

65. "European Finding Bolsters Case for Referendum Made by Government," *Irish Times*, May 19, 2004.

66. Arthur Beesley, "Coalition Defends Proposals on Citizen Rights," *Irish Times*, May 22, 2004.

67. Arthur Beesley, "Voters Urged to Aid Genuine Migrants,'" *Irish Times*, June 4, 2004.

68. Mark Hennessy, "McDowell Insists His Action Heads Off 'Threat,'" *Irish Times*, May 19, 2004. Silvia Brandi observes that the minister seized on and exaggerated the possible implications of the *Chen* case, in part by failing to acknowledge that Ms. Chen's residency remained contingent on her access to private health insurance and having sufficient resources, which meant the decision limited who might be able to avail of it. Brandi, "Unveiling the Ideological Construction of the 2004 Irish Citizenship Referendum: A Critical Discourse Analytical Approach," *Translocations, the Irish Migration, Race and Social Transformation Review* 2, no. 1 (Summer 2007): 26–47.

69. For example, "what Dan Boyle of the Green Party correctly called 'the back door to EU citizenship' is actually the key issue. . . . We do have obligations to our EU partners." Martin Mansergh, "Opinion: Back Door to EU Citizenship Is the Key Issue," *Irish Times*, April 24, 2004.

70. Marie O'Halloran, "Higgins Pours Scorn on Birth Figures," *Irish Times*, April 23, 2004. Similarly, Aisling Reddy, the director of the Irish Council for Civil Liberties, argued there was no need for harmonization of laws in this area and challenged many of the government's other assertions. Carol Coulter, "Civil Rights Group Voices Concern at Citizenship Referendum," *Irish Times*, May 14, 2004.

71. Beesley, "Coalition Defends Proposals on Citizenship Rights." Note that this is not a direct quote but rather Beesley's paraphrase of Hanafin's remarks.

72. O'Halloran, "Citizenship System 'Being Abused.'"

73. Brian Lenihan, "Opinion: Citizenship Change Common Sense," *Irish Times*, May 28, 2004.

74. "McDowell Changes Arguments on Referendum," *Irish Times*, April 9, 2004.

75. Michael McDowell, "Opinion: We Must Be Able to Manage Migration in a Sensible Fashion," *Irish Times*, April 24, 2004.

76. Government discourses on citizenship generated a range of counterarguments. For instance, Fintan O'Toole, in a provocative column for the *Irish Times*, suggests that "we are, even by the most negligible definition, extremely bad at being citizens." O'Toole, "Opinion: Racist? No, This Poll Is Far Worse," *Irish Times*, April 27, 2004.

77. See Ong, *Flexible Citizenship,* for discussion of the idea that "in an era of globalization, individuals as well as governments develop a flexible notion of citizenship . . . [as a strategy] to accumulate capital and power" (6).

78. *Opinion,* para. 128.

79. "This is not a case of people 'improperly or fraudulently invoking community law' . . . but rather one of people who, appraised of the nature of the freedoms provided for by Community law, take advantage of them by legitimate means." Ibid., para. 122.

80. Ibid., para. 126.

81. Ibid., para. 127.

82. Some women undoubtedly did make such calculations, but chapter 2 argues that migrant women's pregnancies cannot be reduced to a single explanation or cause.

83. For discussion, see Judith Butler, "Contingent Foundations: Feminism and the Question of 'Postmodernism,'" in *Feminists Theorize the Political,* ed. Judith Butler and Joan W. Scott, 3–21 (New York: Routledge, 1992).

84. "The state is to deploy citizenship as a labour market incentive to ensure a steady supply of cheap and fit workers to meet the needs of foreign and domestic capital." John A. Harrington, "Citizenship and the Biopolitics of Post-Nationalist Ireland," *Journal of Law and Society* 32, no. 3 (2005): 448.

85. Mancini and Finlay, "'Citizenship Matters,'" 586.

86. Thanks to Patrick Greaney for drawing this point to my attention.

87. Thus, the minister argued, "One sure way that Ireland would risk racial and ethnic discord would be a public perception that our generous and open system is being exploited by people who are not willing to abide by our laws and rules." "Minister Defends Citizenship Referendum," *Irish Times,* March 29, 2004. Similarly, "A note of a meeting between the Minister and two of the Masters in October 2002 appears to bear out Mr. McDowell's insistence that in proposing the referendum he is motivated by a desire not to fuel racism. He promised the Masters decisive action to ease the pressure on maternity services caused by the high number of asylum seekers arriving late in pregnancy, as the existing difficulties were 'fuelling racism thinking' among the public, the note says." Brennock, "Citizenship Tourists 'a Tiny Group.'" Documents released concerning the meetings between the minister and the masters showed that "Mr. McDowell said his concern about the situation was that the difficulties in maternity hospitals would fuel racist thinking" ("Masters Urged Tighter Controls on Immigration," *Irish Times,* April 22, 2004). On June 10, a day before the vote, "the Minister said the greatest contribution to racism and xenophobia would be if it was perceived that the government could not control immigration." Carol Coulter, "Referendum: Yes Campaign," *Irish Times,* June 10, 2004.

88. Mark Brennock, "FF Says Amendment Is 'Sensible' Response to Citizenship Situation," *Irish Times*, May 24, 2004.

89. Brandi, "Unveiling the Ideological Construction," 32.

90. According to Michael Breen, Amanda Haynes, and Eoin Devereux, who surveyed coverage of the referendum by the *Irish Times* and the *Sunday Tribune* from January 1 to June 11, 2004, "loophole was used in fifteen articles." Michael Breen, Amanda Haynes, and Eoin Devereux, "Citizens, Loopholes, and Maternity Tourists: Media Frames in the Citizenship Referendum," in *Uncertain Ireland: A Sociological Chronicle, 2003–2004*, ed. Mary P. Corcoran and Michael Peillon (Dublin: Institute for Public Administration, 2006), 66.

91. Oran Doyle, "Citizenship and Equality," in *The Citizenship Referendum: Implications for the Constitution and Human Rights* (Trinity College, Dublin: The Law School, 2004), 117.

92. For example, "In a statement last night Ms. Harney [the Tanaiste or Deputy Prime Minister] denied that the Government's proposal was racist, and urged 'calm and considered debate.' She regretted claims that the proposal is designed to encourage racist tendencies, saying she hoped its opponents do not lower the entire level of democratic debate by simply denigrating the proposal, or those of us in favour of it, as "racist." . . . It cannot possibly be racist to favour more scope for law-making by the Oireachtas [Parliament] on the details of the important issue of citizenship. Since the Government has announced our decision we have heard no reasoned views against the substance of the proposal, but objections to the process and, regrettably, some personal accusations passing off as argument.'" Mark Brennock, "Tanaiste Staunchly Defends Citizenship Poll Plan," *Irish Times*, April 20, 2004.

93. Harrington, "Citizenship and the Biopolitics of Post-Nationalist Ireland," 445.

94. "Instead, the government and the vast majority of the people who supported the referendum did it 'on a basis which is decent and free from improper motives.'" Brandi, "Unveiling the Ideological Construction," 36.

95. McDowell, "Proposed Citizenship Referendum."

96. Tormey, "'Everyone with Eyes Can See the Problem,'" 69–98.

97. Ibid., 69.

98. Ibid., 86. Like other scholars, Tormey is careful to note that economic, nationalist, and other concerns also shaped the process.

99. As Tormey concludes, "Dramas of the abuse of Irish hospitality, phantasms of excessive/instrumental fertility, and the spectre of a proliferation of immoral and unworthy character were phenomenologically animated by the bodies of black immigrant mothers." Ibid., 87.

100. Lentin and McVeigh, *After Optimism?*, 54.

101. Radhika Mongia has analyzed how the legal fiction of formally equivalent sovereign nation-states, who together comprise the global, has provided the means to perpetuate inequalities grounded in histories of global capitalism and colonialism. Moreover, she describes how state systems for controlling immigration particularly enable these outcomes. See Mongia, "Historicizing State Sovereignty: Inequality and the Form of Equivalence," in *Comparative Studies in Society and History* 49, no. 2 (2007): 384–411; and Mongia, "Race, Nationality, Mobility: A History of the Passport," *Public Culture* 11, no. 3 (1999): 527–56.

102. McVeigh and Lentin, "Situated Racisms," 18.

103. Growing numbers of nation-states are harnessing their diasporas for strategic ends, including to create desirable futures.

104. Aristide R. Zolberg, "The Next Waves: Migration Theory for a Changing World, *International Migration Review* 23, no. 3 (Autumn 1989): 409. Shachar and Hirschl say that "securing membership in a given state or region—with its specific level of wealth, degree of stability, and human rights record—is a crucial factor in the determination of life chances" (253). See Ayelet Shachar and Ran Hirschl, "Citizenship as Inherited Property," *Political Theory* 35, no. 3 (June 2007): 253–85.

105. Some people are born into a citizenship status that greatly enhances opportunities and possibilities (through no merit of their own), while others are born into citizenship status that does the opposite (through no fault of their own).

106. Shachar and Hirschl, "Citizenship as Inherited Property," 274. In a different article, Shachar describes citizenship "in affluent political communities as a complex form of property right that perpetuates not only privilege but access to a disproportionate accumulation of wealth and opportunity, while at the same time insulating these important distributive decisions . . . from considerations of justice and equality" Ayelet Shachar, "Children of a Lesser State: Sustaining Global Inequality through Citizenship Laws," in *Child, Family, State,* ed. Stephen Macedo and Iris Marion Young, 345–97 (New York: New York University Press, 2003), 349. See also Ayelet Shachar, *The Birthright Lottery: Citizenship and Global Inequality* (Cambridge, Mass.: Harvard University Press, 2009).

107. Shachar, "Children of a Lesser State," 383.

108. A reproductive futurism framework usefully sheds significant light on the interconnections among sexuality, emigration, immigration, and nation-making—in Ireland and elsewhere too. For example, in the face of widespread unemployment in the 1950s, emigration soared, dividing families and communities. These "family experiences of emigration were identified as part of the rationale for the internationalization and modernization of the Irish economy," including opening Ireland to global capital starting in the late 1950s. Breda

Gray, "Putting Emotion and Reflexivity to Work in Researching Migration," *Sociology* 42, no. 5 (2008): 938. The success of this economic strategy was measured by young people's fates: would future generations be able to remain in Ireland or forced to emigrate?

6. From Childbearing to Multiple Sexuality and Migration Struggles

1. Carol Coulter, "McDowell Plans a Range of Moves on Immigration," *Irish Times,* June 14, 2004.

2. This statement makes clear that the minister's architecture of migration control, which worked through equating pregnancy with illegal migration, was by no means natural, reasonable, accepted by everyone, or unassailable. Rather, the rationales and technologies of migration control emerged—as they always do—through political processes, individual decision making, and contingencies.

3. The *Zambrano* decision, discussed later, revealed that the minister's concerns were prescient.

4. "Deported Nigerian Woman Leaves Irish-Born Child," *Irish Times,* August 26, 2004.

5. Coulter, "McDowell Plans a Range of Moves." It took the minister more than six months to announce his plan for regularizing the status of these migrant parents; in the meantime, he pushed ahead with deporting some of them, with their citizen children, which generated serious questions and concerns.

6. The new citizenship rules came into effect on January 1, 2005; until that date all children born in Ireland continued to acquire citizenship at birth.

7. Coakley and Healy, *Looking Forward, Looking Back,* 26. Other important conditions were continuous residence in Ireland since the birth of the citizen child and active involvement in the child's upbringing.

8. Ibid.

9. Ibid., 48. Moreover the requirement forced migrants to "disregard your spouse" and become "single parent[s] not by choice." Ibid., 48.

10. "The immigrants spoken to here invariably came to Ireland with the express understanding that they had a good case for consideration under the refugee application guidelines." Coakley and Healy, *Looking Forward, Looking Back,* 43. Moreover, they were aware that what happened to them impacted on family members still in their countries of origin, including family members living under conditions of danger, scarcity, or turmoil. The asylum process, however, with its overly bureaucratic construction of eligibility, combined with developments such as the *L&O* decision and the citizenship referendum, rendered migrants vulnerable to deportation, and "served to invalidate" their experiences in a manner at sometimes undermined their "very sense of themselves." Ibid.

11. Ibid., 48.

12. Quoted in ibid.

13. Applications could be submitted regardless of a parent's legal status in Ireland at that moment.

14. Coakley and Healy, *Looking Forward, Looking Back*, 27.

15. "Notice to non-national parents of Irish-born children born in the state before 1 January 2005 who were granted permission to remain in the state under the IBC/05 scheme. Arrangements for the processing of applications for renewals of permission to remain in the state for persons granted permission to remain under the IBC/05 scheme," Department of Justice, *Equality and Law Reform*, July 2007, accessed January 12, 2012, www.inis.gov.ie/en/INIS/IBC05 Renewal.pdf/Files/IBC05Renewal.pdf. For information about the renewal process in 2010, see ibid.

16. Coakley and Healy, *Looking Forward, Looking Back*, 46.

17. Liam Coakley and Claire Healey, "Ireland's IBC/05 Administrative Scheme for Immigrant Residency, the Separation of Families and the Creation of a Transnational Family Imaginary," *International Migration* 50, no. 2 (2012): 20.

18. See "Explanation of Reasons for Refusal of Visa," Irish Naturalisation and Immigration Service, accessed January 1, 2009, www.inis.gov.ie/en/INIS /RefusalExplainJuly08.pdf/Files/RefusalExplainJuly08.pdf.

19. Coakley and Healy, *Looking Forward, Looking Back*, 27.

20. Coakley and Healy, *Ireland's IBC/05 Administrative Scheme*, 20.

21. Liam Coakley, *Irish Born Child Administrative Scheme for Immigrant Residency 2005 (IBC/05): The Impact on the Families of Status Holders Seven Years On.* New Communities Partnership Paper (2012), 23, www.newcommunities.ie /download/pdf/ibc_05_report_27_march_2012.pdf.

22. "The Zambrano Case and Parents of Irish Citizen Children," Citizens Information, June 15, 2011, accessed November 11, 2011, http://whatsnew.citizens information.ie/2011/06/15/the-zambrano-case-and-parents-of-irish-citizen-children/. The case concerned a Colombian family living in Belgium whose children were Belgian citizens.

23. Pamela Duncan, "Over 850 Non-EU Parents Get Residency," *Irish Times*, January 24, 2012.

24. See *Bode (A Minor) v. Minister for Justice, Equality, and Law Reform*, December 2007, [2007] IESC 62, section 22.

25. Lentin and McVeigh suggest that the IBC/05 scheme "seems more probably connected to the huge cost of potential court cases by migrant parents than to humanitarian reasons." See Lentin and McVeigh, *After Optimism?*, 54.

26. The 2010 MIPEX report finds: "With the least favourable family reunion policies in Europe or North America, Ireland shows little respect for the family

life of its non-EU residents and discourages their integration once arrived. . . . Families enjoy better security and rights in most European countries because of EU law (2003/86/EC), whereas Ireland opts out. Irish politicians have been unable to pass the Immigration, Residence and Protection Bill, despite wide consultation. . . . Few families in Ireland can reunite. Beyond refugees, others are at the mercy of the Minister. . . . Family members that succeed in being reunited still suffer the most unfavourable conditions for integration in the 31 MIPEX countries." See Migrant Integration Policy Index, accessed May 2, 2012, www.mipex.eu/ireland.

27. Kieran Allen describes that a key feature of the Irish neoliberal state is that it "outsources" government by hiring consultants who are not democratically accountable but make decisions on crucial aspects of society. This trend is certainly evident in the government's approach to immigration control, and the IOM has become one such important independent "consultant" that has shaped Irish migration management. See Allen, *The Corporate Takeover of Ireland* (Dublin: Irish Academic Press, 2007), 71.

28. International Organisation for Migration, *International Comparative Study of Migration Legislation and Practice* (Dublin: Stationery Office, April 2002), 97, 98.

29. "Uproar at Ruling over Refugee in 'Sham Marriage,' " *Irish Independent,* August 31, 2007.

30. As Nasc observes, "The government has provided no evidence that marriage is being exploited for immigration purposes." See "Nasc, the Irish Immigrant Support Center, Concerns with Immigration, Residence and Protection Bill," accessed August 29, 2008, www.nascireland.org.

31. Kitty Holland notes that "this was introduced despite a directive from the EU introduced three years ago, 2004/38/EC, which says non-EU family members of EU citizens should be automatically permitted to work and live in the EU." Holland, "Thousands of Couples Get Deportation Notice Letters," *Irish Times,* August 30, 2007.

32. Many ended up without legal status, which made them deportable or else caused them to voluntarily leave the country.

33. See *Metock and Others v. Minister for Justice, Equality, and Law Reform,* C-127, European Union, European Court of Justice, July 25, 2008.

34. These events vividly illustrate the changing ways that migrants may or may not be able to transit among legal statuses, based on the sexualities and intimacies of marriage—and the power of the state *and* supranational bodies such as the ECJ to establish the rules concerning such transiting.

35. Tracy Simmons, "Sexuality and Immigration: U.K. Family Reunion Policy and the Regulation of Sexual Citizens in the European Union," *Political Geography* 27 (2008): 218.

36. Three of the four *Metock* couples married after the man was refused refugee status; in the fourth case, the marriage occurred before refugee status was refused.

37. Jamie Smyth, "Few Legal Means to Restrict Rise in Bogus Unions," *Irish Times*, August 17, 2010.

38. Povinelli, *Empire of Love*.

39. The case is *Izmailovic and Anor. v. Commr of An Garda Siochana and Ors* [2011] IEHC 32 (January 31, 2011), and it involved a Lithuanian woman married to a failed asylum seeker from Egypt. The quote concerning the ruling comes from Máiréad Enright, "Operation Charity in the High Court," *Human Rights in Ireland*, February 14, 2011, www.humanrights.ie/index.php/2011/02/14/operation-charity-in-the-high-court/.

40. Smyth, "Few Legal Means"; and Jamie Smyth, "Minister Says Law to Tackle 'Sham Marriage' on Way," *Irish Times*, June 10, 2011.

41. For example, Helena Wray, "An Ideal Husband? Marriages of Convenience, Moral Gatekeeping, and Immigration to the U.K.," *European Journal of Migration and Law* 8 (2006): 303–20, and other writings about the British state's strategies for policing marriages that involved spouses from the Indian subcontinent.

42. The Irish Naturalisation and Immigration Service (INIS) website guidelines for spouses or partners seeking to join spouses or partners in Ireland reveal the kinds of intimacies that are expected. For instance: "The following documentation might also be useful for visa applications where spouses have not lived together since their marriage. In order to provide a full account of the relationship history: copies of a range of emails/letters sent since the relationship began; copy of telephone bills showing record of calls made to each other; copies of tickets showing when your Irish spouse visited you; holiday photos (digital format is best, especially if it shows the date the photo was taken). If there are cultural differences in terms of courtship and marriage this should be explained and evidence of this should be submitted, for example, a signed declaration from a religious or cultural leader. If you have children together then the birth certificates could be included in the application. Evidence of financial support: Copies of money transfers if your Irish spouse has been financially supporting you." See INIS, "Information about Visa Application and Immigration Procedures," at www.inis.gov.ie/en/INIS/Pages/Join%20Family#NON_EEA_Family_Member_of_EU_Citizen.

43. For example, Luibhéid, "Pink Tide."

44. Anne Mulhall, "Queer in Ireland: 'Deviant' Filiation and the (Un)holy Family," in *Queer in Europe*, ed. Lisa Downing and Robert Gillette (Aldershot, U.K.: Ashgate, 2011), 103.

45. GLEN, Dublin, "Submission to the Joint Committee on Justice, Equality, Defence, and Women's Rights Re: Immigration, Residence, and Protection Bill 2008," March 2008.

46. The All-Party Oireachtas Committee on the Constitution, "Oral Hearings, Family Issues, 2005," accessed June 10, 2008, www.constitution.ie/oral-hearings/family-issues_presentations-21042005/.

47. GLEN, "Same Sex Couples and Immigration Provisions in Ireland," May 2011, accessed November 27, 2011, www.glen.ie/attachments/Same_Sex_Couples_and_Immigration_Provision_in_Ireland.PDF. According to GLEN, the Civil Partnership and Certain Rights of Cohabitation Act 2010, which came into effect January 1, 2011, means that same-sex couples can register as civil partners in Ireland, which confers most of the rights and obligations of civil marriage, including migration rights. Also recognized for purposes of conferring migration rights: relationships between same-sex couples that have been recognized in other regions (e.g., Canada recognizes same-sex marriage). There is also a provision for recognition of de facto relationships, involving people who have not registered as civil partners but are in a committed relationship. Application of the rules further depends on the nationality, legal status, and current residence of each partner.

48. See INIS, "Spouse of an Irish National/Civil Partnership with an Irish National," accessed November 27, 2011, www.inis.gov.ie/en/INIS/Pages/WP07000024. The site opens with wording in red: "NOTE: Applications from persons where it is deemed that they are seeking such permission to simply gain entry to the State or where they seek such permission simply to continue their length of stay in the State for whatever reason, such applications will be refused and the appropriate and necessary action taken to remove the individual from the State. Any misinformation given during the application process will result in the application being refused immediately."

49. Mulhall, "Queer in Ireland," 104. Mulhall is paraphrasing Michael Cronin's useful analysis.

50. Jo Doezema, "Forced to Choose: Beyond the Voluntary v. Forced Prostitution Dichotomy," in *Global Sex Workers: Rights, Resistance, and Redefinition,* ed. Kamala Kempadoo and Jo Doezema (New York: Routledge, 1998), 42.

51. Rutvica Andrijasevic, *Migration, Agency and Citizenship in Sex Trafficking* (Basingstoke, U.K.: Palgrave Macmillan, 2010), 9.

52. Elizabeth Bernstein, *Temporarily Yours: Intimacy, Authenticity, and the Commerce of Sex* (Chicago: University of Chicago Press, 2007), 149, 156.

53. "Domestic Workers Launch Week of Action to Call on the Government to End Their Exploitation," Migrant Rights Centre Ireland (MRCI), April 30, 2012, accessed May 2, 2012, www.mrci.ie/press-centre/domestic-workers-launch-week-of-action-to-call-on-the-government-to-end-their-exploitation/.

54. MRCI, *Private Homes, A Public Concern: The Experience of Twenty Migrant Women Employed in the Private Home in Ireland* (Dublin: MCRI, 2004), 29.

55. Siobhan Mullally, "Guest Post on Migrant Domestic Workers and Migration Law in the EU," January 27, 2012, Human Rights Ireland, accessed May 2, 2012, www.humanrights.ie/index.php/2012/01/27/guest-post-on-migrant-domestic-workers-and-migration-law-in-the-eu/.

56. By contrast, resorting to an identitarian model means not just that these kinds of connections remain underplayed or even ignored but that the larger norm—and the history of its emergence and transformation—remains unproblematized.

Conclusion

1. Judith Butler, *Frames of War: When Is Life Grievable?* (London: Verso, 2009), 32. While *Frames of War* is focused on U.S. wars, Butler substantively addresses migration issues too, arguing that the treatment of migrants is conditioned by a framework of "the war at home."

2. Ibid., 28.

3. Düvell, "Irregular Migration," 22; and John Torpey, *The Invention of the Passport* (Cambridge: Cambridge University Press, 2000), 7–11.

4. On renationalization, see Saskia Sassen, *Losing Control? Sovereignty in an Age of Globalization* (New York: Columbia University Press, 1996), 59, 60, 62. In regard to statecraft, Jonathan Ping offers the following succinct definition: "The state as such is an organization that recreates itself through statecraft. . . . The creation of a state *which holds supreme legitimate authority within a territory* is theoretically the goal. The reality of the political, economic, and natural environment, however, transforms the theoretical goal into an ongoing project." See Jonathan H. Ping, *Middle Power Statecraft: Indonesia, Malaysia, and the Asia-Pacific* (Aldershot, U.K.: Ashgate, 2005), 17. A statecraft perspective usefully does not presume in advance that states have a necessary or predetermined form, and it points to the labor of continually maintaining and recreating the stateness of the state—which means that labor is always in process, incomplete, and subject to intervention.

5. For example, Emma Quinn writes, "Between the mid 1990s and mid 2000s the government placed a deliberate emphasis on addressing the asylum situation and developments in the immigration arena have lagged behind somewhat." See Quinn, *Organisation of Asylum and Migration Policies in Ireland*, x.

6. In making this argument, I am extrapolating from Ann Stoler's suggestion that sexualities and intimacies are often believed to manifest "inner" qualities of the person. See Stoler, *Carnal Knowledge and Imperial Power*, 9.

7. Inda, *Targeting Immigrants*, 24–26.

8. For example, see Anne McClintock, "Family Feuds: Gender, National-ism and the Family," *Feminist Review* 44 (Summer 1993): 61–80.

9. As Boucher and Collins explained, "The Irish political and business classes incorporated social interests, initially the trade union movement and later the community and voluntary sector, into an elite community of social partners who were directly involved in policy-making. This elite community of social partners has fashioned new forms of institutional regulation that selec-tively draw on liberal British, neo-liberal American and neo-corporatist Euro-pean models" (297). See Gerry Boucher and Gráinne Collins, "Having One's Cake and Being Eaten Too: Irish Neo-liberal Corporatism," *Review of Social Economy* 51, no. 3 (September 2003): 295–316. See also Rory O'Donnell, "The Partnership State: Building the Ship at Sea," in *Contesting the State: Lessons from the Irish Case,* ed. Maura Adshead, Peadar Kirby, and Michelle Millar (Manchester, U.K.: Manchester University Press, 2008), 73–99. Aihwa Ong also explores the ways that new articulations between states and other institu-tions have emerged under conditions of globalization.

10. For discussion of how statuses relationally define one another, see, for example, Yen Le Espiritu, *Home Bound: Filipino Lives across Cultures, Commu-nities and Countries* (Berkeley: University of California Press, 2003), 47–48; Bonnie Honig, *Democracy and the Foreigner* (Princeton, N.J.: Princeton Uni-versity Press, 2003); Gary Okihiro, *Margins and Mainstreams: Asians in Ameri-can History and Culture* (Seattle: University of Washington Press, 1994); and Soguk, *States and Strangers.*

11. On the desirability of the migrant as a worker to whom no social welfare costs attached, see, for example, Steve Loyal, "Welcome to the Celtic Tiger: Racism, Immigration and the State," in *The Ends of Irish History? Critical Reflec-tions on the Celtic Tiger,* ed. Colin Coulter and Steve Coleman (Manchester: Manchester University Press, 2003), 74–94. See also the text of the *L&O* deci-sion where several justices explicitly contrast pregnant migrants who are pre-sumed to be engaged in a form of illegal migration and welfare sponging with hardworking, contributing labor migrants.

12. In this context we can understand why subsequent figurations of migrant illegality that centered on workers who entered legally but became illegal "through no fault of their own" gained some degree of sympathy, eventually leading the government to issue "bridging visas" to several thousand of them.

13. Filipina nurses started to arrive in the late 1990s; from 2000 onward the Irish government explicitly targeted them as a reserve army of nursing labor. By 2002 Ireland was the third-largest importer of Filipina nurses (after Saudi Ara-bia and the United Kingdom). Because of their classification as highly skilled workers, they could bring their spouses relatively quickly (subject to certain conditions), but the spouses could not work; thus, they remained dependent on

the migrants who were working in Ireland. In 2002 Filipina nurses and various NGOs lobbied to change the policy, and in February 2004 the government did change the policy—largely in order to retain Filipina migrant nursing labor rather than having them remigrate to other countries such as the United Kingdom, which did allow the spouses to work.

14. Note that the habitual residence condition has been modified though not abolished in recent years; the state now relies on five criteria to determine social welfare eligibility: length and continuity of residence in Ireland or another country; length and purpose of any absence from Ireland; nature and pattern of employment; person's main center of interest; and future intention of the person as they appear from all the circumstances. As Barrett and his colleagues describe, "In this way, there is a degree of discretion built into the system of determination of habitual residence which provides scope for differential treatment of immigrants and natives." See Alan Barrett, Corona Joyce, and Bertrand Maître, *Immigrants and Welfare Receipt in Ireland,* IZA Discussion Paper 5516, Bonn, February 2011, 5. In terms of the differential treatment of migrants, see Crosscare, Doras Luimní, and NASC, *Person or Number? Issues Faced by Immigrants Accessing Social Protection* (Limerick: Crosscare, Doras Luimní and NASC, 2012).

15. Deirdre Conlon notes that policies targeting migrants inevitably introduce questions about "the lines and connections between [citizen] individuals, their families, and the framework of the state in Irish society" (108). See Conlon, "Ties That Bind: Governmentality, the State, and Asylum in Contemporary Ireland," *Environment and Planning D: Society and Space* 28 (2010): 95–111.

16. See Ngai, *Impossible Subjects*; and De Genova, "Migrant 'Illegality' and Deportability in Everyday Life," including his argument that "'illegality' . . . both theoretically and practically, is a social relation that is fundamentally inseparable from citizenship" (422).

17. Alicia Schmidt Camacho, "Ciudadana X: Gender Violence and the Denationalization of Women's Rights in Cuidad Juarez, Mexico," in *Terrorizing Women: Feminicide in the Americas,* ed. Rosa-Linda Fregoso and Cynthia Bejarano (Durham, N.C.: Duke University Press, 2010), 275–89; see especially 286–87.

18. Ong, "Cultural Citizenship as Subject Making," 263.

19. Mulhall, "Queer in Ireland," 100.

20. Finola Kennedy writes that the Irish language version of the constitution, which is the legally binding version in cases of dispute, uses the word "teaghlach," which means both family and household. See Kennedy, *Cottage to Creche,* 7. In a 2002 case, two Polish Roma sought residence in Ireland based on the fact that they were the grandparents of an Irish child and lived in Ireland with their son and daughter-in-law. Their solicitor argued that they fit within the Irish language definition of the family, even though they did not fit the

English-language definitions contained in immigration and asylum law. Ultimately they lost. See "Definition of What Constitutes Family Is Key Issue in the Case," *Irish Times,* January 11, 2002. See also House of the Oireachtas, "Family Issues: Presentations," April 21, 2005, accessed May 23, 2012, http://debates.oireachtas.ie/CNJ/2005/04/21/00004.asp.

21. An extensive scholarship examines how immigration controls are founded on histories of racism and end up reinforcing racist suspicion toward people of color, regardless of their legal status.

22. Breda Gray usefully points out that "integration" is never a preset, predetermined program; rather, we need to explore why "integration" emerges as a problem to be solved, the changing nature of the definition of integration as a problem, and the rationalities and technologies that are employed to (try to) resolve the problem. See Gray, "Migrant Integration Policy." Once the Irish government moved away from denial about the permanence of migration, it came to view integration as a necessary strategy for properly "managing" migration. Policies focused only on those who were expected to remain in Ireland long term—those who were recognized refugees in particular. Asylum seekers were manifestly excluded from integration strategies, as were undocumented and short-term migrants. Key government reports on migrant integration strategies include Interdepartmental Working Group on the Integration of Refugees in Ireland, *Integration: A Two Way Process* (Dublin: Department of Justice, Equality and Law Reform, 2003); National Economic and Social Council, *Managing Migration in Ireland* (Dublin: NESC, 2006), esp. chapter 9, "Fostering Integration"; and Office of the Minister for Integration, *Migration Nation: Statement on Migration Strategy and Diversity Management,* 2008, accessed May 27, 2012, www.integration.ie/website/omi/omiwebv6.nsf/page/AXBN-7SQDF91044205-en/$File/Migration%20Nation.pdf. Further information is available through the Office for the Promotion of Migrant Integration at www.integration.ie. A series of national action plans against racism, and national action plans against poverty and social exclusion, were part of the integration strategy, although with very significant limitations. Gray's critique of official integration strategies seems worth quoting extensively: "Integration policies pay little or no attention to the dividing practices of the politico-legal system which divide people into citizens, refugees, emigrant citizens, immigrants on visas and work permits, regular or irregular migrants. The racialised and gendered workings of the global labour market and economic policies by which nation-states are positioning themselves optimally in relation to globalising capitalism also remain outside of the integration policy frame. Moreover, integration policies as they are currently being formulated ignore the 'dissimilar, heterogeneous, and unpredictable' nature of identity formation and the fact that identities are produced in a context where cultural meanings and practices

increasingly transcend national borders.... Integration polices ... can be seen as nationalist practices of belonging that reproduce national boundaries of inclusion and exclusion. They rely on assumptions about migration and the territorialized nation-state that Mary Chamberlain identifies with a modernity marked by Empire, capitalism and industrialization." Gray, "Migrant Integration Policy," 135–36. For a different take on these issues, see Ronit Lentin and Elena Morea, eds., *Migrant Activism and Integration from below in Ireland* (Basingstoke, U.K.: Palgrave Macmillan, 2012).

23. Gray, "Migrant Integration Policy," 120, 135. See also Ronit Lentin, "Turbans, Hijabs, and Other Differences: 'Integration from Below' and Irish Interculturalism," *European Journal of Cultural Studies* 15, no. 2 (May 2012): 226–42.

24. Scholarship on migrants and transnationalism has grown significantly, as marked by the publication of "Going Transnational," special issue, *Irish Journal of Sociology* 19, no. 2 (2011). Scholarship on migrants' use of media to create and maintain transnational ties, and on religious identities in transnational frameworks, is especially evident. In addition, scholars have explored migrant activism as a route to transnational and local belonging. For discussion of transnationalism among migrant parents with Irish born children, see Chatháin, "Transnational Migrants' Negotiations of Formal and Informal Citizenship"; and Coakley, *Irish Born Child Administrative Scheme for Immigrant Residency 2005 (IBC/05): The Impact on the Families of Status Holders Seven Years On,* New Communities Partnership Paper (2012), 23. There is also a growing scholarship that situates Irish emigration in a transnational framework. Finally, some work has begun to explore the importance transnational identities among Irish people of color.

25. Katy Hayward, "'For Mutual Benefit': Irish Official Discourses on Europeanisation and Hibernicisation," *European Studies* 28 (2010): 95.

26. Harrington, "Citizenship and the Biopolitics of Post-Nationalist Ireland," 426. Moreover, Harrington argues, the citizenship referendum was a mechanism through which Irish elites signaled their willingness to be "good Europeans" in a manner that disavowed connections with the "peoples of other post-colonial territories.... Citizenship would mediate racism by embodying Irish Europeanness directly, rather than being the symbol of a deeper cultural belonging." Ibid., 447.

27. Robbie McVeigh, "United in Whiteness? Irishness, Europeanness, and the Emergence of a 'White Europe' Policy," *European Studies* 28 (2010): 255.

28. Ibid., 251.

29. Fatima El-Tayeb describes that the whiteness associated with Europeanness is not transhistorical and self-evident but instead needs to be historicized and specified. As she notes, groups and nationalities that in the United

States might be characterized as white are not necessarily so in Europe, either historically or under current conditions of globalization. See Fatima El-Tayeb, *European Others: Queering Ethnicity in Postnational Europe* (Minneapolis: University of Minnesota Press, 2011), xiv. See also David Theo Goldberg, "Racial Europeanization," in *Ethnic and Racial Studies* 29, no. 2 (March 2006): 331–64. On whiteness and Irishness, see, for example, Suzanna Chan, "'Kiss My Royal Irish Ass': Contesting Identity: Visual Culture, Whiteness, Gender and Diaspora," *Journal of Gender Studies* 15, no. 1 (2006): 1–17; Garner, *Racism in the Irish Experience*; Lentin and McVeigh, *Racism and Anti-Racism in Ireland*; and Angeline Morrison, "Irish and White-ish: Mixed 'Race' Identity and the Scopic Regime of Whiteness," *Women's Studies International Forum* 27, no. 4 (2004): 385–96.

30. El-Tayeb, *European Others*, xxviii. See also "Women's Rights, Gay Rights, and Anti-Muslim Racism in Europe," special issue, *European Journal of Women's Studies* 19, nos. 1–2 (2012), as well as Judith Butler, "Sexual Politics, Torture, and Secular Time," *British Journal of Sociology* 59, no. 1 (2008): 1–23; Jin Haritaworn, "Colorful Bodies in the Multikulti Metropolis: Vitality, Victimology, and Transgressive Citizenship in Berlin," in *Transgender Migrations: The Bodies, Borders, and Politics of Transition,* ed. Trystan T. Cotten (New York: Routledge, 2012), 11–31; Jennifer L. Petzen, *Gender Politics in the New Europe: "Civilizing" Muslim Sexualities,* Ph.D. diss., University of Washington (Program in Near and Middle Eastern Studies), 2008 (UMI no. 3328436); Tamsila Tauqir, Jennifer L. Petzen, Jin Haritaworn, Sokari Ekine, Sarah Bracke, Sarah Lamble, Suhraiya Jivraj, and Stacy Douglas, "Queer Anti-Racist Activism and Strategies of Critique: A Roundtable Discussion," *Feminist Legal Studies* 19, no. 2 (2011): 169–91. Analyses of other connections among national, European, racial, and sexual identities include Damani J. Partridge, *Hypersexuality and Headscarves: Race, Sexuality, and Citizenship in the New Germany* (Bloomington: Indiana University Press, 2012); and, from a different angle that is not engaged by this book, Ali Nobil Ahmad, *Masculinity, Sexuality, and Illegal Migration: Human Smuggling from Pakistan to Europe* (Farnham, U.K.: Ashgate 2011).

31. Stoler, *Carnal Knowledge and Imperial Power,* 53.

32. On the jailing of mainland Chinese women who give birth in Hong Kong, see Te-Ping Chen, "Hong Kong Cracks Down on 'Birth Tourists,'" *Wall Street Journal,* October 27, 2012, A16.

33. Mancini and Finlay, "'Citizenship Matters,'" 593.

34. See Federation for American Immigration Reform (FAIR), "Birthright Citizenship," www.fairus.org/issue/birthright-citizenship, accessed December 17, 2012. The reference to Ireland is in note 1. Note that these arguments about migrant women's childbearing in the United States rely mainly on a one-sided selection of anecdotes for support.

35. For a brief article about the change, see Keldkurat Katz, "Birthright Citizenship Abolished in New Zealand," *Free Republic,* www.freerepublic.com /focus/f-news/1552467/posts, accessed December 17, 2012.

36. IOM, *International Comparative Study of Migration Legislation and Practice* (Dublin: Stationery Office, 2002), 5. For critical questions about the IOM's global impact on migration policies, see Ishan Ashutosh and Alison Mountz, "Migration Management for the Benefit of Whom? Interrogating the Work of the International Organization for Migration," *Citizenship Studies* 15, no. 1 (February 2011): 21–38. Other important transnational bodies include the European Court of Justice and other European level bodies.

37. Gary Gates, *Irish Men and Women in Same-Sex Partnerships in the United States* (Los Angeles: Williams Institute, March 2008).

38. Indeed, since 1958 the Irish state has been engaged in programs of economic development that depend on opening Ireland to the global. See Gerard Boucher, "Official Discourses on Managing Migration," in *Globalisation, Migration, and Social Transformation: Ireland in Europe and the World,* ed. Bryan Fanning and Ronaldo Munck (Farnham, U.K.: Ashgate, 2011), 135–136.

39. For discussion of the idea that Irish people owe a historical duty to contemporary migrants into Ireland, based on Ireland's own sustained history of emigration, see Garner, *Racism in the Irish Experience,* 159–60. For a critique of the limits of the "historical duty" argument, see Gray, "Remembering a 'Multicultural' Future."

40. For example, Lentin, "Illegal in Ireland, Irish Illegals." See also the Migrant Rights Centre Ireland's "Justice for the Undocumented" campaign materials, which consistently draw out connections between undocumented Irish in the United States and undocumented migrants in Ireland, www.mrci.ie/our -work/justice-for-undocumented/, accessed December 17, 2012.

41. Boucher, "Official Discourses on Managing Migration," 136.

42. Joseph Carens is the paradigmatic proponent of open borders. See Carens, "Aliens and Citizens: The Case for Open Borders," *Review of Politics* 49, no. 2 (1987): 251–73. Others ground their arguments for open borders in Marxian economic logics; for example, Nigel Harris, *Thinking the Unthinkable: The Immigration Myth Exposed* (London: I. B. Tauris, 2002); and Teresa Hayter, *Open Borders: The Case against Immigration Controls,* 2nd ed. (London: Pluto Press, 2004). Still others argue for open borders based on neoliberal economic principles. For a good overview, see Jonathan Seglow, "The Ethics of Immigration," *Political Studies Review* 3 (2005): 317–34.

43. For an excellent overview, see Stephen Castles, "Development and Migration—Migration and Development: What Comes First? Global Perspectives and African Experiences," *Theoria: A Journal of Political and Social Theory* 56 (2009): 1–31.

44. Ibid., 2.

45. Bill Jordan and Franck Düvell, *Migration: The Boundaries of Equality and Justice* (Cambridge: Polity Press, 2003), 140. See also David Miller, *National Responsibility and Global Justice* (Oxford: Oxford University Press, 2008).

46. This idea is elaborated in Shachar's book *Birthright Lottery*. She introduced the argument in an article that she cowrote with Ran Hirschl, "Citizenship as Inherited Property." See also Jacqueline Stevens, *States without Nations: Citizenship for Mortals* (New York: Columbia University Press, 2009).

47. Martin Manalansan, "Queer Intersections: Sexuality and Gender in Migration Studies," *International Migration Review* 40, no. 1 (Spring 2006): 224.

48. Lisa Duggan, *The Twilight of Equality? Neoliberalism, Cultural Politics, and the Attack on Democracy* (Boston: Beacon Press, 2003), xiv. See also Penny Griffin, "Sexing the Economy in a Neo-liberal World Order: Neo-liberal Discourse and the (Re)Production of Heteronormative Heterosexuality," *British Journal of Politics and International Relations* 9, no. 2 (2007): 220–38; and Colin Danby, "Political Economy and the Closet: Heteronormativity in Feminist Economics," *Feminist Economics* 13, no. 2 (April 2007): 29–53.

49. Aihwa Ong argues that elite migrants seek to create possibilities for mobility across borders by strategically mobilizing interlocking regimes of capital, state, and family. See Ong, *Flexible Citizenship*. Denise Brennan's work explores how poor women seeking to migrate legally from the Dominican Republic strategically cultivate ties with foreign sex tourists that may lead to marriage proposals—which would enable them to legally migrate. Ironically, in this context marriage rather than sex work represents women's last-ditch efforts at survival. See Brennan, *What's Love Got to Do with It? Transnational Desires and Sex Tourism in the Dominican Republic* (Durham, N.C.: Duke University Press, 2004); and Caren Freeman, *Making and Faking Kinship* (Ithaca, N.Y.: Cornell University Press, 2012); as well as the broad scholarship on transnational family forms and on migrant social networks that are organized through sexualities and intimacies.

50. Luibhéid, *Entry Denied,* conclusion. This issue resonates with the debates about how migrants, especially those without legal status, are—through their presence, work, and activism—challenging nation-state constructs of citizenship. See, for example, Baker-Cristales, "Mediated Resistance"; and Anne McNevin, "Contesting Citizenship: Irregular Migrants and Strategic Possibilities for Political Belonging," *New Political Science* 31, no. 2 (June 2009): 163–81. There can be no doubt that these effects are real and significant. Yet, to create possibilities for regularizing their status, currently irregular migrants must generally demonstrate that they possess the qualities that are deemed desirable in citizens (hard working, good morals, and so on). This reinforces the existing system although it also somewhat complicates, disrupts, and potentially changes it over the long term.

51. Cohen, "Punks, Bulldaggers, and Welfare Queens," 27, 25.

52. For example, see Duggan, *Twilight of Equality?*; Jasbir Puar, *Terrorist Assemblages* (Durham, N.C.: Duke University Press, 2007); and Varela, Dhawan, and Engel, *Hegemony and Heteronormativity.*

53. For example, see Amy Lind, ed., *Development, Sexual Rights, and Global Governance* (New York: Routledge, 2010); Alexander, *Pedagogies of Crossing*; Natalie Oswin, "The Modern Model Family Home in Singapore: A Queer Geography," *Transactions of the Institute of British Geographers* 35, no. 2 (April 2010): 256–68; Kate Bedford, *Developing Partnerships: Gender, Sexuality, and the Reformed World Bank* (Minneapolis: University of Minnesota Press, 2009); and Penny Griffin, *Gendering the World Bank: Neoliberalism and the Gendered Foundations of Global Governance* (New York: Palgrave Macmillan, 2009). For discussion of the paradoxical conjunctions between queering sexualities and neoliberalism, see, for example, Duggan, *Twilight of Equality?*

54. The scholarship about the affective dimensions of citizenship may offer promising possibilities; for example, Carol Johnson, "The Politics of Affective Citizenship from Blair to Obama," *Citizenship Studies* 14, no. 5 (October 2010): 495–509. The extensive queer works that theorize connections among sexualities/intimacies, affect, and citizenship struggles seem especially promising. Geraldine Pratt has explored how to mobilize affective responses to Filipina migrant mothers working in Vancouver, Canada. See Pratt, *Families Apart.*

55. Undoubtedly, some pregnant migrants were queer women, but that is different from suggesting that pregnant migrants as a category are queer.

56. For example, Martin Manalansan has explored how feminist migration scholarship that is focused on women's reproduction, childbearing, and carework across borders may inadvertently reinforce heteronormative models of gender, sexuality, affect, and life course—and suggests ways to queer such work. See Manalansan, "Queering the Chain of Care Paradigm."

57. Anderson and Ruhs, "Guest Editorial, Researching Illegality and Labour Migration," 176.

58. Framing events as a struggle among diverse actors over where to draw boundaries between citizens and migrants, and among migrant statuses, allowed me to discuss events without claiming to "represent" migrants' experiences. Instead, migrants in this text exist primarily as people who are engaged in struggles that are partly documented here and in other academic sources but who also have lives beyond the inscriptions of the state or this text.

59. Note that there is already some excellent scholarship about how the Irish state has addressed emigration, return emigration, and new immigration as overlapping concerns; for example, Gray, "Migrant Integration Policy."

60. As Homi Bhabha describes, nationalism is at once pedagogical and performative. See Bhabha, "DissemiNation: Time, Narrative and the Margins of

the Modern Nation," in *Nation and Narration,* ed. Homi Bhabha (London: Routledge, 1990), 291–322.

61. Warmest thanks to Ronit Lentin for suggesting that I document interactions on public buses in Dublin.

62. Tormey, "'Everyone with Eyes,'" 86.

63. Ibid., 69.

64. For example, see Siobhan Somerville, "The Queer Geopolitics of Birth: Jus Soli in Global Perspective," paper presented at the American Studies Association Annual Meeting, November 18, 2012, San Juan, Puerto Rico.

65. Nayan Shah, *Stranger Intimacy: Contesting Race, Sexuality, and the Law in the North American West* (Berkeley: University of California Press, 2012), 262.

66. Natalie Oswin has explored how the postcolonial state in Singapore harnessed heteronormativity in order to fulfill state desires for and projects associated with "modernity, development and progress" (139). In the process, she argues, not just gays and lesbians but also "the single, the uneducated, the unskilled migrant worker and many others who have been deemed incapable of creating and sustaining a 'quality' population" have been queered (ibid.). Her insightful analysis is directly applicable to the Irish situation, and to the arguments advanced in this book. See Natalie Oswin, "Sexual Tensions in Modernizing Singapore: The Postcolonial and the Intimate," *Environment and Planning D: Society and Space* 28 (2010): 128–41.

67. Povinelli, *Empire of Love,* 10.

Index

Refugees (cont.)
   integration, 198, 281n22; Irish
   refugee regime, 15, 20, 36, 104, 140,
   153, 159, 229n35, 236n15, 260n86;
   status, 8, 20, 59, 60, 67, 76, 80, 81,
   82, 88, 90, 93, 96, 98, 119, 153,
   221n60, 224n91, 236n19, 241n71.
   See also Asylum seekers; Geneva
   Convention; Legal status: as
   changing
Repatriation, 11, 136, 137, 230n37,
   256n15
Reproductive futurism, 149–50, 151,
   161, 168, 173, 174, 266n30. *See also*
   Heteronormativity; Pregnancy;
   Pregnant migrants; Residency
   through a child
Residency through a child, 9, 39–53,
   67, 72, 74, 75–80, 83, 111, 192, 194,
   243n89; as a clearer and quicker
   process than asylum, 76, 78, 79; as
   generated by state policies, 17,
   80–81; as incentive for illegal
   immigration, 1, 17, 159, 160, 161,
   166, 173 (*see also* Birthright
   citizenship; *Chen* case;
   Citizenship Referendum;
   Fajujonu case; IBC/05 scheme;
   L&O case; Pregnant migrants;
   Zambrano case)
Residents against Racism, 22, 41, 154
Responsibility: and citizenship, 112,
   113; for deciding refugee claims, 57
   (*see also* Dublin Convention); and
   immigration policy, 202 (*see also*
   Minister for justice); and migrant
   motherhood, 69–70; migrants as
   irresponsible (*see also* Illegal
   immigrants; Pregnant migrants);
   migrants as responsible, 84,
   112–18; and neoliberalism, 7, 196

Returned emigrants, 11, 24, 192
Right to life. *See* Abortion
Roma, 44, 61, 232n63, 280n20
Romanians, 12, 39, 80, 104, 146,
   220n55
Rubin, Gayle, 4, 189
Russia, 263n125

Same-sex couple migration, 28, 175,
   180, 185–87, 198, 201
Sexual exploitation, 39, 62, 63, 65, 66,
   67, 182–83, 184, 188. *See also*
   Trafficking
Sexualities and nationalisms. *See*
   Birthright citizenship;
   Citizenship Referendum;
   Fajujonu case; Heteronormativity;
   Heterosexual marriage migration;
   Immigration controls and sexual
   norms; *L&O* case; Pregnant
   migrants; Residency through a
   child; Same-sex couple migration;
   Women's bodies and national,
   racial, and imperial boundaries
Sexuality and economy, 33, 34, 36, 37,
   193. *See also* Heteronormativity;
   Immigration controls and sexual
   norms
Sex workers, 5, 16, 187–88, 238n43
Sham marriage. *See* Marriage fraud
Stratified reproduction. *See*
   Racialization: of reproduction;
   Pregnant migrants
Subjectification: 5, 7, 9, 21, 27, 28, 63,
   87, 89–90, 91, 93–110, 161, 173, 178,
   197, 198; definition of, 90
Subsidiary protection, 59–60, 93

Trafficking: of children into Ireland,
   64; as distinct from smuggling, 63,
   66; of forced labor into Ireland,

65; Irish laws and policies concerning, 64–67; UN definition of, 62–64; victims being treated as illegal migrants, 66–67; of women into Ireland, 65

Transnationalism: and economic fields, 142, 179; and families, 68–71, 179–80, 183; and medical tourism, 70; and migrant identities, 198; and migration strategies, 67–71; and motherhood, 69; and nation, 5; and reproductive struggles, 147; and sexuality struggles, 201, 208; and trafficking, 62–67

Travellers, 17, 35, 126, 133–35, 227n19, 258n55; Traveller women, 17, 35, 126, 133–35, 249n58

Ukraine, 184

United States: illegal Irish in, 25, 84, 202; images of Irish emigrants, 23; influence on Irish immigration policy, 3, 64, 200, 201; links with Irish abortion politics, 127–28; struggles over pregnant migrants, 3, 200, 201; U.S. migrants in Ireland, 1, 12, 186; visa lotteries, 25

Vincentian Refugee Centre, 22, 23, 56

Welfare, 27, 48–49, 78, 87, 88–91, 94, 110–12, 116, 117, 118–19, 120, 121, 178, 192, 194, 196, 201, 205, 245n11, 246n28, 279n11, 280n14; asylum seekers as welfare scroungers, 24, 42, 48–49, 50, 51, 57, 82, 92, 93, 113,

116, 117, 118, 139, 140, 193, 195, 246n21; and migrant subjectification, 90–123; as racializing, 97. *See also* Direct provision; Habitual residence condition

Welfare officers, 76, 79, 92–93, 115, 116, 117

Wives, 18, 34, 40, 41, 61, 81, 89, 101, 181, 182

Women and parenting, 39, 78, 96–97, 101, 111, 117, 118, 120, 130, 134, 150, 154–55, 157, 177, 178, 179, 194. See also *Fajujonu* case; IBC/05 scheme; *L&O* case; Transnationalism: and motherhood

Women's bodies and national, racial, and imperial boundaries, 16–17, 31–33, 35–36, 37, 41, 47–50, 52, 127–28, 130, 132, 138, 142, 143, 144, 150, 154, 160, 161, 168, 171, 172, 174, 193, 194, 198, 199, 204. *See also* Abortion; Birthright citizenship; *Chen* case; Citizenship Referendum; Heteronormativity; Immigration controls and sexual norms; Irish sexualities; *L&O* case; Ms. O; Pregnant migrants: as national threat; Racialization: of reproduction; Racism: sexualized and gendered racism; Reproductive futurism; *X* case

Women's high emigration rates, 35, 36, 37

X case, 126, 130–32, 141–43, 144

Zambrano case, 179, 180, 194

EITHNE LUIBHÉID is associate professor of gender and women's studies at the University of Arizona. She is author of *Entry Denied: Controlling Sexuality at the Border* (Minnesota, 2002) and coeditor, with Lionel Cantú Jr., of *Queer Migrations: Sexuality, U.S. Citizenship, and Border Crossings* (Minnesota, 2005).